An unforgettable
Journey

ISBN: 978-1-968970-97-0 Paperback
ISBN: 978-1-968970-98-7 Ebook
ISBN: 978-1-968970-99-4 Hardback

Rev. date: 09/25/2025

Walter R. Somerville Jr.

An unforgettable Journey

EDIFYING TIMES

Growing Up in Impoverished Environment

Rising to Achieve Visionary Legacy Public Service

Touring Abroad Inspired by Curiosity and Education

My Memoirs
EDIFYING TIMES

To my late mother and father

I think they would be proud of my fifty-four years of public service to the American people and especially the way I am living my life.

Also, I am forever grateful to my adorable wife, Jean Renwick Somerville, for encouraging me to record my memoies.

Contents

Introduction

When growing up, I did not know what I wanted to be or who I wanted to be like. I grew up in a sheltered environment, with my parents, schoolteachers, and neighbors. I heard and read about doctors, lawyers, and many other professional people but I did not think I would be able to become an educated person like them. The family resources were just not available. I listened to sports' broadcasting on the radio when it was about Joe Louis boxing matches and Brooklynn Dodgers baseball games. Could I become a boxer or baseball player? My father bought me some boxing gloves for Christmas. Sparring with a friend in the neighborhood convinced me I could not become a professional boxer. But what about baseball? Around the age of thirteen, when I entered ninth grade at Dunbar high school, I began playing baseball. My interest in sports continued to grow. I was lucky enough to work part time at Bugle Field Baseball Stadium when the Baltimore Elite Giants baseball team played their games there. Members of the team taught me much about various baseball skills, especially pitching and infield positions. Their coaching prepared me for competitive baseball with hopes of becoming a professional baseball player, but that did not come true.

I entered public service in 1951 and served nearly fifty-four years in service to my country. During that time, I advocated making a positive difference in the lives of ordinary people. That was my unyielding focus while working until I retired, as a federal Senior Executive Service (SES) official, from the coast guard on September 30, 2004. Since transitioning from retirement to another phase of my life's journey, I have maintained that advocacy focus by establishing a scholarship fund at the University of Maryland University College.

Some people look for another job after they retire. That is not what I did. I often tell everyone that I spend my spare time doing what comes naturally, enjoying sports and traveling with my wife to countries we had never visited. We enjoy an educational experience enriched with historical knowledge.

I was born in Macon, a small city in eastern North Carolina. My parents were the most caring and nurturing couple you could ever meet. My mother was a housewife who cared deeply for her husband and children. She never worked outside the home. My father was a sharecropper who worked in North Carolina and was always seeking a better place to live and raise our family, which eventually became six children—two girls and four boys.

Shortly, after my sister and I were born, my parents moved to Sykesville, Maryland, where my father had another job as a sharecropper. My brother and another sister were born there. My family then migrated to Baltimore, Maryland, where my twin brothers were born.

We lived in a substandard house until my father moved the family to another house with indoor plumbing, modern appliances, a piano,

and other things people normally take for granted in their homes. The house was purchased conditionally—rent with an option to buy. My father paid the rent until he exercised the option to buy the house in the 1960s.

I grew up in Baltimore and attended the public schools there. And as a teenager, I developed a passionate interest in playing baseball. I also worked wherever I could to earn money to help pay the bills. We lived in an impoverished neighborhood, commonly referred to as the ghetto, for many years, as this was all my father could afford.

My father worked two jobs most of the time. He was a laborer on the Western Maryland Railroad, and in the evenings, he had a second job working at a laundry. The laundry was just a block away from where we lived. I observed all of this and often wondered what I could do to help my father in some way. This worried me even when I enrolled in the United States Air Force, for four years, in 1951. I was convinced that my family could and should enjoy a better life.

While in the air force, I volunteered for a tour of duty in South Korea. I completed one year there and then returned to the United States. I was honorably discharged in 1955. I reenlisted for another four years. The four years were spent working at the Air Force Reserve Center in Baltimore, Maryland, not far from where I lived. I attended college at night, working toward a bachelor's degree in business and economics. I completed one and a half years of credits toward the degree. My enlistment was extended for one year, and I was honorably discharged in 1960.

A couple of months after discharge, I went to work as a civilian in the federal civil service as a GS-5, an Air Force Reserve technician, at Andrews Air Force Base. I met a coworker there who left the base to take a job at the Federal Aviation Agency (FAA). Apparently, he valued the work I had done at the base because he arranged for me to get a job at the FAA.

It was there that I became a personnel management specialist. And from the work I performed in that job, I developed a strong desire to become a personnel officer in the federal government. This motivated me to continue my evening college studies.

I transferred to the Office of Economic Opportunity (OEO), where I worked for two years. I returned to the FAA to assist in establishing the Department of Transportation (DOT), authorized by Congress in 1967. All the while, I continued my college studies and received a bachelor's degree in 1970.

After the DOT was established, I went to work as a senior personnel management specialist in the DOT Office of the Secretary.

In 1970 I accepted a position in the United States Coast Guard as chief, Civilian Equal Employment Opportunity division. Since this was a promotion to a GS-15 position but not in the professional personnel field, I accepted the position with the intention of serving just long enough to qualify for retirement at age fifty-five. At that time, I would have worked long enough in the federal government to qualify for maximum retirement benefits.

My potential retirement goals changed when I reached age fifty-three and was appointed to a Senior Executive Service (SES) position in September 1983 as chief of civil rights, the military equivalent of rear admiral in the United States Coast Guard.

I assumed the awesome responsibilities as the coast guard's director for the program. These responsibilities included policy, budget, resources acquisition, and support to the field for all civil rights activities throughout the service. These responsibilities also involved overseeing the coast guard's civil rights obligations for administering a $67 million Boating Safety grant program.

In addition to carrying out these responsibilities for twenty-one years, I led coast guard efforts in establishing new programs and developing innovative strategies for the coast guard to reach out to minority organizations and communities to enhance recruiting and create mutually strategic partnerships for business purposes.

Up until I moved into this new position, the coast guard had limited contact with minority organizations and communities. There was a

consensus among coast guard leadership that this needed to change. It was time to challenge the coast guard's organizational culture to become more receptive to working with minority organizations. The commandant believed that their contributions would offer an external resource of value to the coast guard. Collaboration with minority organizations would not only enhance recruiting in minority communities but also would enhance military readiness and add value to operational mission performance. It was an honor for me to accept this awesome responsibility for leading coast guard efforts in developing strategic relationships with minority organizations.

For twenty-one years, I served under the direction of six commandants. Each of them possessed personal views about civil rights and what the concept should mean to the coast guard. Given coast guard practices, each of their tours of duty was limited to four years of active military service.

I am grateful for their support of my vision for civil rights in the coast guard and their participation in the programs and strategies initiated during their tenures as commandant. This meant a lot to achieving successful outcomes. Many of the programs and strategies the coast guard pursued were administered over a period exceeding the four-year tenure of any one commandant.

For this reason, I purposely have refrained from citing names, except for names of those principal parties who participated in the decision-making process of the activities that comprise relevant events. Many persons shared in the implementation phases of those events. I am grateful to them for that, but I did not want to write about every facet of their efforts, lest I unintentionally misrepresent the contributions of any one person.

When I retired from the coast guard, I left with a continuing quest for knowledge and new experiences that would enable me to remain active and filled with curiosity.

I established a scholarship program at the University of Maryland University College to help those in need. Education is imperative in our society today, and I wanted to reinforce that notion by setting up a scholarship fund as a living legacy.

Sports and sporting events have always been favorites of mine. I played baseball in high school and at the semipro (sandlot) level, hoping to join the Major League, which did not happen. I still follow sports, especially basketball and baseball. I purchased partial season tickets for both of these sports. And I have become an avid fan of the Wizards and the Washington Nationals here in Washington, DC.

My wife and I have traveled to several countries abroad. Our travel experiences have introduced us to new knowledge, customs, traditions, and events that we would not normally get from reading books. You have to be "there" to acquire appreciation for other peoples of the world.

A Tribute to My Mother

Mama, as I called her, was my shoulder to cry on. She called me "Lil Bra." She always made me feel special, regardless of the circumstances. Growing up and when I was a teenager, she was always there for me. She ensured I attended school and participated in church activities. These two activities meant so much to her. They were grounded in my mother's humane value system.

As a faithful member of her church, she would prepare me and my siblings for church every Sunday. On most Sundays, Mama would spend most of the day in church, often staying to have lunch there. Mama had lots of friends at church. She enjoyed being around them and chatting during lunches and other events at the church.

Sundays were her days to do just what pleased her outside the house. On a routine Sunday, we didn't expect her to come home until late afternoon. And she often went back to church for evening events. She looked forward to attending the Easter sunrise service held at the old Orioles baseball park, then located at Alameda and Thirty-Third Streets in Baltimore.

Except for church, Mama spent most of her time at home. She was a friendly lady who loved to be around people. She loved to listen more than she talked. But some things set her apart from the typical housewife.

She loved to wear hats. For Easter, we kids would get new clothes to wear to church; Mama would always get a new hat. She had numerous hats and always wore an attractive hat to church.

Mama also loved to play Bingo. The state of Maryland held its annual state fair in the fall in Towson, Maryland, several miles from where we lived. When we could muster transportation to get to the fair, Mama and most of the family would attend. The first thing Mama wanted to do when we got to the fair was to find the tent that had Bingo games. She would look for an open seat and play until we'd seen everything we wanted to see at the state fair and returned to get her to leave for home.

She was often lucky enough to win some Bingo games. Winners were given stuffed animals for prizes. When she won prizes, she would leave the event very happy about her success. She really enjoyed herself at the state fair, especially getting the stuffed animals. She often gave some of the stuffed animals to neighborhood children.

Mama was a spiritual person. She strongly believed in the tenets of religious teachings. She often talked about visiting the Holy Land. Mama was normally the last person to go to bed each night. She would sit at the dining room table, reading the Bible and praying before going to bed. I once asked her why she prayed before bed, and she said, "So your daddy and your brothers and sisters will have the strength and courage to carry on."

After I moved away from my parents' home, I often visited them to talk about old times and to see how they were doing in their new home. Whenever I called to let Mama and Daddy know I was coming over, mostly on the weekends, Mama always had a special meal waiting for me—salmon cakes and strawberry tarts. I loved to eat Mama's cooking, and she knew that. My mother passed away in 1989, at the age of eighty-two. She was a phenomenal woman.

A Tribute to My Father

Daddy was a gentle man, someone you could talk to. He would listen to everything you had to say. Very seldom would he interrupt to editorialize on anything. When I talked with him, he always smiled and most times said, "That's good boy."

He loved baseball. The Brooklyn Dodgers were his favorite team. We would listen to the Dodgers games when they were broadcast on the radio. We didn't have a television until after I enlisted in the air force.

He was the disciplinarian of the house. When he would come home from work, he would ask my mother what had happened during the day. My mother would tell him things and let him know if she thought follow-up disciplinary action was warranted. Daddy would always have talks with my brothers or sisters before he would mete out punishment. Whatever the case, he normally talked to the sisters, but for the boys, he often used a more aggressive yet compassionate discipline.

My daddy did all the shopping for groceries and other household items. It's amazing how he did all these things when he never owned a car. He didn't have a checking account. He paid all his bills in person, with cash, even purchases that most people would transact through the mail. It's a good thing that streetcars ran just about everywhere in the city. This was Daddy's mode of travel to anywhere he wanted to go.

Daddy frequently went hunting for rabbits, and he often took me. While he was hunting, I would pick strawberries in the close-to- home-yet-isolated spot. It was not a large area as you would expect to see in a forest. It was a hunting site on the outskirts of the city, with trees, tall grass, bushes, creeks, and wild strawberries. It was located near the old Morgan State College, before it was rebuilt—an out-of-the-way place.

When we returned home, if we were lucky enough to have caught and picked anything, Mama would prepare a delicious meal with it.

Daddy was a "homemade" horticulturist. His house had a nice-size backyard, with a lawn in the front. He planted flowers and raised various vegetables in the backyard. He had the most beautiful flowers. He grew tomatoes, cucumbers, onions, and string beans, often enough to cook. In the front of his house, the lawn was always meticulously manicured. We would sit on the front porch overlooking the lawn and talk about how well the grass was kept.

Daddy did not have discretionary money, but he always found ways to ensure everyone was happy on Christmas. We could always expect a live Christmas tree, with presents for everyone beneath it. As we opened our gifts, he would sit on the couch with Mama and smile at our reactions.

Daddy was not only my father, but he was my savior. I always did my best to please him. Daddy always suggested that I would make a good lawyer. I tried very hard to please him. As a matter of fact, after I graduated from the University of Maryland, I took the LSAT exam, necessary before attending law school.

At that time I was working for the personnel officer in the Federal Aviation Agency. I told him that I had taken the LSAT and that I was considering attending law school. I told him I was considering two options: (1) continue working and attend law school at night, or (2) resign from the GS-14 position I held at that time and attend law school full time. If I did the former, it would take about seven years to graduate from law school; the latter would take three to four years.

The personnel officer strongly counseled me to do neither but to continue my career in the federal government. He advised that with my outstanding work record to date, there was reason to believe I could rise much higher in the federal government. Besides, he said, if I elected to go to law school and later tried to reenter the federal government, the best I could hope for would be a lower grade, perhaps at the GS-9 or maybe GS-12 level at the highest.

Given this counseling, I was convinced that getting a law degree was not a good idea for me. That was part of the reason I didn't attempt to become a lawyer, as Daddy had hoped, but under the circumstances, I think he might have said, "That's OK, son."

For a long time my daddy also called me "Lil Bra," as Mama did. But for some reason, when he met Jean, my wife, he started calling me Walter. Daddy really adored Jean.

Daddy was my mentor and role model. A devoted family man, he was a tender and affectionate father. He always said the right things at the right time. His sage advice and inspiring praise guided me throughout my life. His teachings challenged me to reach for higher ground. Daddy was the quick in my step, the heart in my soul, and the strength in my conviction. He passed away in 2000 at the age of ninety-five. He was an inspiration to me. I shall always remember him as my mentor and loving hero.

My family was honored that the coast guard commandant Admiral James Loy took time out from his busy schedule to attend Daddy's funeral ceremony in Baltimore. After the funeral, and when I returned to work, Admiral Loy came to my office to talk about Daddy and extend more condolences.

Chapter 1

Growing Up in Macon, North Carolina, 1930–1932

I WAS BORN ON FEBRUARY 17, 1930, IN MACON, NORTH CAROLINA. Macon is located in Warren County in the northeastern part of the state. My oldest sister, Nancy, has said that when I was born, the city of Macon was noted mostly for its tobacco and cotton crops and chicken and pig farming.

Mama, Daddy, Nancy, and I lived in a big house with my grandfather James Somerville, grandmother Anna Somerville, uncle James Somerville, uncle Robert Somerville, aunt Mary Somerville, aunt Effie Somerville, uncle William Somerville, and aunt Nancy Somerville. My father was the sixth child of seven brothers and sisters in the Somerville family. James and Anna Somerville, my father's parents, were the patriarch and matriarch of the family.

None of my aunts and uncles living in the house was married. Each family or unmarried person had a separate room. For example, my mother, father, Nancy, and I lived in one room of the big house. The house had eight rooms, along with a kitchen with a steel stove for cooking and a parlor for lounging. The house had no indoor plumbing or running water. Biological functions were cared for outside the house (in outhouses) during the day. Chamber pots were kept inside for us at night. Water was pumped from a well dug outside of the house. If warm water was desired for bathing or other purposes, it was heated in a stainless-steel container on a steel stove furnished with wood and coal. The house had a bathtub. It was customary for everyone in the house to bathe on Saturday.

My mother, Bettie Lou (Hunt) Somerville, was born in Wise, North Carolina. Her parents were Nicholas and Anna Hunt. She was the second of six children—they were Nicholas, Mama, Melvin, Lafayette, Flossie, and Jessie.

Mama attended elementary school in Wise, completing the eighth grade. After marriage and with my father's insistence, she became a traditional housewife. She didn't work outside the home; she took care of our family. Her daily routines involved washing on a washing board on Mondays, ironing on Tuesdays, and doing odds and ends throughout the rest of the week, except for Saturday and Sunday. On Saturday, she went to the local country store with my father to buy food items that could not be grown on the farm and nonfood supplies. Saturday also was a special cooking day. She cooked the meals we ate on Sunday. On Sunday she spent most of the day in church. My mother was a religious person, owing to her Baptist faith and religious teachings. She was a loyal member of Locust Grove Baptist Church, where she met my father and eventually married him.

My father, Walter Raleigh Somerville, was born in Macon, North Carolina. He attended elementary school in Wise, North Carolina, and he also completed the eighth grade. He was called upon early to work and help provide for the Somerville family. He was the breadwinner of our family; as mentioned, he didn't allow my mother to work.

My father raised vegetables and chickens on the family farm. To earn money, he worked during the week as a laborer, picking cotton and tobacco and raising pigs. The wages were minimal but enough for the family to get by after purchasing staples and other items at the country store on Saturdays.

My father was the disciplinarian of the family, although with only two infant children, he did not have much to do in that regard until later in life, when my sister and I were joined by four siblings. My father also attended church regularly. He was an active member of Pine Grove Baptist Church. His church and Locust Grove Baptist

Church, in Wise, where my mother attended, often held Sunday services together.

While living in the big house with so many relatives and not being able to plan for the future of our family, my father decided we should leave North Carolina in the early 1930s—this was after I was born. We didn't own much of anything, so it was not too difficult for my family to pack up and go.

Chapter 2

Growing Up in Sykesville, Maryland, 1932–1936

WE MOVED TO SYKESVILLE IN CARROLL COUNTY, MARY LAND. I'M not certain what mode of transportation took us there, but my sister Nancy recalled that a man named Mr. Bennett persuaded my father to come to Sykesville to work for him.

Mr. Bennett must have been a generous man. He put us up in a two-room house with a wood stove. It had no indoor plumbing, just an outhouse consisting of an ash pile. My mother's first impression of the house was a negative one, as the house had been neglected. It was covered with weeds and other debris and looked as though no one had lived there for some time.

My mother was so unhappy with the house and the situation we found ourselves in that she broke down and cried. What were we in for now? Thank goodness my father worked on the house, cleaning it up and clearing away the weeds and debris, and it soon became acceptable to my mother. My father must have been happy with this, so much so that he was able to get our family established in this new location. Of course, I was too young at the time to understand what was going on, but my sister, who was a few years older, quickly grew to like our new home and its surroundings.

Daddy went to work every morning at Mr. Bennett's house, where he tended the cattle. He returned home for lunch and then went back to Mr. Bennett's farm to work for the remainder of the day. This was his daily routine, Monday through Friday. It was not the most interesting job, but it served its purpose at the time, which was for Daddy to provide for his family as best he could.

The house we lived in was a small two-room dwelling—a big kitchen and one bedroom. Outside we had a chicken coop, pigpen,

vegetable garden, and fruit trees. The house had a porch that wrapped around it. A water pump was there for drawing water. It was a place to live but nothing special. Nancy enjoyed growing up there.

A one-room schoolhouse was within walking distance, and I started there in 1935 when I was five years old. My sister often told the tale that I was so familiar with some of the livestock on the farm that a pig once followed me to school. (This tale may be worth telling, but there is no evidence that it's true.)

The church was close to our house, as was the main highway. The family went to church every Sunday. My father was a deacon at the church. We had church friends, including the Shepherds. The Shepherd family had children, and so my sister would sometimes spend the night at their house. This was a good thing for our family because it freed up more room in the house for my father, mother, and me. We had no car. Routine travel was by a horse-driven wagon.

My mother would sew, prepare three daily meals, wash clothes, iron, and perform the other chores around the house. While she was doing all these necessary things, my sister and I were around getting on everybody's nerves, inside and outside the house.

The family grew while we lived in that house. My brother James was born in the house on November 17, 1933. My sister Bessie was born in 1936. Our family quickly outgrew the house.

Chapter 3

Growing Up in Baltimore, Maryland, 1936–1951

IN 1936, RIGHT AFTER BESSIE WAS BORN, MY FATHER MOVED TO Baltimore when he got a job working for the Western Maryland Railroad. My cousin John Somerville, known as Bossy, arranged for Daddy to get the job. John was kind enough to let us live with him on East Madison Street in Baltimore until my father found a place for our family to live.

We joined the Faith Baptist Church, two blocks away, on Ashland Avenue and Bond Street, shortly after we moved to Baltimore. My mother enrolled Nancy and me in Dunbar Elementary School at the beginning of the school year in 1936.

The school was located at North Caroline and McElderry Streets, about two blocks away from where we lived with cousin Bossy. In 1937, we moved into a house in the 1200 block of North Dallas Street, about six blocks from where we were staying. In 1940, my family moved to North Bethel Street, about three blocks from our North Dallas Street residence. Richard and Roland, a set of twins, were added to the family the same year.

The house at 1404 North Bethel Street was a two-level dwelling with an unfinished basement. It had three bedrooms with a bathtub on the upper level. The bathtub was situated in the same area as one of the bedrooms. Only cold water was available for use in the bathtub. On the first level was a living room and a kitchen/dining room combination. A piano sat in the living room. In the kitchen area, there was a stove and an ice box. The stove was made of steel and was fired up to heat up with coal. The ice box was cooled with blocks of ice that my father purchased daily from the ice man, who came around on a horse-driven wagon.

The house had a backyard that was part cement and part dirt. The toilet/outhouse was located in the backyard. This is where everyone in the family had to go for a bowel movement throughout the year—summer, fall, winter, and spring—regardless of the weather conditions. Going to the outdoor toilet was a horrible experience. If there was one thing I disliked about the house, it was the outdoor toilet.

The house had a large basement that spanned the length and width of the first-floor level, but it was dark, cold, and dreary, with dim lighting and a dirt floor. My father would preserve peaches and apples in jars and store them in the basement for fermenting. The fruit jars were opened for eating around Christmas. On occasion, Christmas gifts for us were purchased early and hidden in the basement until my father surprised us with the gifts.

The 1400 block of North Bethel Street was unique, as it was a dead-end section of the street. The only entrance was off East Oliver Street. At the east corner of East Oliver and North Bethel Streets was an all-purpose store owned by a Caucasian family. Halfway down the block on the east side was a one-block street, Llewellyn Avenue that ran east and west. Llewellyn Avenue had a cobblestone surface.

On the northeast corner of Llewellyn Avenue was a grocery store owned by a Jewish family. This is where my father did most of his shopping, buying items on credit. He would charge anything, from costing a penny to much more in value, when he did not have the cash to purchase things outright. The store owner allowed my father to maintain a running tab that was paid off once a week.

At the south end of Bethel Street was Hoffman Street. Hoffman Street was also a dead-end street. The only way to exit Bethel Street was to turn east on to Hoffman Street. An Italian family lived on the southeast side of Hoffman Street. Directly across from Hoffman Street was a railroad track; it was south of Hoffman Street. The railroad track was partly partitioned off by a wire fence that ran the length of Hoffman Street.

On the west side of Bethel Street were houses that stretched about three-quarters the distance of the street, which was approximately one and a half times the length of a football field. A dirt plot made up the remaining portion of the street, and we spent a lot of time playing games there, such as shooting marbles for keeps. There were no houses on the east side of Bethel Street, just a paved walkway in some sections of the street.

In the back of our house was an alley that ran the length of Bethel Street, from Oliver Street on the north end to Hoffman Street on the south end. We often used the alley when walking to and from to our house because it was closer than entering and leaving from the front entrance on Bethel Street.

This area is where I lived from 1940 until I joined the United States Air Force in June 1951. Nothing much changed during the eleven years I lived on North Bethel Street.

The 1400 block of Bethel Street was my playground, but there were pros and cons associated with it. No one living on the block owned a vehicle during most of the time I lived there. The only vehicles that routinely traveled this dead-end street during my early years were horse-driven wagons selling merchandise (ice, fruit and vegetables, etc.) and visitors from outside the neighborhood who may have had cars. There was very little traffic. This allowed us to spend lots of time playing in the street. When I was growing up, we played handball and touch football, using just about the entire street as the playing area.

One Christmas my father bought me a set of boxing gloves. Another boy around my age and I would put on the gloves and box in the middle of the street. The neighbors would look out from windows and doorways or come out on the stoops to cheer us on. Our boxing became such a hit that we passed the word up and down the block to let the neighbors know when we planned to box together again.

Boxing was very popular then because that was when Joe Louis could be heard boxing on the radio.

Our touch football games were a big hit with all the neighbors. Guys my age—or sometimes older—came around to play. We would choose up sides and play the game, using the entire block from East Hoffman

Street to East Oliver Street as our playing field. The neighbors crowded along the sidewalk to watch the game and cheer on the teams. Playing the game sometimes filled an evening or even entire weekends when I had nothing else to do or when Mama allowed me to play outside the house.

Shooting marbles on the dirt was another treasured pastime. This activity became so popular that hundreds and hundreds of marbles were exchanged between the best marble shooters in the neighborhood. There were times when I had so many marbles that there was no place to keep them in the house. I exchanged them with friends for candy or something else of equivalent value, just to get rid of them. Then I would win them back from shooters less skillful than me.

We also played handball using most of the Bethel Street area. The neighbors would come out to observe the game, as they did when we played touch football. We used one of our hands to hold the ball and then hit it with the other hand, trying to place it where no one could catch it. We then ran the designated bases, from home plate to first base to second base to third base and back to home to score a run. The object of the game was to catch the ball and throw it to the base before the "batter" could reach the base. There were very few home runs, with the exception of the guys with great strength, who would get lucky and hit the ball over the outfielder's head.

These outdoor games attracted lots of neighbors who seemed to enjoy watching us play. There was probably not much more to do during most of the time I lived on Bethel Street, but playing these games was lots of fun. Persons living as far away as ten to twelve blocks would come to play or watch the games. The 1400 block of Bethel Street was the place to be if you enjoyed such games.

I did lots of things to earn money when I was growing up. On Saturdays when I was young, my mother would require my sister and me to scrub the floors of the kitchen and dining rooms. They were covered with linoleum, so this was not difficult to do. My sister and I, however, would tussle over which one of us would use the better cloths. My mother always took pleasure in observing our banter. Nancy scrubbed one half, and I scrubbed the other. After we finished our chores, Mama would give us money to go to the movies.

I liked to go to the Dunbar movie theater, about seven blocks away on Central Avenue. I got there when the movie opened around eleven o'clock and stayed until just before it closed or until the beginning of the last movie for that day. In between shows, I would find a good aisle seat, and when the theater got crowded, I would offer my seat for sale. I did this so frequently that I had "regulars" who came to the movies on Saturday, looking to buy a seat from me. When I sold one seat, I would stand in the back and wait for someone to leave; then I would take that seat and hold it for sale to someone else who was willing to give me some small change.

I got to know the manager of the theater and he allowed me to do what I was doing. On a good day, I would take home about two dollars or more from selling seats. Of course, I gave half of the money to Mama because during those days, my family was going through some hard times. Two dollars was a lot of money in my early days.

I had a shoeshine route that I worked on the weekends. My father built me a shoeshine box, which I still have. It's a treasured collection. I used it for many years when I was working my shoeshine route, which stretched from Asquith Street and Harford Avenue to Gorsuch Avenue, a distance of two or more miles.

During those days there were many bars and taverns located on Harford Avenue, the distance I walked. I would go in every bar and

tavern and offer to shine shoes. Many men would give me business because if there was one thing that pleased them, it was a well- shined shoe. All of my clientele were white men. During those days, very seldom would you see a woman in a bar or tavern because most of the customers stood up at the bar and drank whiskey poured in a shot glass.

Most of the men I serviced were very friendly, and they would give me good tips, especially if they had been drinking very much. This was in 1944 and 1945, when discrimination was an accepted way of life in most urban cities, but most of my clientele were very nice to me. The most troubling situation I faced was when half-drunk white men would rub my head and call me *boy*. This didn't bother me at the time because I didn't know what discrimination was in those days, and I was happy if the men gave me a nice piece of change. I was pleased about the money

I earned and paid less attention to their behavior and actions. I did very well with shining shoes.

I was about fourteen during the summer of 1944. My father asked my cousin, who lived up the street from us, if he would get me an easy job during the summer. My cousin was a foreman on a construction project not too far from where we lived. He agreed to give me a job working on his project.

We left home very early in the morning, before sunup. I can't recall if we walked to the construction site or rode. When we got there, my cousin called all the workers together and told them what their tasks were for the day. He asked me to take a shovel and go with him. I started out with him, but I did not know what I would be doing, especially since he had told my father that he would find a light job for me. When my cousin walked off and left me by myself, I put down the shovel and walked all the way back home without telling him I was leaving or why.

Later that evening, my cousin came to see my father and asked why I'd left the work site. Of course, my father didn't know, so he called me in and asked me. I said that I had anticipated hard labor, despite their thinking that I would be given something light to do.

"That was my intent," my cousin said, "but you left in such a hurry that I didn't have a chance to get you started. I only wanted you to carry water to the men when they needed a drink."

I said, "That wasn't clear to me because you asked me to pick up a shovel and follow you."

"I gave you the shovel in the presence of the other workers because I didn't want them to think you were getting off easy while they worked at hard jobs," my cousin said. "I didn't want them to see you getting any special treatment."

"I don't want to do that kind of work," I said. "I don't want to go back, regardless of what might be in store for me."

This experience convinced me that working as a laborer was not what I wanted to do for a living. It enlightened my understanding of what my father was doing in his job, working as a laborer with the Western

Maryland Railroad. And I resolved at this early age to do whatever I could to make things easier for my father. But I still didn't want a laborer's job.

When I was fifteen, just after school let out for the summer break, I got a part-time job at the Holtite Manufacturing Company, a rubber-producing industry. I had persuaded one of my female friends, Dickie, to change the numbers on my birth certificate from 1930 to 1929. Dickie was the only person in the neighborhood who owned a typewriter. She made the change for me so it appeared I was sixteen—old enough to get a job.

I worked at Holtite that summer, earning seventy-five cents an hour, which was big money at that time. When school resumed in the fall, I continued to work there, though I don't know how I convinced my parents that I should continue working instead of going back to school. It might have been that I was helping out with household expenses, and that took some of the financial pressure off my father. I knew Daddy could use my help. This was just after the end of the recession in 1945, when my father was working two jobs to take care of the family. It was a brief absence from school for me, however; I returned in the fall of 1946.

I worked part-time at a drugstore during my last two years in high school. The drugstore was located at the corner of East Preston and North Caroline Streets. This was about four blocks from where I lived on North Bethel Street.

My tasks at the drugstore including working at the counter, selling merchandise, and cleaning up just before the store closed. I worked about two hours after school and more hours on the weekends when I wasn't playing baseball.

The fun thing about this job was that I got to eat a lot from the drugstore soda fountain—candy and ice cream. My favorite was the chocolate nut sundae, made with vanilla ice cream, walnuts, and chocolate syrup. Every night before I left for home, I would prepare a huge chocolate nut sundae to take with me. My family members waited for me to get home so that I could share the sundae with them. I knew that would leave me a very small portion, so before I left work, I would have a sundae at the store just for me. The take- out was for the family.

Going to School in Baltimore, Maryland: 1936–1948

From 1936 to 1948, I attended the Baltimore Public Schools. I attended Dunbar Elementary, Junior High and Senior High, except for six months at Carver Vocational High School from January to June 1946.

All of the Dunbar schools were located on the same grounds at Caroline and McElderry Streets in Baltimore. Carver was located across town in West Baltimore. I started out in Dunbar Elementary in the first grade. Walking to school was very convenient for me because the school was only three blocks from where we lived. In 1937 we moved to the 1200 block of North Dallas Street, which was about six blocks from where we had formerly lived and nine blocks from Dunbar Elementary School. Because we had very little discretionary money, I still had to walk to school. In 1940, we moved to the 1400 block of North Bethel Street, about twelve blocks from the school.

Elementary school left me with very few memories. We studied reading, writing, and arithmetic. I remember our history teacher, Ms. Fisher. She was a very small woman, about five feet tall, but she was very professional and was strict with discipline. She taught us Lincoln's Gettysburg Address, which we had to memorize and recite in class. If we missed anything or got a word wrong, Ms. Fisher would sit us in the corner of the classroom as punishment until the class period was over. Then she would say, "Go home, study the address, and be prepared to recite it in class correctly tomorrow."

In addition to the Gettysburg Address, I learned more from this teacher than I did from any other in the elementary school. Ms. Fisher was known for applying discipline by taking a ruler and tapping students on their hands if they got out of line for any reason.

I must have done well in all my classes in elementary school because I was selected to skip the second half of the sixth grade and advance to the lower half of the seventh grade. In Dunbar, class grades were split into two parts, lower half and upper half. For example, there was class 1-A lower half and 1-B upper half. We had to successfully complete both halves before passing on to the next grade, which would be the second grade, lower half. This progression in passing from one grade to the next was true for all grades at Dunbar and Carver, from first grade to the twelfth.

To skip a half grade and advance to the next grade, I was required to attend summer school, held at Morgan State College (now Morgan State University) in Baltimore. Getting to the college was a physical challenge because it was located about one mile from where we lived and I did not always have money to ride the local public bus, so I had to walk most of the time. We studied advanced courses during the summer session. I successfully completed summer school and was advanced to the seventh grade at the beginning of the school year.

The junior high school—grades seven through nine—was located on the same grounds but in a different building. During this time my grades were noteworthy, as I was once again was chosen to skip the upper half of ninth grade (9-B) and advance to the lower half of tenth grade (10-A). As before, I had to attend a summer school program at Morgan State College, which I successfully completed and passed on to 10-A.

At that time, I was fourteen. I ran track in the Dunbar High School program. I ran the sixty-yard dash, competing against other high schools in the Baltimore, Annapolis, and Washington, DC, areas. I completed the tenth grade, both A and B levels, and then I dropped out of school to work at the Holtite Manufacturing Company. As I've mentioned, I wanted to help my father with household expenses because he was working two jobs—at the Western Maryland Railroad and at the laundry. Even working two jobs did not enable my father to bring home enough money to take care of the family, which had grown to eight persons. Since I was the second oldest child, I felt a responsibility to help out.

In January 1946, after I had saved some money, I returned to high school at George Washington Carver Vocational High School. Because I was changing schools, I had to reenter in the tenth grade (10-B). That didn't matter to me because I had developed an interest in baseball. This would give me three years of baseball instead of two, had I entered in the eleventh grade.

During my time at Carver, I took up tailoring. I tailored a pair of pants. My grades were so good that the English teacher told me I should go back to Dunbar, which was considered an academic school that provided all the necessary courses to prepare students for college.

I played baseball during the half year I was at Carver and stood out as a pitcher. I was so popular that the coach, Zodi White, praised me and treated me as a very special student. He too advised me to go back to Dunbar, where I could not only exercise my baseball skills but also take classes that would prepare me for college.

The reason I went to Carver was because the school was noted for having an excellent sports program, much better than Dunbar and Douglass, the academic schools. Carver was a technical school, and few Carver graduates went on to college. Nevertheless, I enjoyed my brief time at Carver, although we never won an intramural championship. I did, however, benefit from the playing baseball because I perfected my pitching skills and had a chance to play third base as well.

I returned to Dunbar High School at the beginning of the 1946–47 school year. I reentered in the eleventh grade, 11-A, and took advanced classes in mathematics. My math teacher was named Enolia Williams. She took an interest in me and offered to tutor me after school on the theory and practical aspects of math at the eleventh-grade level. She invited me to spent weekends at her home, subject to my parents' approval of course. My parents agreed. I spent several weekends at my math teacher's home, studying math. I developed a good relationship with her, and she remained my tutor until I graduated in June 1948.

Spending weekends with my math teacher had some pros and cons. The pros were that it afforded me an opportunity to gain proficiency in math, and this became my favorite subject in high school. Also, staying with her gave me an opportunity to be away from home and be privileged to use indoor plumbing. This was great because my parents' house still did not have indoor plumbing.

The cons were there too, but they were accepted with pleasure since I was an adventurous teenager. My teacher assigned me chores. Inside the house I cleaned and mopped the floors; outdoor chores involved cutting the grass with a push mower. The lawn had a slight hill, which made it doubly hard to navigate the lawn mower. But this didn't bother me, as I wanted to show my teacher how manly I was.

As I look back, I wonder now if she had an agenda. She tutored me at no expense, but on the other hand, I mowed the lawn without remuneration. My conclusion is that this was a win/win situation, as my teacher benefited but so did I. We each made a contribution to the well-being of the other. I believe Enolia Williams had as much influence as my parents in keeping me in school until I graduated.

During eleventh and twelfth grades, I played baseball. Dunbar played intercity schools (Carver and Douglas), Bates in Annapolis, and high schools in Washington, DC. The Washington, DC, high schools included Armstrong, Dunbar, Phelps, and Cardozo. Playing the Annapolis and Washington, DC, schools gave the players a chance to travel outside of Baltimore. This was a treat for many of us because we had not experienced life in the locations we visited to play baseball. Playing baseball opened up a whole new world for me. It inspired me to study hard, keep up my grades, and, above all, stay in school so I could play baseball, the one sport I truly loved.

In my junior and senior years of high school, I could hardly wait for baseball season to arrive. Playing baseball gave me a thrill I will always cherish. I pitched many games and played third base with a passion. Playing two positions enabled me to play in just about every game.

My expertise was in pitching, which I did very well at my age. I learned many of my techniques from being around the Baltimore Elite Giants, the black professional baseball team that played its home games at Bugle Field in Baltimore. The players on that team taught me how to throw four different pitches (fast ball, curve, drop ball or sinker, and "in-shoot" or slider). This made my pitches very effective because most high school players had never seen these kinds of pitches. As a result, I struck out many batters. During my senior year, I pitched a no-hitter against Douglas High in Baltimore. Dunbar won the Negro High School city championship in 1948, the first in the history of the school. It was an honor for me to be a part of this history, and especially the contributions I might have made with my pitching and playing third base as a member of the Dunbar baseball team.

Playing Baseball in Baltimore, Maryland: 1944–1950

I developed a great interest in baseball when I was fourteen. I started going to baseball games at Bugle Field in Baltimore, where the Baltimore Elite Giants played in the Professional Negro Baseball League.

Players on the Elite Giants team were my professional teachers. They taught me the basic techniques and an understanding of how baseball should be played. Their pitchers taught me how to grip and throw a baseball with such deceptive spin that it would be very difficult to hit. Their infield players taught me how to handle and field baseballs hit hard to them. They taught me how to field and release the ball to effectively throw out a player running to first base. They taught me how to field a ball and initiate a throw to second base to start a double play and how to receive a throw from a player and release it to first base to complete a double play. What I learned was that playing the game was not as easy as it looked when sitting in the grandstands. A baseball player has to not only know the game but be prepared to play it at a highly skillful level in order to be effective in every aspect of the game, as well as the position played.

I was lucky to have had such professional players teaching me how to pitch and play the infield. Among some of my teachers playing for the Baltimore Elite Giants (BEG) were Joe Black (pitcher), Junior Gilliam (second baseman), Pee Wee Butts (shortstop), Roy Campanella (catcher), and several others. It is interesting to note that several BEG players went on to play in the National and American Leagues. Some of the players were even selected to join other outstanding Major League players in the renowned Hall of Fame.

There is one story involving Roy Campanella that I think is worth mentioning. It just happened that I was fielding balls in the infield when the players were taking batting practice. I was stationed around third base. Roy was batting. He hit a "hard to handle" baseball down the third-base line that I attempted to field with my cheap baseball glove. When the ball hit my glove, the glove disintegrated, with pieces flying all over the field.

Roy came down to see if I was all right. He said, "Boy, you need to get a better glove if you intend to play baseball." I was speechless. Then he asked, "When will you be back at the park?"

"Just about every time the team plays," I told him.

The next time I saw Roy at the park, he gave me a gift—the best-looking glove anyone could ask for. I thanked him profusely. When I showed it to my family they were surprised and overjoyed to see what Roy had given me. I showed it to everyone I could and played with it throughout my entire amateur baseball career, even when I was pitching. What the BEG players taught me at Bugle Field was amazing.

The ball field was located at Federal Street and Edmonson Avenue, about a mile from where I lived, and I normally walked there and back. In order to get into the ball park, I got there early enough to be selected to pick up the soda and beer bottles the patrons discarded under the bleachers, or I stood outside the ball park until a foul ball was hit out of the park. Retrieving a foul ball and turning it in to the gatekeeper served as free admission to see the ball game.

I liked being selected to pick up discarded bottles and cans because not only could I see the entire game, but I earned a few dollars as well. It also afforded an opportunity to mingle with the ball players and catch balls in the infield and outfield during batting practice before the game started. The downside to this was that if I wanted to get paid, I could not leave until the game was over and all the bottles and cans had been picked up from under the bleacher seats. Then there was another downside. Getting home could be a costly matter if the game wasn't played during the early daylight hours. Games played later in the day or evening meant I'd have to spend some of the money earned to catch a bus due to the late hour.

Interacting with the professional baseball players before the games at Bugle Field gave me a profound interest in baseball that has lasted until today. The players taught me how to play the game as a professional player would. I learned to play infield positions (second base, shortstop, and third base). But most important, I learned how to pitch by throwing breaking balls, allowing me to perfect the skill of pitching at an early age. I believe I was the only fourteen-year-old in the Baltimore area who could throw as many different kinds of pitches as I could. That's why the coaches at Dunbar and Carver High Schools and the manager of the sandlot Dolphin AC baseball team approached me to play for their organizations.

I began playing sandlot baseball with the Dolphin AC in 1945. Richard Doswell was manager of the sandlot team. He was a very generous man. He ensured that his players were taken care of not only on the baseball field but also in their daily lives. Richard was a dessert chef at a local restaurant. At times he would take me and other players to his job at night and allow us to help him prepare jelly doughnuts to be sold at the restaurant the next day.

He would prepare sandwiches and hamburgers and bring them to practice sessions to encourage our players to come to practice on time. He was committed to having the best amateur baseball team in Baltimore. He recruited players from the high schools and any other places where he could identify amateur players who had demonstrated good baseball skills. Most of his players were recruited from Dunbar High School. Among the players recruited from Dunbar were a catcher, a first baseman, a second baseman, several pitchers, and outfielders. He managed the players as if they were professionals.

Our team practiced during the week after school. We played games on Sundays. If I wasn't pitching, I played third base. Most of our games were played in public parks: Druid Hill Park, Clifton Park, Carroll Park, Swan Park, and Waverly Park in Baltimore City. We played in the Monumental Unlimited Baseball League, which was part of the Bureau of Recreation, Baltimore City Amateur Athletic Association.

In 1945 this league was composed of eight teams; in subsequent years it expanded to include many more teams. In addition to the Baltimore City teams, we occasionally played teams located in the surrounding suburbs. Most of the players on our team and the opposing teams were of high school age or a few years older. Our games started at two o'clock on Sunday afternoon for the early games or after four o'clock for the later games, which were considered the most important games of the day. We played at least twelve games a year, usually more, in league play, including double- headers occasionally.

The Dolphin AC team won the Baltimore Amateur Athletic Association (BAAA) championship in 1945. Recognition of this accomplishment was acknowledged by the white commissioner of the newly created Division of Amateur Sports in Baltimore City. The presentation of the trophy—a large sterling silver loving cup—was given to our manager by the *Baltimore Afro-American* editor, who stated, "My only wish is that this trophy is going to the best team in the city, not just the best colored team."

The white commissioner responed, "The challenge by the *Afro* editor is certainly a fine opportunity for the people of Baltimore to show what real brotherhood and Christianity mean. However, we, as a public institution, find it difficult to take the lead in such an undertaking. That leadership must come from private minds and interested organizations, like the BAAA."

The commissioner's statement was not only optimistic but powerful at that time, when there was authorized segregation. I applaud his commitment to opening up a discussion on ending segregation in sandlot baseball in Baltimore City. (*Note*: The *Baltimore Afro-American* newspaper was founded by John Henry Murphy Sr., an African American, in August 1892, to cover news events in the African American community.)

Our baseball manager was very passionate about baseball. He had contacts in eastern Maryland and Washington, DC, and he often arranged for us to travel to those locations to play games as well. When playing outside the city, we sometimes would travel in straw- filled trucks, if that was the only way to get to where we were going, because none of us, except for the manager, had a car at that time.

I played sandlot baseball from 1945 to 1949. During that time, I enjoyed some noteworthy experiences. I acquired the nickname Beaver on one occasion, when I pitched a no-hitter in Druid Hill Park before a large crowd of people. The news went viral throughout colored neighborhoods. This was a rare event for most people in colored communities to hear about, especially those who knew me as a baseball player in Baltimore City. A fan commented, "I knew you were a good pitcher, but I didn't know you were that good."

On the day of the no-hitter, I broke a bat. Because of that, some people thought I should be given an analogous code name. I had broken bats before. The manager gave me the nickname of Beaver, an animal that chews wood, a metaphor for breaking bats. Since then, people have publicly referred to me as Beaver throughout colored communities in Baltimore City. My family members and friends in Baltimore City still address me as Beaver.

I graduated from Dunbar High School in 1948. And in 1949, before the end of the school year, the Dolphin AC team played an exhibition game against the Dunbar High School baseball team. The game was played in Bugle Field, the home of the National Negro League Baltimore Elite Giants.

To play this game was very special for me. I had recently graduated, and this was the same year that Dunbar won the intramural colored high school city championship. I persuaded the Dolphin AC manager to get a game with Dunbar High School. I thought it would be fun to play the school from which I had just graduated. Besides I had never played in a ball park where people paid an admission fee to watch the game.

I urged a number of people to watch the game. My father and one of my sisters attended the game. I purchased tickets (as many as I could afford) for relatives and friends, so they could watch me pitch. The entrance fee was not much, a very small charge at that time. We had great attendance at the game—former Dunbar classmates who had not yet graduated, family members, and friends who followed the Dolphin AC baseball team when we played in public parks, and other people who enjoyed sandlot baseball.

To add excitement to the game, the Dolphin AC manager selected me as the starting pitcher for the Dolphins. The Dunbar baseball coach selected another member of the Dolphins, who had not yet graduated, as the starting pitcher for Dunbar. The pitcher for Dunbar did an excellent job; he did a much better job than I did.

When I started pitching, I was very excited. The first pitch I threw was called a ball.

The ball was thrown so errantly high that it went over the batter's head and landed against the backstop. Eventually, I settled down and started throwing some strikes but still did not do well enough to finish the game. My manager took me out when he observed that I was pitching a bad game. I think he did the right thing, especially if the Dolphins were to win.

The Dolphin AC team eventually won the game. Winning the game spoke well for sandlot baseball, as that level of play was considered only a step above high school baseball.

Moreover, Dunbar had a reputation of producing some good baseball players. For this reason, the Dolphin AC manager had recruited several members of Dunbar's baseball teams to play for the Dolphins over the years.

I really loved playing baseball, especially pitching. I loved it so much that I worked hard at trying to prepare myself to become a professional baseball player. My manager told me that there were two professional baseball team scouts, one from the Philadelphia Phillies and another from the Brooklyn Dodgers, who were interested in what they had heard about my pitching. I don't know whether they ever came around to watch me, but it was an honor to know that interest in my pitching had risen to the professional level, even though no one personally contacted me. Playing baseball at the professional level was a dream unfulfilled.

Realizing a Daughter Born in Baltimore, 1947

Before I graduated from high school, I fathered a daughter. I was just seventeen years old when the baby was born. She was a wonderful child. Her mother named her Thomasine Angeline Walker, taking her mother's maiden name. I was so young at the time—the father of a baby, still finishing my last year in high school and not having a job to support the baby.

My parents, while shocked and somewhat disappointed in me, took it reasonably well, as you would expect parents to do after learning of such an unjustified development in their son's life. They supported the baby as much as they could with the help of the mother's parents and grandparents and scolded me to finish school and do what a good father is expected to do in raising a newborn baby.

I continued to pursue my interest in baseball, hoping I would get an offer to join the Major League, but that never happened. Prior to graduating from high school, my sandlot baseball manager, Richard Doswell, was grateful enough to give me money from time to time to help out with expenses for the baby. I managed to get through high school and work a short while before joining the United States Air Force, all the while providing some money for the baby as she was growing up. I felt more comfortable in caring financially for the child when I was on active duty in the air force because I took out an allotment, which was sent to the child's mother every month until I got out of the service in 1960.

I regret that I did not see as much of Thomasine as I would have liked during her formative stages. My parents and sisters and brothers, however, did see much more of her than I did. My parents treated her as if she were a member of the family.

When Thomasine finished high school and started working for the US Postal Service, she would stop by my parents' house while delivering mail, and eat her lunch there.

As life evolved, I became closer to Thomasine, especially during family reunion outings. Of course, by that time she had developed into an accomplished young lady. I was fortunate enough to attend some of the important events in her life. I walked her down the aisle when she married Andrew Adams. I attended her indoctrination when she preached her first church sermon ("My Prodigal Child") to become an ordained minister. I attended her graduation from Towson State University when she graduated with a bachelor's degree in 1998.

Thomasine went on to get a master's degree a few years after graduating from the university. She has devoted her life to helping others, with a spiritual emphasis on everything she does. Thomasine accepted a position of chaplain at Johns Hopkins Hospital in Baltimore. She epitomizes a caring and Christian generation of God.

Thomasine has a son from a previous marriage, Lamont Gilliam. He was born in 1966. Lamont is her pride and joy. He enlisted in the United States Army. He made a career of it and now is honorably retired. During the time he spent in the service, he pursued a vigorous education program, obtaining a master's degree in psychology. Since retirement, he has continued his education, working toward a PhD in psychology. His goal is to become a college professor of psychology. With his demeanor and temperament, he would do well in that profession. Lamont is a very creative individual. He also is looking for other ways to make a contribution to our great society and the betterment of humanity.

Working after High School Graduation, 1948–1951

My first full-time job was working for the B&B Auto Supply Store, delivering auto parts. Before I started, I obtained a driver's license after taking lessons from the Easy Method Driving School. The driving instructor would pick me up and take me out on a driving (learning) experience. I must have had about three lessons before I was able to get my driver's license. I was employed with the B&B Auto Supply Store for a short time and then went to work for the Londontown Manufacturing Company, makers of the London Fog rainwear. Londontown paid more money and also provided steady employment. My job was to assist in the manufacturing, stocking, and packing of trench coats. I drove a delivery truck, delivering packages to the post office for shipping and also delivering orders within the city.

Working at this company was my first opportunity to acquire appreciation for what it was like to have a "real job" that paid competitive wages. I also developed a good working relationship with the owner of the business, Mr. Myers, and the company manager, Mr. Margolis. During my time working at the company, I made it possible for most of my friends to purchase the popular London Fog trench coat at a discounted price.

I enjoyed working and playing baseball at the time. But I began to realize that the Londontown job was not going to last. After all, it was only a small business operation. Also, I didn't think my chances of becoming a professional baseball player were all that good. What was I to do in the long run, considering that I had a child that must be cared for at this time? The jobs I'd had thus far would not take me very far. So I started considering other options.

The best thing that ever happened to me was when my father suggested I join the military and become a man. This was a powerful message at the time because my wish was to get a college degree and then a job working as a personnel officer. I still don't know why I wanted to become a personnel officer, but that's what I thought I wanted to do. My father, on the other hand, thought I would make a good lawyer.

My friend Alvin Coleman, who lived around the corner from me, also was thinking about the future. Alvin was the same age as I was. As a matter of fact, we shared a birthday. He was a good friend from high school.

Standing six feet tall or more, Alvin was a good basketball player. He excelled in that sport. At the time, he had no hopes of becoming a professional basketball player. He was very popular in the neighborhood. He owned a yellow Buick convertible.

Alvin and I had talked several times about the prospects of being drafted into the army. Neither of us cherished that thought. So one day, we went downtown, took the Armed Forces Qualification Test (AFQT), passed it, and enlisted in the United States Air Force.

I don't know about his family, but my father was elated when I told him the news. Being in the military service would get me off the streets and give me an opportunity to do something meaningful with my life.

Chapter 4

Serving in the United States Air Force, 1951–1960

AFTER ENLISTING IN THE UNITED STATES AIR FORCE FOR FOUR YEARS, the recruiter gave us several days to get our affairs in order and then report for basic training. We reported to the air force indoctrination station on June 28, 1951, where we were sworn in as new recruits.

I thought about what I had done and then came to the realization that for the next four years, I would be bound by following the directions of the senior people in the United States Air Force. What I got myself into remained to be experienced. I was somewhat curious but anxious about the future.

We were sent to Sampson Air Force Base in Ithaca, New York, for eight weeks of basic training. The air force must have needed recruits very badly because this new facility had just opened and the training was reduced from sixteen week, as it was conducted at Lackland Air Force Base in San Antonio, Texas, to eight weeks at Sampson. This was fine with me because I was ready to get started as a specialist of some sort in the service.

We spent a very busy eight weeks at Sampson AFB. The first thing we had to do was memorize our Air Force Service Number (AFSN). I believe I learned mine the first night I was there and have never forgotten it, even to this day. When I talk to Alvin now—he is married and living in Spain—we begin our conversations by stating our names and reciting our eight-digit AFSN, a badge of honor.

After successfully completing basic training, I was sent off to a USAF administrative training school at the New Mexico Highlands University, located in Las Vegas, New Mexico. This is when Alvin and I were separated. He must have had a different test score battery because he was sent to an air traffic controller technical school. He enjoyed the training and his career as an air traffic control operator so much that he stayed in the service long enough to retire in that career field.

I attended the administrative training program at the university for twelve weeks. I learned to type and was taught other college courses that related to administrative management. After successfully completing the program, I received a diploma in administrative management and some college equivalency credits for courses completed at the university.

Afterward, I was sent to my first duty station at Hamilton AFB in San Francisco, California. There, I met two airmen, and we became very good friends. One airman was a Caucasian, John Terranova, an Italian from Connecticut, and the other was a Native American from the Northwest, although I can't remember his name. We were very good friends and hung out together until I got orders to go to Korea in November 1952.

An interesting story is associated with my getting those orders. The air force squadron had a daily roll call, and at that time we received the orders of the day. One day, the first sergeant read the assignments and ordered a number of airmen to pack their duffel bags and get ready to ship out to Korea. One of the airmen selected shared my barracks. He had just gotten married and told me that he did *not* want to ship out at this time. He wanted to spend some quality time with his new bride. I told him that I would take his place if he could get the first sergeant to agree.

He appealed to the first sergeant, who granted his request, since I had volunteered to take his place. This was possible because the airman most likely had the same technical specialty as I had. This was fine with me. Despite leaving my new friends, I wanted to travel to see as much of the world outside of the United States as I could during my time in the USAF. Given the arrangements just made, I had talked myself into going to Korea during a time of war, although it politically was called the Korean Conflict because United States participation in a war had not been authorized by Congress. When I told my family and high school sweetheart about the orders, they all cried—they could not envision what lay ahead for me.

Performing Tour of Duty in Taegu, Korea, 1952–1953

In November 1952, I boarded a navy ship, USS *General M. C. Meigs*, along with over five thousand other US troops at a port in San Francisco, California. As we sailed under the Golden Gate Bridge as we left San Francisco, I was filled with anxiety and anticipation, not knowing what to expect but also wondering what would happen when I got there. I had very limited training, certainly not as comprehensive as the US Army or the marines. After all, I was just an airman in the United States Air Force.

We sailed for thirty days over the waters of the great Pacific Ocean. There were times when all I could see was water that appeared to meet the sky—no land in sight at all. On board the ship, we slept on bunks, three to five high, in vertical arrangement. I was on the third tier in the compartment where I stayed.

My daily routine was simple throughout the trip: I would eat breakfast and then get in line for lunch and then do the same for dinner. There were so many troops aboard the ship that I was afraid the food would run out before everyone was served; of course that never happened. I took care to make friends with the cooks aboard the ship, as they would bring food back to the sleeping quarters after they finished up for the day.

On the way to Korea, the ship stopped in the Philippines and Guam to restock food and take on other provisions needed to complete the voyage. The troops were not allowed to leave the ship when we stopped, so we stood on deck, exchanging waves with the people who came out on land to greet us.

There was hardly anything to do during the day as we were sailing except watch the water beating against the hull of the vessel. And from time to time, when the ocean was rough, the water would forcefully gush up against the ship. The water surge hit the ship so strongly that it felt as though a whale or other large ocean creature was trying to overturn the boat. Sometimes the water would rush over the ship, causing the troops to return to their quarters in order to avoid the powerfully rushing water.

Besides watching the water, the only other thing taking place was gambling. A group of guys would gather daily and play cards— mostly Blackjack—for money. I watched but did not play because I had very little money to spare.

When the ship crossed the International Date Line in the Pacific Ocean, all members aboard the ship were given a certificate indicating that we had crossed it. I didn't know what that meant but thought it must have been an important development, given that it was worthy of a certificate denoting the accomplishment. (The International Date Line is an imaginary line of navigation on the surface of the earth that runs from the North Pole to the South Pole and demarcates the change of one calendar day to the next.)

After thirty days of sailing, the ship docked at a port in Fukuoka, Japan, where we all debarked. We were assembled on a large outdoor field, according to predetermined arrangements. After taking care of preliminary issues, I was directed to a certain location along with other airmen. Our dog tags were checked to be sure we were who we were supposed to be. Then we were led to a cargo aircraft. We boarded the aircraft and were flown to our duty assignments in South Korea. My duty assignment was located in Taegu, Korea, known as K-2, the 154th Fighter-Bomber Squadron.

All of us who were scheduled to go to the same duty station were placed on a bus and driven there. My duty assignment was engineering clerk, working directly for the engineering officer, the commander of the 154th Fighter-Bomber Squadron. The mission of the squadron was twofold: (1) train/indoctrinate newly arriving pilots on the T-33 jet, a trainer aircraft, and (2) fly sorties (scheduled flights) on the F-84 fighter-bomber jet, to serve as escorts for other military aircraft or drop bombs in enemy territory.

We were given an orientation about the squadron, which was primarily a training location for pilots. The pilots reported there to get checked out on T-33 fighter-bomber training aircraft, prior to piloting the F-84 fighter-bomber aircraft that flew escort for larger air force bombers, as well as carried bomb payloads destined for enemy attacks. Pilots training on T-33 aircraft carried napalm bombs, designed for training purposes only. Napalm training bombs were not used for attacks on enemy lines.

My responsibilities can be broken down into two major categories. One was as record keeper in the squadron, working for the engineering officer, who was the squadron commanding officer. I kept records on all the personnel assigned to the squadron and also equipment (including aircraft, parts, etc.). The other responsibility was very important. It entailed getting up early in the morning around two o'clock to prepare a report on all the sorties flown and casualties, if any, that had occurred the day before. This information was compiled and reported to our parent command and subsequently to the 8th Fighter-Bomber Wing, the organization that was over all the air force squadrons, groups, and commands in the Korean Theater of Operations. The formatted information had to be sent before four o'clock every morning. Because of the size of our squadron, having two hours to collect all the required information was not a problem. The toughest part of the job was getting up so early in the morning and then trying to go back to sleep in the tent we called home.

I was equipped with all my belongings. I had my metal eating utensils, including a tin plate, which was strapped around my waist and secured with a leather belt. I was supposed to carry this paraphernalia everywhere I went. We ate breakfast, lunch, and dinner at a designated time every day, except on some days when I was working on my morning report, so I had to eat at an awkward time. Most of the meals were C-rations or canned foods, except for Coca-Colas, which were provided by the Coca-Cola Company as their contribution to the war effort.

Of course, I didn't carry my eating utensils into downtown Taegu. I went to town a very few times, as there was not much to see or do there, so going there was not worthwhile. A squadron bus would make runs into town at a certain hours during the day to drop off airmen and then bring them back to the squadron, always before it got dark. Downtown Taegu was off limits at night. When we went into town, we were encouraged to take our side arms. We always went in groups. The Koreans in town were friendly, so there were no problems. The local Koreans referred to the African Americans as *number twos* and the Caucasian Americans as *number ones*. Even the native Koreans working on the base referred to Americans the same way.

Other unpredictable events occurred, like air raids. When the air raid sounded, mostly at night, everyone in the tent had to grab his belongings and rush to the bunker that was set up for air raid safety. While we had air raids most nights before the cease-fire in Korea, I don't recall ever seeing or being told that the North Koreans dropped bombs in the area near where I stayed. At least no one was harmed. If anyone had been harmed, I would have had to report the situation to higher headquarters in my daily morning report.

There was little to do in the squadron except just hang around. Of course, everyone had his assigned responsibilities. The busiest airmen in the squadron were the aircraft mechanics who had to keep the T-33 trainer and F-84 fighter jets in good operating condition. The pilots were assigned sorties that they had to perform daily. I watched the jets take off and land most days when I had nothing else to do.

My job was not as boring as it may sound. The pilots and nonflying airmen organized a softball team on which I played third base. We had fun playing the game. We played among ourselves on a makeshift diamond in the squadron, and we played other US military services in close proximity to us, as far north as Seoul, which was about 250 miles from Taegu (K-2).

We organized an intermural softball league, playing the marines and army soldiers. We could not always keep on schedule because the squadron events of the day took priority over everything else, especially for the pilots who had to fly sorties up around the danger zones in and around Seoul.

Unlike in the States, the enlisted airmen and officers were allowed to fraternize. That's why we were able to organize sports events. We had gatherings for fun. The pilots would take a case of beer up thousands of feet in the atmosphere to cool it, and then we would drink it. What a creative way to have fun and socialize during a time of war!

The engineering officer for whom I worked was a pilot. He didn't fly sorties in combat during the war, but he had to fly a certain number of hours every month in order to get flight pay. He flew the T-33 to get in his flying time.

On several occasions, he would invite me to go along with him on a flight in a T-33, one of the training jets. The jet had two seats, one in the front and one directly in back of the pilot. I would sit in the back seat.

The engineering officer allowed me to operate the instruments, under his supervision, several times; I was actually flying the T-33 jet aircraft.

On one occasion, the engineering officer exposed me to a maneuver I will never forget. He took the jet up thousands of feet and asked me if I was prepared to undertake a "three-G maneuver." A *G maneuver* is when the aircraft descends downward at a certain speed, causing your body to feel the force of gravity, three times the weight of your body.

The engineering officer called for a three-G, and I said, "Let's go for it." The jet took a dive, such that I had never felt anything like it in my life. At three G's, the force pressing on my body was three time my weight. I was able to withstand the three-G force while in the jet, but when we landed, I had a headache lasted far too long to forget the experience. The experience was thrilling, but my body told me that I was not trained or prepared to be a jet pilot, at least until I went through the rigorous pilot-conditioning program.

This experience did not deter me, however, for I accumulated ten to fifteen hours of flying time, flying in the trainee's seat with the engineering officer, during my twelve-month tour of duty in Korea.

Getting mail in Korea was a special thing, knowing that someone back home was thinking about you. All the airmen would assemble daily at a certain time for mail call. And to hear your name called was an extra-special thing. My name was called frequently. My sweetheart wrote me every day, and I would occasionally receive letters from family members and friends.

We often talked about some of the things written in our letters and especially what people had to say about being away from us. We often talked about similar comments in letters we received, as well as things we wrote in the letters we sent home. One airman said he wrote to his wife, "Paint the ceiling the color you like because you will be looking at it for a long time when I get home." Getting mail from home was a big deal. Airmen would become popular in the squadron when they received mail regularly.

After being in Korea for six months, everyone was given time off to leave the war zone. We were flown to Tokyo, Japan, for a full week for "Rest and Recuperation" (R&R). While there, I stayed at a Japanese hotel and spent most of the daylight hours touring the city, taking in the sights.

After completion of our R&R, we were flown back to Korea. During the return flight in a cargo aircraft, something occurred that required the pilot to direct us to put on our life jackets, as we were flying over the Sea of Japan. This momentarily aroused fearful thinking. Having to put on a life jacket generated a problem for me because I did not know how to swim. I don't know why we were asked to do that, but everything turned out all right, and we returned safely to our squadron in Korea.

After R&R, we knew that our tour of duty was half over. Most airmen kept a calendar above their bunks that showed the number of days remaining before they would be eligible to ship out back to the United States. The calendar was called the FIGMO calendar, somewhat vulgar in its definition, but it stood for "Funk You I Got My Orders." This inferred that when the 365 days had expired, the airman had completed his tour of duty and was expected to receive orders to ship back to the good ole' USA. I can't recall anyone being disappointed when that time arrived. If there had been, I would have known, because I usually delivered the written orders to the airmen to travel to their next duty station in the United States.

I was in Korea from November 1952 to November 1953, so I was there in July 1953 when the cease-fire took place. Very little celebration took place when the cease-fire occurred. Some of the squadron's pilots again took cases of beer several thousand feet in the air to get it cold so we could drink and celebrate. All members of the 154th Fighter-Bomber Squadron were awarded the Syngman Rhee Medal for service in Korea during the conflict. Dr. Rhee was president of South Korea at that time. We also received the National Defense Service Medal, a United States citation for service in Korea.

My time was up in November 1953. I departed Taegu and was flown back to Hamilton Air Force Base, California. There, I was given orders to go on leave before reporting to my next duty station, which was Amarillo, Texas.

I hopped a space-available flight on an air force bomber that took me from Hamilton AFB to Andrews AFB, Maryland. That was the coldest flight I have ever experienced. I was flying in the hull of the aircraft, where the bombs would normally be stored. And, of course, there was no heat in that part of the bomber. On top of that, the plane was flying at about thirty thousand feet most of the way. We stopped once to refuel. I could not complain about anything because the flight was based on space available, and this bomber was the only plane scheduled to fly from the West Coast to the East Coast at the time my orders would permit me to fly on a space-available flight. It was a new experience for me. At age twenty-three, I could take it, and what's more, it didn't cost me any money. When we landed at Andrews AFB, Maryland, and I departed the plane, I was fine.

Getting Married While in the United States Air Force, 1953

The first thing I did when I arrived at home in Baltimore was to make arrangements to marry my high school sweetheart. She wrote me nearly every day when I was in Korea. We had written about getting married nearly every day I was abroad. There was not much more to talk about other than to just do it, as we had agreed.

We got married on November 20, 1953, in the sanctuary of the church my wife attended. It was a small wedding. The witnesses were Nancy, my oldest sister, and her boyfriend. Hardly anyone knew about the marriage except her family and mine. We moved in with her parents until it was time for me to report to my next duty station in Amarillo.

Due to an unresolved conflict about career planning and our outlooks for the future, my wife and I decided to separate in 1967. I moved to Washington, DC, where I was working. And we were divorced in 1969.

Performing Tour of Duty in Amarillo, Texas, 1953–1955

I reported to Amarillo Air Force Base in December 1953. This was my first trip to Texas; Amarillo was a new environment. In 1953 segregation was lawful. The military armed forces were integrated, but the local communities were not.

African Americans had limited social life in Amarillo. On base, we could mingle but not in town. There were no movies for African

Americans to attend, other than the outdoor movie, requiring a car to get there. And many African Americans did not have cars on the base. There was one tavern that welcomed African Americans, so many of us would flock there on the weekends.

The air force base sponsored bus rides to and from town during scheduled hours for all airmen who wanted to go to town. The last bus would depart for the base at a certain hour, and if you weren't there to meet it, you could be left without a ride back to the base. I spent most of my time on the base working in the administration, or orderly, room, as it was called in military service, keeping records on airmen assigned to the squadron or organizational unit.

One interesting thing concerning life in Amarillo, was the livestock there and how they were transported to and from various locations. This was the first time I had ever seen cattle being herded into Cadillac automobiles and driven as though they were being chauffeured. Of course, most airmen did not have cars, and to see cattle being driven in luxury cars was an eye-opener for me but maybe not for cattlemen living in Amarillo.

I purchased my first car in 1954. It was a 1952 Buick. I expected a visit from my wife during the summer of 1954. When she arrived in June, after school had let out for the summer, we lived off base in an African American community. I had a duplex unit during the time she was there. And with a car, I could drive to and from work at the base. The car came in handy. We drove around the Amarillo city area. We frequently visited the outdoor movie, the only place African Americans could see a flick. My wife stayed until late August, until it was time for her to return to Baltimore, where she taught elementary school. She rode the Greyhound bus back to Baltimore and later told me the long bus ride was a grueling trip.

With the car, I explored other parts of the country. Some of my airmen friends and I got in the car one evening and drove south of the border to Juarez, Mexico. It was an adventurous trip, driving through parts of New Mexico and then into Mexico, where we spent a short time.

What I recall vividly was that we purchased a bottle of tequila; we wanted to see what it tasted like. What a mistake—for me, anyway. I took one sip, and that was enough for me. We didn't stay in Mexico very long. Shortly after we got back to the base, I developed a headache that must have lasted for two days. I was convinced of the potency of the Mexican tequila. That is the only time I ever drank tequila. Leave it alone—especially if it is being sold across the border in Mexico. But on the other hand, maybe we bought a bad bottle because we purchased it at a kiosk on the sidewalk.

Driving from Amarillo, Texas, to Baltimore, Maryland, 1954

I encountered another interesting experience with my car. Just before Christmas 1954, I drove to Baltimore. Another airman from Baltimore had planned to go with me, but at the last minute, he changed his mind. I was so determined to go home that I did not let that change my mind.

I took off by myself, driving from Amarillo to Baltimore, over 1,600 miles. It was a successful trip, but I was lucky—someone must have been looking over me all the way. I had a map. Following Route 66 to Route 40, I drove all the way to Baltimore, stopping only briefly on the side of the road to catch a nap when I got too sleepy to drive. After a brief nap, I continued on my way. I had planned thirty-two or more hours for the trip, so for nourishment, I had a supply of No Doz tablets and lots of gumdrops.

I traveled through eight states—Texas, Oklahoma, Missouri, Illinois, Indiana, Ohio, Pennsylvania, and Maryland. I drove through the Ozark Mountains in Missouri, where there was no speed limit set for drivers. I drove at a speed that reached nearly ninety miles an hour or more. When I departed the Ozarks and headed for the Illinois border, the generator in the car gave out on me. Luckily, it was daylight. This happened not too far from a repair shop, just at the foot of the Ozark Mountains. I was able to get a new generator and continue on my trip to Baltimore.

I never will forget the scary experience of driving through the Ozark Mountains at night. The car was running out of gas. I came upon a filling station and stopped to get gas. I had to go to the bathroom, so I asked the manager of the station if I could use the bathroom. He told me that colored people could not use his bathroom and that I should find a place to stop along the road in the mountains and do what I had to do.

I started to leave without getting gas there, but common sense told me that there might not be another place available before the car ran out of gas. So I purchased a full tank of gas and went on my way, stopping at an opening along the road to take care my other business. That was the only place I stopped where there were problems getting gas and using the facilities.

I drove on through Illinois, Indiana, and Ohio until I reached Cumberland, Pennsylvania. At that point I was so tired I didn't know what to do, but I was determined to continue driving until I reached home in Baltimore. When driving through the Cumberland Mountains, I took the road that was icy, hoping that driving on partially ice-covered roads would help keep me awake. This did the trick, but was it scary. When I left Pennsylvania, approaching Maryland, I was tired and sleepy, but determined to finish the trip without stopping again for a nap.

Driving on Route 40, heading for Baltimore, my speed was seventy miles per hour in a fifty-miles-per-hour speed zone. A state trooper pulled me over and asked me where I was going. He observed my air force uniform, and I told him I was going home. I said I had left Amarillo Air Force Base, heading for Baltimore, and had been driving for over thirty hours nonstop.

"I'm going to give you a warning ticket to remind you that you need to drive safely or you won't reach Baltimore alive. Driving for thirty hours alone is dangerous for anyone person."

What he said made sense, and I agreed with him. He gave me a warning ticket, with no fine involved. This incident woke me up at a time when I sorely needed it. From then on, I drove safely to Baltimore.

When I arrived, I drove to my parents' house and went straight to bed. I didn't wake up for hours. When I did wake up, my mother said she kept checking on me. She told me that she was concerned that it was an unusually long time before I woke up.

The nonstop driving time from Amarillo to Baltimore was thirty-two hours, an experience I won't forget, nor one I would want to repeat, especially during the time of segregation in the United States. I think by wearing my uniform, patriotism was on my side.

After spending my leave in Baltimore, I left my car there and returned to Amarillo by train. Shortly thereafter, I was honorably discharged in June 1955 and returned home to stay.

Reenlisting in the United States Air Force, 1955–1960

My home stay, after discharge from active duty in the air force, did not last very long. I reenlisted in the air force in August 1955 for another four years. At that time, the air force was offering reenlistment bonuses, and this, in part, motivated me to sign up for another tour. The reenlistment bonus enabled my wife and me to purchase a house for the first time.

I was lucky enough to get a duty station in Baltimore at the Air Force Reserve Center, located not too far from where we lived. I spent my entire enlistment time there, including a one-year extension, working as an administrative clerk.

In 1957 I enrolled in college. I began taking evening classes, using the GI Bill to pay expenses, at Morgan State College. I majored in business and economics. I accumulated a year and a half of college credits before being honorably discharged from the air force in August 1960.

After discharge, I began working at Andrews Air Force Base in Camp Springs, Maryland. Several years later, I resumed college studies at the University of Maryland. It wasn't until June 1970, however, that I completed all the requirements for a BA degree from the University of Maryland University College, with a concentration in business and economics.

Chapter 5

Working in Federal Civil Service

Working in Federal Civil Service Technical Jobs, 1960–1970

FOLLOWING DISCHARGE FROM ACTIVE DUTY, THE COMMANDING OFFICER at the Air Force Reserve Center advised me to consider taking a similar job to the one I'd performed at the reserve center but as a federal civil service employee at another reserve center. The job he referred to was an Air Force Reserve technician position, located at the 459th Air Force Reserve Troop Carrier Wing at Andrews Air Force Base, Camp Springs, Maryland.

I applied for the job in September 1960 and received a favorable response. I took the required written test and passed it. And Chief Master Sergeant Lawrence Sneed, supervisor of the position, offered me the job the same day. The starting salary was that of a GS-5 in the federal civil service at the time. Taking this job required that I enlist in the Air Force Reserve for four years. I worked on the job at Andrews Air Force Base for two years, until seemingly better options developed.

Then, due to excellent performance on the job and at the advice of my supervisor, I applied for and received another job offer at the Federal Aviation Administration (FAA). Also helpful in this regard was that I had built a reputation of competence and dependability among friends and other enlisted and officer personnel in the Air Force Reserve working at Andrews Air Force Base. I had shown great potential to work at a level higher than the job I'd been performing at the base. My work associates strongly supported my transfer to a higher-level position at the FAA.

The transfer to FAA was facilitated by Captain Jack Cranage (a civilian Air Force Reserve officer) who had transferred earlier from the base to the FAA. He paved the way for me to follow him there.

At this new location I was able to move into a management position as a personnel staffing specialist. I owe this important promotion from technician to professional management to the mentoring of Ms. Eleanor McClellan, the FAA personnel division secretary, who taught me how to maneuver successfully among peers and superiors in the federal government. Eleanor was a great mentor. She had my back during the time I worked at the FAA. She possessed a high level of professional intelligence and knew how to work the federal career employment system. I credit her excellent ability to influence superiors above her pay grade to make favorable decisions that enhanced my career appreciably.

I was given three special assignments while working at the FAA. As a personnel staffing specialist, I served as recruiter for mobile lounge operators at Dulles International Airport. I recruited the first person to operate a mobile lounge at the airport.

Another job assignment was recruiting high school graduates in the Baltimore area to work for the FAA in clerical and secretarial positions. For two summers, I arranged to have an office located in the Social Security Administration building in Baltimore. I invited high school graduates from Dunbar, Douglas, and Carver High Schools to come for an interview. I recruited some excellent candidates, who eventually were accepted for employment by managers at the FAA. I followed some of the new recruits throughout their careers and was pleased to learn that several of them achieved senior management positions in various agencies in the government.

Additionally, an interesting assignment that came my way was by the direction of the FAA administrator Najeeb Halaby. Mr. Halaby summoned me to his office in 1963 and asked me to serve as the administration's Equal Employment Opportunity (EEO) officer. This position was established for the first time in the FAA as well as in other federal agencies. I was overwhelmed that he had asked me, but frankly, I did not know what was expected of me. I accepted the position anyway, but then I went to see my boss, Mr. Nelson Jump in the civilian personnel division to get some advice on what was expected in such a position. He explained that President John F. Kennedy was concerned about the dearth of blacks servicing in the federal government and wanted to employ more.

Given this guidance, I reached out to those managers in the FAA who had potential vacancies to fill. I wanted to know what could be done to recruit candidates to fill their vacancies with the kind of workers they desired. One of those managers told me that he would like to have a person just like me—a hard worker, industrious, and reliable. I realized that the FAA had asked me to take the EEO job because I was the only black professional working as a personnel manager in the FAA. They assumed that I had contact with other blacks that the white recruiters did not. Of course, this was not true. I did not stay in the EEO position or at the FAA long enough to make a difference because I transferred to another agency.

In 1964, at the urging of Mr. Tom McKenna, formerly with the FAA, I transferred to the Office of Economic Opportunity (OEO). The OEO was established by President John F. Kennedy to address poverty throughout the country. Mr. McKenna was the first personnel director hired by the OEO. He offered me a promotion to come work for him. I worked there as a middle-level personnel manager until I transferred back to the FAA in 1968.

When I left the OEO to return to the FAA, I served on an advance team organized to establish the Department of Transportation, a new department created by Congress to consolidate all transportation agencies in one department.

When the Department of Transportation was set up and began operating as a department of government, I accepted a personnel management position in the Office of the Secretary of Transportation, at the advice of Mr. Gene Weithoner, a senior manager in the department.

In November 1970, I went to work as a senior management official for the United States Coast Guard, which had been transferred from the Department of the Treasury to the Department of Transportation.

It was amazing that I moved up the ladder so fast in the federal civil service system, from a GS-5 in 1960 to a GS-15 in 1970. I attribute this surprisingly quick rise in such a competitive environment to the tutoring of my mentors in all the civilian organizations in which I served. They not only coached me along the way but also spoke up for me when I could not speak up for myself. The value of a mentor cannot be overstated or measured in finite terms.

Chapter 6

Working as a Civilian in the United States Coast Guard

Managing Coast Guard Civilian Equal Employment Opportunity Program, 1970–1983

IN OCTOBER 1970, MR. BILL HUDSON, UNITED STATES COAST GUARD Chief of Civil Rights, offered me a job as chief of the civilian Equal Employment Opportunity (EEO) division, under his supervision. This offer came after I had been tentatively selected to the position of assistant division chief of the civilian personnel division in the Office of the Secretary of Transportation. This civilian personnel division offer was intriguing to me because my goal was to become a personnel director in a federal agency. And this position would have put me on the path to achieving that goal.

There was a problem, however, in that the incumbent of the position was planning to leave but would not give an anticipated departure date. He was delaying his departure in hopes of getting more than the organization was willing to offer him at the time. Consequently, I was unsure when or if the position would be available. The position was only a GS-14 level job but held great expectations that I would eventually become the chief of the division, with a promotion to the GS-15 level.

Before accepting the civilian EEO position at the GS-15 level, I had to consider other relevant things on my mind. The position was not a priority stepping stone, leading to the goal I had in mind for the future. Moreover, working in the EEO field at that time was considered a dead-end career compared to working in other occupations of employment in the federal government. The perception was that when marginal employees could not hack it in other occupations, they were placed in EEO positions, rather than removed from their current positions and terminated for poor performance.

Even though this perception existed, there was a renewed interest in the value of the EEO program in the Department of Transportation, brought about by the Honorable John Volpe, the newly appointed secretary of transportation.

Secretary Volpe had vowed to employ more blacks in higher-level positions in the organization during his tenure. EEO practitioners had an important role in making that happen. This optimism generated lots of interest among senior managers in other occupations in the Office of the Secretary of Transportation, so much so that many of them were clamoring to work in the EEO field, assuming they possessed the requisite qualifications to work in EEO management positions.

Given the developing excitement generated by the vision of the new secretary of transportation, I was compelled to reexamine my negative observations associated with working in the EEO field. And coupled with the promise that I would be a strong candidate to head up the Civil Rights program after the departure of the current chief, I accepted the promotion to chief of the civilian EEO division in November 1970, a GS-15 position, which resulted in a substantial increase in salary. Although I could not look so far ahead at the time, this decision led to the most rewarding career I could ever have in the federal government.

In November 1970, I went to work as the chief, civilian Equal Employment Opportunity division, United States Coast Guard. Accepting the position placed me in a division with the authority and responsibility for leading the coast guard's nationwide responsibility for ensuring equal employment opportunity for approximately seven thousand civilian employees, disbursed in headquarters and other field facilities throughout the contiguous United States, Alaska, and Hawaii.

I had a small full-time headquarters staff of seven equal- opportunity specialists and a secretary to support the overall operation. In addition, since the civilian EEO program was in its infancy, part-time civilian and military personnel who were employed in facilities outside of the headquarters office were assigned to support the full-time staff of headquarters EEO specialists.

The headquarters staff had no direct control over the collateral duty personnel. This meant that the collateral duty personnel were left to operate at their own discretion outside of Coast Guard Headquarters. When equal opportunity issues required attention outside of headquarters, and no collateral duty personnel were available in a given field location, the headquarters staff had to determine how to address the situation.

This occurred often for a simple reason: The primary duties of collateral duty personnel came first. They were evaluated on how well they performed their primary duties, the jobs that they were hired for and were being paid to perform, not their voluntary EEO duties, which required 10–20 percent of their time at the maximum. Furthermore, supervisors of collateral duty personnel, in many instances, did not look favorably upon temporary EEO work performed by the employees they supervised.

EEO issues were frequently mishandled or simply ignored because the collateral duty personnel were unavailable or didn't know how to effectively address the situations. In some instances, supervisors of collateral duty personnel did not treat EEO as an important activity, thus requiring the collateral duty personnel to concentrate exclusively on their primary job assignments, lest they be given marginal performance evaluations. Getting things done in this environment, especially outside of headquarters, where there were no full-time EEO specialists, was fraught with challenges, as well as there being little appreciation for the contribution the EEO program made to the success of the various coast guard missions.

In assuming this new responsibility, the first thing I observed was that something needed to be done to elevate the standing of the EEO program throughout the organization and demonstrate its value to mission performance.

Studying Coast Guard Organization and Decision-Making

Process

Before tackling these seemingly unmanageable problems, I needed to learn more about the coast guard. What was the purpose of the coast guard? Why did the coast guard exist? What made up the coast guard? How was the coast guard organized? How were decisions made in the coast guard? These and many other questions begged answers before I would feel comfortable working in the coast guard.

I decided very quickly that in order to be successful as a division manager, I had to understand the complex organization of the service, know who the power brokers were at the division levels, and know how policy decisions were made. I immediately learned as much as I could about the coast guard's organization by reading literature dealing with the creation and history of the coast guard and studying organization charts and diagrams.

The US Coast Guard is a top-down organization—policy was made in Coast Guard Headquarters and executed by operational commanders outside of headquarters, in the field. The commandant was the only operational commander in headquarters. The commandant was a four-star admiral, the highest rank in the organization. The vice commandant and the chief of staff, both three- star admirals, did not have operational responsibilities but were the second-highest ranking officers in headquarters. The vice commandant served at the pleasure of the commandant, and the chief of staff coordinated all business conducted in headquarters, including planning, organizing, and overseeing the overall coast guard budget. Other lower ranking rear admirals with one or two stars (lower half and upper half, respectively) served as program directors or office chiefs and were responsible for policy making in their particular areas.

The chief of civil rights, a civilian employee, served as policy maker in that area, with the equivalent rank of senior rear admiral. By possessing the equivalent rank of rear admiral, the civilian chief of civil rights was the fourth-highest ranking officer in Coast Guard Headquarters, behind the commandant, vice commandant, and chief of staff. All office chiefs reported to the chief of staff, with the exception of the chief of civil rights, who reported directly to the commandant. The protocol status of the chief of civil rights was senior to all rear admirals in the coast guard. This was established by fiat of the secretary of transportation to ensure that the chief of civil rights could perform the duties of that office without interference or influence by anyone in headquarters or field organizations in the coast guard.

The civil rights organization consisted of the Office of the Chief and three additional divisions—external civil rights, military civil rights, and civilian equal employment opportunity.

I served as the chief of the EEO division, reporting to the chief of civil rights. Responsibilities of the EEO division included developing, recommending, and overseeing implementation of coast guard policies approved by the chief of civil rights and/or the commandant. On rare occasions controversial policies were approved by the commandant in order to emphasize the importance of such programs.

Given the organizational structure of Coast Guard Headquarters, the chiefs of offices in headquarters played a key role in developing and interpreting policy, as well as participating in the decision- making process, which in many instances involved controversial operational issues not routinely settled by operational commanders in the field.

The coast guard is a very complex organization. Unless you worked at the senior level in the organization, you likely would not appreciate this complexity, especially how the headquarters and field organizations work so efficiently together to accomplish the various missions of the coast guard.

The top to bottom field organizations in the chain of command were uniquely structured. At the top of the field commands, headed by vice admirals, were two area commands, the Atlantic area command and the Pacific area command. The Atlantic area command had operational responsibility for all activities performed by the coast guard east of the Mississippi River, primarily in the eastern United States, from Florida to the Eastern Seaboard. The Pacific area command covered the western United States, reaching from Alaska to other western states and to Hawaii.

Supporting the area commands were officers below the rank of rear admiral, who headed up air station commands, consisting of cargo aircraft; search-and-rescue resources and helicopters; fleets of coast guard cutters, ranging from large to medium to patrol boat commands; buoy tenders; and ice breakers.

Coast guard ice breakers were shared with the National Science Foundation to assist in conducting research in icy and frigid waters in the Northwest and in and around Alaska. On occasion, ice breakers were used to assist foreign-flag vessels that were stuck in icy waters in frigid environments.

Reporting to the area commands were operational units, such as coast guard districts, headed by rear admirals. The coast guard districts in the Atlantic area command were located in Boston, Massachusetts (First District); Saint Louis, Missouri (Second District); New York City, New York (Third District); Portsmouth, Virginia (Fifth District); Miami, Florida (Seventh District); New Orleans, Louisiana (Eighth District); and Cleveland, Ohio (Ninth District).

The coast guard districts in the Pacific area command were located in Alameda, California (Eleventh District); San Francisco, California (Twelfth District); Seattle, Washington (Thirteenth District); Honolulu, Hawaii (Fourteenth District); and Juneau, Alaska (Seventeenth District).

There were two maintenance and logistic commands (MLCs), headed by rear admirals. The MLC located in Portsmouth, Virginia, provided support for the units and activities within the Atlantic area command. The MLC located in Alameda, California, provided support for units within the Pacific area command.

There were several coast guard training commands. The coast guard academy, headed by a rear admiral, was the educational arm of the coast guard. Its mission was to recruit and educate high school graduates to become the future leaders of the coast guard. Located in New London, Connecticut, the academy enrolled approximately three hundred new students each year, with the expectation of graduating around 150, depending on the needs of the service. The retention rate for the students was around 50 percent due to the rigid physical and academic requirements. A full complement of freshmen, sophomore, junior, and senior students in any given year totaled approximately eight hundred, near the maximum number of students the academy could effectively house in any given year.

The tall ship *Eagle*, the nation's flagship, was stationed at the coast guard academy, under the supervision of the superintendent of the academy. It was used to train coast guard cadets and other officers in the service.

The Yorktown, Virginia, training command, headed by a captain, was another training command for officers. This command was an indoctrination facility that trained persons who joined the ranks of the coast guard as college graduates, direct commission, and/or enlisted service members. These members were exposed to a dedicated number of weeks of training and orientation, designed to develop their physical, mental, and knowledge capacity to operate as junior coast guard officers.

There were two enlisted training commands, headed by captains, one located in Cape May, New Jersey, and the other in Petaluma, California. The Cape May command was a boot camp for newly enlisted members of the coast guard. The mission of the Petaluma command was to prepare junior and senior enlisted personnel to take on more responsible roles as leaders in their organization.

The coast guard operated a small boat school in Oregon for training enlisted personnel to develop skills in maneuvering small boats, especially small boats newly manufactured and assigned to perform coast guard search-and-rescue missions. Training was carried out on the Columbia River, one of the most difficult rivers, because of its tremendously rough water, to navigate in the United States, if not in the world. Because of the quality of training provided there, friendly countries from around the world would send some of their boat coxswains to the school for training.

Field commands also included several Marine Safety Office (MSO) commands strategically located throughout the area commands; coast guard group commands, located within each of the district commands; Coast Guard Yard (ship building and maintenance), located in Curtis Bay, Maryland; the aircraft repair and supply command (AR&SC), located in Elizabeth City, South Carolina; and small- boat stations, located within each of the district commands.

MSOs were headed by a captain, commander, lieutenant commander, and/or lieutenant, depending on the size and scope of the unit's operation.

Coast Guard Yard and AR&SC commands were headed by captains.

Small-boat stations were headed by junior officers and, in some cases, senior enlisted personnel, depending on the size and scope of the unit's operation.

The area commander reported to the commandant of the coast guard, who also was an operational commander. The district, air station, coast guard cutters, buoy tenders, and ice breaker commands reported to the respective area commanders within their operational jurisdiction. The small-boat commands reported to district commanders. The Coast Guard Academy and training commands reported to the chief of personnel, as those commands were designated headquarters commands.

The MLC, AR&SC, and Coast Guard Yard commands reported to the chief engineer, as those commands were designated headquarters commands.

The MSOs reported to the chief of marine safety, as those offices were designated as headquarters offices. The buoy tender commands reported to the chief of navigation and boating safety, as they were designated headquarters commands.

Some of these organizational components may have changed due to reorganization since I retired in 2004.

Understanding the organizational structure and decision-making processes of the United States Coast Guard was important for getting things done in military service. This would be especially true when addressing challenges and opportunities confronting the Civil Rights program. Without a working knowledge of the organization, I doubt that I would have been able to work successfully as a civil rights leader in the coast guard.

As a subordinate agency to the Department of Transportation (DOT), the coast guard implemented the civil rights guidance provided by that organization.

As I've mentioned, the United States Coast Guard is a complex organization, so how could the civil rights organization operative effectively and efficiently within the coast guard while at the same time meeting DOT requirements. Understanding the complex coast guard organization is the beginning salvo. When you couple this with other issues that need to be addressed, such as integrating civil rights practices into coast guard operational missions, then you might imagine the challenges facing the Office of Civil Rights.

Examining Coast Guard Operational Missions, Human Resources, and Civil Rights Challenges

The US Coast Guard had five operational missions:

1. Marine law enforcement; this included drug interdiction, guarding our shores, and protecting our fishing rights within two hundred miles offshores from the United States.
2. Maritime safety; this involves inspecting ships and cargo bound for the United States and developing and enforcing regulations to ensure safety at sea and in the United States waters.
3. Search and rescue; this involves aid and assistance to sea craft and individuals stranded at sea and in United States waters and emergency rescue operations.
4. Ice breaking; this involves breaking ice, facilitating travel in frozen conditions, and National Science Foundation research in extreme frozen-water environments.
5. Boating safety; this involves licensing and inspecting boats that travel in United States waters to ensure safety and compliance with coast guard regulations. It also provides support and assistance to over thirty thousand members of the Coast Guard Auxiliary to support their boating-safety missions, which includes teaching boating safety classes and assisting coast guard operations.

(Descriptions of these five missions may have changed since I retired in 2004.)

The military members of the coast guard, consisting of approximately six thousand officers and thirty-six thousand enlisted personnel, treated these activities as their primary responsibilities. Not much attention was paid to understanding and performing functions outside of these primary missions.

Civil rights was not part of the paradigm that drove military members of the coast guard to see the value in performing equal opportunity and civil rights functions along with their primary missions. After all, military members' performance was evaluated on how well they performed their professional duties, not how they dealt with issues involving equal employment opportunity and civil rights. It's no wonder that equal employment opportunity and civil rights activities were not considered to be as important as other operational activities.

Making equal employment opportunity and civil rights part of the primary missions of the coast guard was one of the most salient goals of the Civil Rights program and was the major challenge confronting the civil rights office.

Understanding the organizational structure of the coast guard and how it operated was one issue, but using that understanding to solve problems was another. And there were many problems to take into account.

There was a dearth of minorities, especially African Americans, in the military, both in the officer and enlisted corps. At the coast guard academy, for example, where the academy accepted approximately three hundred new cadets each year, very few were minorities. There was little or no outreach to minority communities to attempt to recruit minorities. The Coast Guard Academy seemed content to consider only those high school applicants who applied for admission to the institution, paying hardly any attention to the diversity of the applicant pool.

What's more, the academy was pleased with the quality of its applicants, given that most of them came with SAT scores over 1300, contributing to the academy's standing as an elite liberal arts college in the academic community. Very seldom did the academy attract more than a handful of minorities to apply for admission, and most of them did not meet acceptance standards. This became a big issue with which the civil rights program had to grapple.

Graduating from the Coast Guard Academy was a big deal. Most of the officers who rose to the ranks of captain or admiral were academy graduates. The academy graduates seemed to get the better job assignments during their careers, thereby affording them the best opportunity to be selected for career-enhancing positions as commanding officers of major coast guard commands; chiefs of staff at area commands and districts; and deputy office chiefs in headquarters. These priority positions became stepping stones for selection and promotion to rear admiral in the coast guard. And to become a commandant of the coast guard, graduation from the Coast Guard Academy was paramount. During my twenty-one years as a Senior Executive Service (SES) officer in the coast guard, not one non-academy graduate achieved the ultimate status as commandant of the coast guard. Only one non-graduate was elevated to the position of vice commandant.

The Civil Rights program should oversee the issue of how to attract, retain, and afford minorities the opportunities to compete for jobs that will enable them to be become rear admirals in the coast guard, as well as how the academy recruits its cadets and creates a wholesome environment so that they can succeed.

Another way to become an officer in the coast guard was to get accepted and graduate from the Officer Candidate School (OCS). College graduates who could meet the coast guard's requirements could join the officer ranks through this process. Most minorities, especially African Americans, chose this route. Graduating from the OCS required completion of a specific number of weeks of orientation and indoctrination at a training facility concerning coast guard culture, traditions, discipline, and other issues to prepare the graduates to take on responsible coast guard duties.

Graduates of the OCS program often were not viewed favorably by their colleagues who graduated from the coast guard academy. This subtle less-than-equal status followed the OCS graduates throughout their careers, often ending in one of two ways: (1) they were either passed over for promotion through a competitive non- selection process, resulting in an honorable separation from the service before they completed enough years of service to retire, with retirements benefits; or if they revived the non-selection process and completed at least twenty years of honorable service, they could retire with full benefits as lieutenant commander, commander or captain. It was seldom that an OCS graduate reached the rank of captain in the coast guard.

Another way to become an officer in the coast guard was direct commission from chief petty officer (E-7), senior chief petty officer (E-8), or master chief petty officer (E-9) to lieutenant in the service. Very few enlisted members took advantage of this opportunity because they did not see this commissioning process as a favorable thing, as there would be a loss of prestige among their peers and often loss of income in going from senior enlisted to a junior officer.

There also was the direct commissioning from warrant officer to lieutenant commander, based on the special needs of the service; that was exercised on a very limited basis. This also applied to the need to reach outside the coast guard officer corps to attract and commission other needed skills, such as pilots or electronic personnel. Normally, persons entering the commissioned officer corps in this manner were considered limited-duty officers and could not be promoted above the rank of commander; of course, there were minimal exceptions. There were very few officers with limited- duty status in the coast guard, most of which were pilots.

In the enlisted ranks, the percentage of minorities, especially African Americans, was not much better. Most of the recruiting offices for attracting enlisted members of the service were set up in nonminority communities, mostly in the suburbs surrounding urban cities. Consequently, there was limited, if any, outreach to potential minority candidates. On top of this, the coast guard recruiters were predominately nonminority members in the service. By and large, if minority candidates did not volunteer at the recruiting offices in the suburbs, the coast guard recruiters did not go looking for them.

Civilian employment throughout the coast guard presented a much different picture. But minority employment improvement was warranted. About seven thousand civilians were employed in a variety of occupations, including white-collar and blue-collar positions. Relatively speaking, the percentage of minority employees compared to nonminority employees was not bad. The problem, however, was that most of the minorities in white-collar positions were employed in clerical, secretarial, or other low-paying jobs.

Most of the minorities in blue-collar positions occupied helper and apprentice positions, with very few as journeymen, supervisors, or foremen. Approximately one-third of the coast guard civilian positions were blue-collar or wage-grade positions.

Compounding the problem was the fact that a large number of nonminority civilian employees in technical, supervisory, and middle-management positions had worked many years for the coast guard and had no intention of leaving their positions until they retired; thus, there was little opportunity to hire new employees or move low- paying employees up into better-paying positions.

In addition to these issues, the civil rights office had the responsibility for overseeing the civil rights obligations of the coast guard's Boating Safety grants program. Over $64 million was appropriated for this program. Part of the mission of the program was to provide boating safety grants to states, nonprofit organizations and US territories to promote boating safety. The responsibility of the Civil Rights program was to ensure that these entities participated in the distribution of the grant money. (The dollar amount may have increased since my retirement.)

Another obligation of the Civil Rights program was to ensure that coast guard operations and activities did not cause hazardous waste problems of any kind in minority communities.

Mandating the Office of Civil Rights Action by Secretary of Transportation

Before the Office of Civil Rights was established, its responsibilities were part of the coast guard's Office of Public Affairs. In the fall of 1970, the secretary of transportation elevated the Civil Rights program to the same status as other operational missions in the coast guard. And he mandated that civil rights be recognized as an important mission and raised to the office level. He directed that a civilian office chief be appointed to head up the office, with the organizational rank equivalent of rear admiral in the coast guard. His intention was that the position would assume the protocol status of the most senior rear admiral in the coast guard. He directed that the chief of civil rights report directly to the commandant of the coast guard.

Much work was needed to give meaning to the newly created organizational entity in the coast guard. This new office consisted of two divisions: the civilian equal employment opportunity (EEO) division and the external compliance division.

The civilian EEO division assumed responsibility for managing all civilian activities related to discrimination complaints and affirmative action to ensure that minorities and women were considered fairly in employment, promotions, and other related personnel practices.

The external compliance division dealt with all external matters concerning oversight of the coast guard's Boating Safety grants program. The Civil Rights program was obligated to ensure that minority organizations were considered fairly in the granting process. Also, coast guard activities were monitored to ensure that coast guard activities did not create hazardous or waste problems in the local communities in which the service operated. The external compliance division had specific civil rights oversight responsibilities, required by civil rights laws, statues, and regulations.

A third military division was later established to manage military affairs, given that the Department of Transportation required the coast guard to develop a program to address equal opportunity complaints by military members. Military members were limited to filing discrimination complaints, as they were not covered under the Equal Employment Opportunity Commission's regulations, as civilian employees were. Nor was there a requirement for an affirmative- action plan for military personnel, although the offices of personnel and civil rights did later develop a military affirmative-action plan, taking into account the need for the coast guard to focus on recruitment, promotion, and retention issues. The first military affirmative-action plan was developed by the Offices of Civil Rights and Human Resources and signed by the commandant, Admiral Paul Yost.

Unlike the EEOC regulations for civilians, there were no specific requirements for military personnel. The Uniform Code of Military Justice (UCMJ) and the commandant's expectations governed the manner in which military personnel should be treated. The UCMJ set forth specific regulations for dealing with military infractions and/ or treatment of military personnel. A military member accused of discrimination against a civilian member or a civilian employee accused of discrimination against a military member (which rarely occurred) could be handled under the EEOC regulations, as these regulations provided remedies only for civilian employees.

But a military discrimination complaint against another military member could not be processed under the EEOC regulations. It had to be handled under certain articles under the UMCJ, mostly under an article related to mistreatment of another service member, misconduct, or a felony of some nature. The accused member had to be read the required rights under the Miranda Act. An article 31 investigation had to be conducted to determine if an Article 15, or court-martial, was warranted.

Complaints of this nature seldom occurred because there were limitations on the nature of complaints that could be filed. Military personnel actions, such as recruitment, training, assignment, promotion, separation, and so forth, were handled by military boards, consisting of more than one person, and most of the boards acted under the direction of the commandant. For this reason, except for charges of sexual harassment or sexual assault, military complaints were resolved at the lowest level, sometimes with the assistance of civil rights service providers, supporting the commanding officers of the military members involved.

To address the DOT and EEOC requirements, the coast guard added a supplement to the DOT regulations, which was all that was needed at this early time. The coast guard set up a system for counseling employees in an effort to resolve their issues, many of which dealt with promotion concerns. By direction of the DOT, formal complaints were filed with their office. Investigations were conducted by their office also. The DOT issued final decisions, which were mandatory for the coast guard to implement when the decisions favored employees. Formal military complaints were also filed with the DOT, with investigations conducted jointly by the DOT and coast guard to ensure compliance with the UCMJ regulations. These processes were revised later as the coast guard began to train its own investigators. Final decisions, however, remained with the DOT.

The coast guard's Civil Rights program eventually grew independent of the DOT by developing its own policies, systems, and processes to accommodate the specific needs of the service for both civilian and military personnel. The coast guard received great praise from the DOT for the innovative actions it took to provide the leadership in developing and implementing such a forward-looking, results-oriented program, arguably the envy of other civil rights and equal employment opportunity programs in the federal government.

Chapter 7

Preparing for Future Leadership Positions in the Federal Government, 1975–1976

IN 1975 THE OFFICE OF MANAGEMENT AND BUDGET (OMB) AND THE Civil Service Commission (now Office of Personnel Management) jointly announced the Federal Executive Development Program (FEDP). This new program was designed to broaden the experience of senior-level managers to meet the growing leadership needs of the future. It was a one-year program consisting of the Senior Executive Educational program at the Federal Executive Institute in Charlottesville, Virginia, followed by rotational assignments in federal agencies to broaden one's background and experience. The expectation, upon completion of the program, was that graduates would be promoted into leadership positions for which they qualified.

I applied for the program. The coast guard granted me a one-year sabbatical leave of absence to participate. This was the first of its kind, planned to prepare senior managers at the GS-15 level to take on leadership responsibilities in the federal government. Applications were solicited nationwide from interested employees. Successful completion of this program was the basis for my selection to chief of civil rights in 1983, although it did not happen until seven years after I completed the program.

Selection for the FEDP was extremely competitive. In addition to examination of the written application, several simulated exercises were part of the examination and selection process. These included an in-box exercise exam (considering judgments on emptying an in- box of office matters); preparing a budget for an organization, given specific objectives and dollars to work with; defending a budget before members of Congress, simulated on Capitol Hill; and an interview by a three-member panel to evaluate your rationale for decisions you made.

Three thousand candidates applied but only twenty-six were selected. Fortunately, I was one of those chosen to participate in the FEDP. The bios of persons who made the cut were circulated widely throughout the federal government and published in their hometown newspapers and in media news stories covered throughout the country. The program was given extensive publicity. It was promoted as an innovative approach for grooming future leaders in the federal government.

The first phase of the FEDP began with the Senior Executive Education program. This program was designed to study leadership and management theories. The course took place from May 4 to June 20 at the Federal Executive Institute, located on the grounds of the University of Virginia in Charlottesville, Virginia. We were mixed with thirty-eight other employees who were at the institute just for the education program.

Upon arrival at the institute, the program director gave us an excellent orientation on what to expect during the program. He encouraged us to not only enjoy what was offered at the institute but to find something to take away from the institute that would remain with us even after we left.

During my spare time, I would jog around the cul-de-sac in front of the entrance to the institute building. As a matter of fact, I liked jogging so much that I continued to jog regularly up until my retirement in 2004. I now walk every day as a form of exercise and relaxation, thanks to the encouragement of the program director at the Federal Executive Institute.

As part of the program, we took the Myers–Briggs personality profile examination to determine our personality traits. Each of us had a confidential session with a trained psychologist or psychiatrist who interpreted the results of the test with us. This was a very informative session, as it provided professional feedback regarding our character traits, based on the findings of the test. It was a very revealing exercise. It enriched my confidence and expectations to become a potential leader in the federal government.

The program involved classroom activities and visits to government entities. We were assigned readings at night, followed by lectures and discussions the next day, led by college professors. In addition, we visited the Richmond, Virginia, City Council in session and the constituency office of a United States senator in Boston, Massachusetts, to observe how these entities of government operated. A graduation ceremony was held for completion of the education program in June 1975. We received certificates of completion from the director of the institute.

After we completed the educational phase of the program, we were encouraged to seek out government agencies to work in areas where there would be an opportunity to broaden our backgrounds and experiences. Finding an appropriate agency for experience development was left to each of us. That was our job, without much assistance from the directors of the FEDP. I chose to focus on research and policy development, management information, and budget formulation and presentation before Congress. These were the areas in which I wanted to acquire new experiences to broaden my background and enhance my knowledge, skills, and abilities.

My first assignment, for three months, was in research and policy development at the Federal Aviation Administration (FAA). I wanted to acquire a better understanding of the role of research and development in an organization. This was one of the areas I thought the FEDP would greatly enhance my knowledge, skill, and abilities and make me a better senior manager in the federal government.

My FAA sponsor created an excellent assignment for me—a job working alongside a group of senior management analysts and policy development professionals. These individuals were overseeing work performed by outside contractors, examining and making recommendations to improve existing FAA operations.

To become more familiar with FAA operations and especially the air traffic control system, I visited the air traffic control center in Leesburg, Virginia. The manager of the center gave me a tour of the facility. He briefed me on the overall operation of the air traffic control system at his center and the issues that concerned him. Also, I talked to several air traffic control operators.

This visit was very informative. I learned quite a bit about the air traffic control operation. It helped me to understand the issues that were worked on by outside contractors and what the FAA was expecting as deliverables from the contractors as finished products.

My FAA sponsor made an effort to expose me to some of the investigative undertaking, under the direction of the Research and Development program of the organization, but he did not give me a specific project to complete. I worked with a group of senior analysts who were managing several projects, worked on by contractors. Those projects were in various phases of dynamic development, ranging from just getting started to near completion.

The actual tasks the analysts asked me to perform involved oversight of data provided by the contractors. I evaluated the data using a checklist of deliverables and provided written and verbal determinations to FAA analysts regarding the status of work performed by contractors. Most of my work had to do with determining if scheduled timelines were being met. This allowed me an opportunity to become familiar with certain work processes and to understand the intricacies of managing timelines for completing research projects, according to contract specifications.

My take-away experience from this assignment was an understanding of how to manage timelines for completing research projects. In addition, this assignment helped me understand how to determine when to contract work that could be better performed by external contractors than by in-house employees. My learning experience was more judgmental than practical application of management theory.

At the end of this assignment, I prepared a summary report on what I had experienced. I acquired valuable experience in understanding the management elements required to direct the operations of a research-and-development activity of a major organization.

A research-and-development organization routinely hires contractors to investigate complex operational issues. Based on their investigative work, outside consultants normally share new ideas, theories, and objective reasoning about business operations not routinely conceived within the organization. The visionary work of consultants may create the basis for formulating new policies, programs, procedures, and operational methodologies that will not only solve complex problems but potentially enhance effective and efficient agency operations.

My next assignment, for three months, was in budget formulation and management at the Civil Service Commission (now the Office of Personnel Management). I worked with the head of the budget activity in the organization. He exposed me to every aspect of budget management, including data collection throughout the agency (headquarters and field regional offices), budget formulation, determining funding priorities, defense of budget decisions, presentation to Congress, monitoring budget execution, and other related budget activities.

This was a very rewarding experience, one that increased my knowledge and bolstered my understanding of how to deal with the OMB and Congress during the budget formulation and approval processes. It was an outstanding assignment. I learned much more than I had anticipated, due largely to the professional people with whom I worked.

Despite the valuable experience I gained from this assignment, one uncomfortable moment transpired. My sponsor asked that I attend a commissioner's meeting with him, where all the regional directors would be present. During the course of the meeting, the commissioner kept looking around the conference table, especially where I was sitting. After a while, the commissioner beckoned to my sponsor and then whispered something in his ear. My sponsor came back to me and asked me to leave the room. He said he would explain later.

After the meeting was over, he told me that the commissioner was leery of my being there, as he thought I might have been a news reporter, and he did not want to have a reporter present. Apparently, the commissioner had expected a closed meeting with his regional directors, none of whom was African American. Given that I was the only nonwhite person in the room, I have often wondered if I was asked to leave the meeting because of my race or for some other reason. I did not press the issue, even though being asked to leave the meeting was embarrassing.

My final assignment was at the National Science Foundation, working in the management division. My tasking was to review how data was collected, managed, and utilized in the various departments. I was asked to examine what was currently going on and to make recommendations on how the entire process could be merged and managed under the direction of the management division.

The primary function of the foundation was to conduct peer reviews of research-project proposals that were submitted for competitive funding.

I interviewed all the division heads at the foundation who conducted any kind of business from which data was collected, integrated, controlled, stored, managed, or shared. Each head of a division seemed to have his own way of collecting and managing data.

I studied how information was collected and considered options for doing things differently. I met with each division head, discussed what I had found, and asked them if there were any reasons they would not be willing to do things differently, such as supporting development of a centralized data collection and management system.

I reviewed with them a variety of options and asked them to offer any new ideas that were satisfying to them. I analyzed the combined data from my perspective, as well as their suggestions. I prepared a preliminary report of the findings. The preliminary report was shared with all the entities involved. I asked them to perform a critical review of the report and provide any suggestions that would put us on a path for developing a centralized process for collecting and managing information at the foundation.

I wanted to get a consensus on the thoroughness, quality, and integrity of the information in the report. In addition, I wanted to know from each of the divisions if it was feasible to consolidate the data collected and manage and store it in a centralized location in the foundation.

I learned that each division head was reluctant to give up control over his current system for managing the data. The head of each division was stringent in his position. I realized that there was no need to press the issue any further; besides, my detail at the foundation was nearing completion.

I wrote my final report, which included recommendations for centralizing the management information operation at the National Science Foundation. I briefed the head of the management division on what I'd done and left the report with him to consider further, at his discretion.

I offered to come back at any time if he thought I could be of service to the foundation. This was a great assignment. I regret it turned out the way it did, but had there been more time and with the hiring of a management information expert to also work on the project, the outcome might have been different. Nevertheless, working on this project was good experience. It taught me how important it was to control information relative to one's own business enterprise. The lesson learned from this assignment was very interesting.

This third assignment completed my agenda in the FEDP. Upon completion in 1976, the chairman of the Civil Service Commission and the director of the Office of Management and Budget presented the graduates with a certificate. Since there was not a new job offer available for me at that time, I returned to my previous assignment in the coast guard.

In retrospect, the objectives of the FEDP were plausible. It was anticipated that graduates of the program would be offered leadership positions for which they qualified, but that was not a guarantee. There was no leadership offer waiting for me. The DOT and the coast guard were unable to place me in another position.

There was a closely held assumption that the parent organization of the individual was responsibility for placing the FEDP graduate in a leadership position. In this regard, the coast guard had only three or four super-grade (now called senior executive service) positions, but none of the people who then held those positions planned to leave. The DOT considered placing me in an SES position elsewhere within the department, but none was available.

Interest in the FEDP faded—and it's no wonder. Placement in a leadership position was circumspect. Limited SES positions were available for FEDP graduates. I believe this is why the initial sponsoring agencies discontinued the FEDP and asked agencies to develop their own executive development programs to meet their future leadership needs.

I obviously was disappointed. I returned to my former position as chief in the civilian Equal Employment Opportunity division in the

United States Coast Guard. What I experienced in FEDP served me well in managing the activities of the division, especially with regard to planning and implementing initiatives to improve the effectiveness and efficiency of managing discrimination complaints and potentially achieving affirmative-action results.

Chapter 8

Getting Married, Seeking the Best Home and Church, 1969–1975

IN 1967 I MET JEAN RENWICK THROUGH ARRANGEMENTS MADE BY her brother-in-law. He mentioned a dance sponsored by his alumni association and asked me to escort his sister-in-law. At first, I was reluctant for several reasons. I was not a good dancer. I didn't know anything about his sister-in-law or what she liked and disliked, and she didn't know anything about me, except for what her brother-in-law might have told her. Furthermore, I recently had separated from my wife and didn't want to get involved in another relationship before getting a divorce.

I finally agreed to take Jean to the dance—but we never got there. Jean's brother-in-law had a sudden emergency, causing him to miss the dance. This left us without a sponsor, which we needed to attend. We decided to meet anyway and to spend the evening together. I went to Jean's house, and when she opened the door, I saw the most beautiful and alluring young lady anyone would want to meet. How lucky was I to meet this single lady?

We exchanged greetings and talked for several hours. We didn't want the evening to end, so we decided to take in an all-night movie. After the movie, I took her back to her house, and we agreed to continue our friendship.

At that time, Jean was raising her five-year-old daughter, Pamela. I got to know her daughter very well, and the three of us spent lots of time together. Jean liked to visit shopping centers. Though this was not my preference, I went along for her company.

After getting to know Jean better, it was apparent that she was not ready to marry any time soon. Her daughter was her priority at the time. Jean wanted to raise her daughter, giving her all the attention necessary to enrich her growth and development through cultural, social, physical, and intellectual experiences.

Over the years, our relationship continued to grow. In 1975, we decided to get married. It was a small wedding. Jean's sister and brother-in-law were our witnesses. The brother-in-law took pictures. We went on a brief honeymoon—two days—to a place called Holt's Farm in Pennsylvania and then returned to DC as a married couple. Since then, our marriage has continued to bloom into a never-ending love affair. And we are forever grateful for the wonderful blessings bestowed upon us.

Jean and I purchased a townhouse in southwest Washington, DC. We made the decision to buy this property after driving all over the DC metropolitan area looking at houses. We reached the point where both of us were tired of looking for a place to live. We were ready to make a decision.

Jean suggested the best place to live was in southwest DC, and I agreed—it was an ideal location for both of us. We would be living in close proximity to where we worked. Jean would be driving east, in the opposite direction of traffic coming into DC, to get to her school. And I could walk to work, which I did until I became assistant commandant for civil rights. Because of my status in the coast guard, I was privileged to have a parking space in the Coast Guard Headquarters garage, so I drove the short distance to work, about one mile away. Another advantage to this location was that the DC's Metro Southwest Waterfront Station was under development. It was located directly across the street from our house.

We joined Christ United Methodist Church, which was within walking distance from where we lived. Although Jean grew up a Presbyterian, and I grew up a Baptist, we decided to join the United Methodist Church. We made friends with many people there. The minister who talked us into joining the church was a nice pastor to work with. Jean participated in church activities as a Bible-reading liturgist. (She still does this at times and also serves on church committees. She has organized a Mahjongg group for women, who meet at the church on Thursdays to play the game.)

I served as an usher and chairperson of the finance committee at the church from 1976 to 1986. Fund-raising was the greatest challenge for the finance committee. We had to raise enough pledges to meet anticipated expenditures each year, which exceeded $100,000. Sources of revenue were church rental fees and occasional special fund-raisers and pledges.

One year we designed and implemented an innovative strategy to get the pledges we needed, along with other income sources, to meet anticipated expenditures for the year. We needed about$85,000 in pledges from a small congregation.

We employed a scheme that depicted a Pony Express delivery. We created Pony Express satchels and placed pledge cards in them. We put enough cards in the satchels for all church members and some for frequent visitors. We had cards for everyone else for whom we had a name and address.

We selected Pony Express delivery riders, whose role was to begin the deliver journey. Satchels were dropped off at homes of individuals we hoped would make a generous pledge. That person was asked to make a pledge, seal it, put it back in the satchel, and deliver the satchel to the next person on the Pony Express delivery address. If a person was, for any reason, unable or reluctant to keep the satchel moving to the next person, that person could call me, and I would arrange for the satchel to be delivered to the next person.

This was an exciting fund-raising drive, and we raised enough pledges to exceed the anticipated amount needed for the year. I believe everyone who participated enjoyed the exercise, and it brought members and friends of the church closer together.

The church was built sometime in 1964 and was financed with a mortgage. As a result of efficient management of the church's finances, the church was able to pay off the mortgage, during my tenure as chair of the Finance Committee. We celebrated this accomplishment with a mortgage-burning ceremony at the church, a significant achievement thoroughly enjoyed by all members and friends of the church.

Also, we had fund-raisers in the form of dinner dances at Fort McNair. Church members persuaded business establishments in the southwest community to participate. They encouraged the business establishments to not only attend our fund-raisers but to contribute some form of a gift to be used as a door prize. The local merchants were very generous in supporting our fund-raisers. They contributed excellent gifts. The gifts were enjoyed by the winners. One year Jean and I won a gift to spend a weekend at the Channel Inn, a motel in the area.

The turnout at the dinner dances was great. We hired a disc jockey to play music, and people in attendance enjoyed the evening of dancing. Fund-raisers were carried out on an annual basis for several years when I was chair of the Finance Committee. They contributed mightily to our fund-raising efforts.

I also served as chairperson of the Administrative Council for one year, directing the work of all committees at the church. After that year, the demands of my full-time job in the coast guard necessitated giving up my leadership role at the church.

Moreover, Christ Church served as an outreach center that was used to introduce the coast guard to the southwest community. The coast guard moved its headquarters office to the southwest quadrant of DC in the early part of the 1980s, not too far from Christ Church. At that time, the coast guard commandant wanted to become an active part of the southwest community. He challenged members of his leadership team to get involved in local community activities to demonstrate to the community that the coast guard was there for their residents. He also indicated that he would like to personally meet some of the leaders in the southwest community.

Since Christ Church was very active in the community, I discussed this matter with Reverend Don Lowe, then the pastor of Christ Church. Reverend Lowe knew most of the leaders in the community. I asked him to invite them to a meeting with the commandant for the purpose of meeting him and to explore ways the coast guard could become an active member of the southwest community.

Reverend Lowe organized the meeting with community leaders to attend, and he and I develop an agenda for discussion, to be facilitated by the commandant and Reverend Lowe. The commandant approved the agenda.

The meeting was held at the church. The commandant did most of the talking, as many of the participants were somewhat awed by meeting a four-star admiral. The commandant and the community leaders exchanged personal information. I offered to serve as the principal contact between the coast guard and the community leaders. The community leaders indicated they would think about how they could work with the coast guard on matters of mutual interest in the southwest community.

The commandant was pleased with the meeting and reported this back to his leadership corps in Coast Guard Headquarters; he asked them to consider ways to get involved in local community activities. Since this was a volunteer task, no meaningful records were kept of coast guard involvement in community activities until the Partnership in Education program was launched years later.

Chapter 9

Working as Senior Executive Service (SES) Official

Being Appointed to Senior Executive Service in the United States Coast Guard, 1983

UP UNTIL 1983, I CONTINUED TO PERFORM MY RESPONSIBILITIES IN an outstanding manner, as was reflected in my annual performance evaluations, prepared by the chief of civil rights. Working as chief of the civilian Equal Employment Opportunity division was a decent job but not challenging enough for me to serve beyond my earliest possible retirement date. I had intended to retire when I reached age fifty-six and had completed thirty-five years of service in the federal government. That would have been in 1986. I did not anticipate moving above the level in the federal government that I had reached thirteen years ago, even though I had completed the FEDP, which was initiated to prepare individuals for leadership positions of the future.

During the past thirteen years, I had applied for promotion to some leadership positions within and outside of the DOT but without success. I had given up on the notion that someone would offer me a promotion to a leadership position. I would opine that those kinds of positions were few and far between and only were given to the best- known and most trustworthy individuals, as determined by the selecting employer. Appointments to SES positions were not based on merit alone but on who you knew and who knew you. While this does not seem to comport with the kind of merit system desired by the OPM, in my opinion, this is the way the system worked when hiring individuals for positions in the senior executive service.

In 1983, I was absolutely surprised when Admiral Jim Gracey (commandant of the United States Coast Guard) promoted me to chief of civil rights, a Senior Executive Service position. The position became vacant when the former incumbent left the position to accept another job as director of civil rights for the Department of Transportation. I knew he had prepared a letter to the commandant strongly recommending me as his replacement.

I did not think much about the recommendation until I received a phone call from the headquarters civilian personnel branch chief. He said he was looking over the information in my personnel folder and that I should update my records. He also asked me to prepare an application for a top-secret security clearance.

"What for?" I asked him.

"Don't you know?" he said. "The commandant has decided to promote you to the chief, civil rights position in the senior executive service."

"You must be kidding!" I said, "I haven't talked to the commandant about the position."

"This is no joke. The commandant would like to effect this action ASAP."

I called the commandant to verify this surprising second-hand information;

He said, "Yes, I want you in the position of chief, civil rights. We can talk later."

(Several years later, the organizational title of chief, civil rights, was changed to assistant commandant for civil rights, representing comparability and protocol standing with titles given to program directors in the coast guard and executives in the DOT.)

I can't begin to explain how honored I was to be selected for an SES position. I never thought this would happen. It exceeded my expectations from the time I entered the federal service as a GS-5 employee back in 1960. As I moved up the ladder from GS-5 to GS- 7, to GS-9, and so on, I thought I would be doing well if I reached the GS-11 level. Then I reached the GS-13 level, and when I reached the GS-15 level, I thought

I had exceeded all expectations, and that was as far as I would go. I had no thoughts of moving up to the SES level, even though I had completed the FEDP. I just didn't think it was in the cards for me.

There were more than 1.5 million civil service employees in the federal government. Only approximately seven thousands of them were members of the SES corps. I was joining the elite of the elite in the civilian federal government. This was emotionally overpowering. It was indeed one of my greatest—but absolutely unimagined— accomplishments in my federal career.

Seven years after completing the FEDP, I assumed responsibility for leading the Civil Rights program in the United States Coast Guard. I knew there was a tremendous amount of work to be done. There were challenges as well as opportunities to confront in this endeavor, but this is what I had longed for—a chance to make a difference is the lives of ordinary people.

The Civil Rights program was perceived as reactive rather than proactive, and this had to change. The program had a reputation as not contributing to the accomplishment of operational missions. The program was not considered an activity on which top-level coast guard leaders (i.e., admirals) should spend their time working to ensure desired civil rights objectives were accomplished. Civil rights responsibilities were vague.

These were some of the issues that I would work on for the next twenty-one years of my career, trying to integrate the Civil Rights program into the operational missions in the coast guard. I was determined to change the negative perceptions of the Civil Rights program. I wanted to reinvigorate the Civil Rights program to show that it added undisputed value to coast guard personnel readiness and mission accomplishments.

Leading Coast Guard Civil Rights and Outreach Initiatives, 1983– 2004

I needed to gain the trust and confidence of all coast guard leaders, especially the admirals and the managers below that level, including the senior officers and enlisted and civilian members of the service. This meant getting to know my peers and other decision-makers. This meant spending time with them to explain the Civil Rights program objectives and the obligations inherent therein to all members at all leadership and decision-making levels. This meant taking tough questions and sometimes serious criticism of civil rights goals and objectives.

Throughout the course of my twenty-one years, I'd traveled extensively to promote the goals and objectives of the Civil Rights program. I prophesied that the program would add value to the operational missions of the service.

My travels carried my throughout all fifty states. I visited every major coast guard facility—area commands, districts, headquarters units (including the Aircraft Repair and Supply Center and the Coast Guard Yard), marine safety offices, small-boat stations, training commands, coast guard cutters (large, medium, and others), air stations, and the chief petty officer school. I scheduled at least four visits a year, making the rounds to as many locations as possible every year. Many field commanders asked me to visit their facilities, and it was an honor for me to oblige.

To prepare for field visits, I consulted extensively with program directors in headquarters to get their take on what their military and civilian personnel in the field wanted to know about civil rights goals, objectives, and desired outcome. How could I change any negative perceptions they might have about the program? My talks were not limited to civil rights issues; I spoke to my audiences as a knowledgeable representative of the commandant. This added creditability to my civil rights objective to integrate the civil rights policies and practices into the coast guard policies, practices, and operational missions.

I developed and maintained an up-to-date briefing book of facts, figures, and other pertinent issues on civil rights, as well as other coast guard operational missions. During field visits, I held all-hands meeting—with groups ranging from as few as ten to over eight hundred military and civilian members—at various field locations.

We met in offices, conference rooms, on the fantails of coast guard cutters, and the like. We exchanged candid information and a variety of interesting views on civil rights issues. Sessions of insightful give- and-take lasted normally one or more hours. Audiences were pleased to see me. They had never had an opportunity to express their views on civil rights with such a high-ranking member of the coast guard, one who was willing to listen to all observations they had to offer. These sessions were a great learning experience for me and for everyone involved.

When I visited the chief petty officer's school, I engaged the members in a teaching experience. I would spend eight hours every year with each new class. Normally, two classes were held every year. During these meetings, I introduced various factual data and solicited comments from the class on how the Civil Rights program was viewed in the field and what needed to be done to change any negative opinions and/or perceptions they held.

The feedback received from military and civilian personnel was very thoughtful and measured, as persons in the audience were speaking to me, the commandant's representative. I appreciated the very revealing and helpful information. This feedback was valuable with respect to developing strategic plans for addressing the negative perceptions that had existed in the field for some time.

My travel was made easy because of the courtesies extended to me, as I held the equivalent rank of rear admiral in the coast guard. At every facility or station I visited, my itinerary was coordinated with the respective commanding officer (CO) of the unit. The CO provided an escort and arranged for whatever travel I needed during the visit to his (or her) facility and subordinate units under their command.

The escort would meet me at the airport with a driver and would take me wherever I wanted to go during my visit. This was a time- saving arrangement, and it enabled me to make all of my planned meetings and speaking engagements on time. Having this assistance available to me, which customarily was provided to admirals, greatly contributed to my successful visits to field facilities. This was one of the admirals' perks that I greatly appreciated.

In addition, my EEO review teams conducted three reviews annually at selected field facilities. As a courtesy to my admiral peers, I participated in close-out sessions when my team members reported on the results of their findings at units headed by admirals. This prevented the potential for admirals to not talk down to my team members and for my team members not to talk up to their superiors in a disrespectful manner, especially when negative findings were the subject of discussion.

During visits to field units where EEO reviews were conducted, the CO often encouraged visits to some of their remote activities. The CO in Kodiak, Alaska, arranged for me to visit a Long Range Aids to Navigation (LORAN) station, located on a nearby mountain.

The warrant officer, who took me there in a jeep, was driving up the mountain terrain when we approached a bear crossing the road. I was startled when I saw the Kodiak bear and the two cubs casually walking across the road we were traveling on. As we came closer to the bear and the cubs, my driver was very calm. He stated that we need to stop the jeep, turn off the motor, and let the bear and the cubs cross the road without interference. I was terrified, to say the least, but tried to be calm for the driver's sake. After they had crossed the road, the driver restarted the jeep and drove up to the LORAN station. Although I appreciated the visit to the LORAN station, my greatest experience was encountering the bears and watching them cross the road without incident.

Staffing of Civil Rights Program and Annual Civil Rights Conferences, 1984–2004

As the Civil Rights program evolved over the years, it was transformed from a centralized headquarters activity to a shared responsibility throughout the Coast Guard. During its inception, the staffing of the program consisted primarily of a small number of equal employment opportunity (EEO) specialists in Coast Guard Headquarters, with none located at field facilities.

Staffing was transformed over the years to a decentralized concept with civil rights and EEO specialists, consisting of military officers (some designated as collateral duty officers) and full-time civilian practitioners, located at all major field locations. As the transformation evolved, I held annual conferences for all civil rights and EEO practitioners, including all military and civilian members working in the program, to keep them apprised of relevant civil rights goals, objectives, and desired outcomes.

A planning and resource staff was part of the headquarters civil rights organization. This staff handled budget formulation and monitored its implementation. It also coordinated planning and management of civil rights conferences.

Civil rights conferences were planned annually to ensure understanding of civil rights initiatives, goals, objectives, and strategies. Field units played an important role in determining the overall design of the agenda and desired outcomes for conferences. This allowed conferees to engage in meaningful discussions on matters relevant to them, as well as matters woven into conference planning by headquarters personnel to ensure understanding of the overall visionary direction of the coast guard's Civil Rights program. Assessment of problems and accomplishments during the past year and plans for the future were evaluated from the field units' and headquarters' perspectives to ensure a service-wide approach to managing the program.

Conferences began with a general overview of the past year's performance and expectations of the conference in session. Conferees participated in workshops to augment their understanding of how to address particular issues to obtain repeatable and consistent outcomes.

The conference proceedings included external speakers as well as senior leaders in the coast guard. On various occasions and depending on the agenda for the conference, our speakers included superintendents of high schools, the principal of the Maritime and Science Technology (MAST) academy, and college presidents. Coast guard leaders always were welcome. The commandant—who always addressed every conference—enlightened the conferees, as did, on occasion, the chief of staff, the assistant commandant for human resources, district commanders, and other office chiefs from headquarters. On several occasions district commanders hosted civil rights conferences in their respective city headquarters.

The annual conference was a yearly highlight of the Civil Rights program. We received many requests from civilian and military members of the coast guard for attendance. Unfortunately, we could not accommodate them all, but we made every effort to ensure that key civil rights service providers and full-time and collateral-duty military and civilian personnel were funded to attend the conference.

Having conferences was necessary to bring conferees up-to-date on important developments. In addition, the conferences provided an opportunity for the conferees to hear from other coast guard leaders, who articulated the value that conferees added to the coast guard's readiness and mission performance.

Developing and Sustaining Relationships in the Coast Guard, 1983–2004

I received invitations to stay at admirals' quarters during my planned visits to their units. It was a privilege to get such offers, which I gratefully accepted when my office planning schedule would permit. I stayed at the rear admiral quarters at the First District, Third District, Seventh District, Eighth District, Ninth District, Eleventh District, Thirteenth District, Seventeenth District, and coast guard academy. In addition, I stayed at vice admiral quarters at the Atlantic and Pacific area commands.

Visiting briefly with these key coast guard leaders was a unique opportunity to get to know them better. At the same time, they wanted to know more about me and what I hoped to accomplish while working in the coast guard. We shared mutual interests and had candid discussions about our respective private lives and professional expectations. Staying at the quarters of these men— meeting their families, eating meals together, having personal chats and business talks—fostered a relationship of immeasurable value.

Furthermore, I noticed that many of my colleagues were tennis players. This was a game worth learning to play. I took lessons at Fort Myers, Virginia, until I could hold my own on the tennis court. After duty hours I occasionally played singles matches at the navy yard with two commandants and with the chief of navigation and boating safety. Playing tennis with the chief particularly paid off, as it precipitated a breakthrough—he initially was averse to accepting any civil rights involvement in the Boating Safety program, but his attitude changed after we got to know each other better. This was important because the Civil Rights program had oversight responsibility for certain aspects of the coast guard's $64 million Boating Safety grant program. We became partners with a commitment to work collaboratively with each other on matters of mutual interest. Playing tennis also created an excellent opportunity to sometimes bring up controversial issues we preferred not to handle in the office. My personal relationship with these officials was greatly enhanced just from playing tennis together.

The admiral in the coast guard planned other occasions to develop a personal relationship. Vice Admiral Paul Yost, the coast guard chief of staff, held a dinner at his quarters to welcome my wife, Jean, and me to the family of coast guard leaders; this was noteworthy. The gathering took place at his home. It gave us an opportunity the meet and chat with the admirals working at Coast Guard Headquarters, as well as others who happen to be in town for business at the time.

At Rear Admiral Richard Ribacki's request, Jean and I shared a Sunday church service with him and his wife. This was another meaningful experience that broke ground in building a relationship and contributed to our trust and confidence in each other.

It was a practice in the coast guard for wives to attend the flag officer conferences, held in the spring and fall of each year, and Admiral Jim Gracey (commandant in 1984) invited Jean to attend. Since Jean was employed full time as an elementary school teacher, it was not practical for her to attend the flag officer conference, as did other admirals' wives; most of the admirals' wives did not have full-time jobs.

Jean, however, took the commandant's invitation seriously. She discussed it with her principal, who thought it was a good idea. She then had to request a leave of absence—ostensibly for educational purposes—from the DC school's assistant superintendent. The authorization was granted, and Jean attended the flag officer conference, along with all the admirals in the coast guard, their wives, two other civilians (a chief administrative law judge and the State Department's foreign policy adviser), and, of course, me.

The commandant was pleased she was able to attend the meeting. He introduced her to the coast guard family. He opened the conference with a message that set the stage for the meeting, and he encouraged Jean to participate freely by offering her thoughts during any discussions that might take place.

The commandant chaired the three-and-a-half-day conference. There was no set agenda, as the commandant indicated that he did not like conference agendas; he wanted to make the meeting a discussion from the hearts and minds of the leaders of the coast guard. During the course of the conference, the men and their wives met together on matters of general interest. The men held closed brainstorming sessions on policy and problem-solving issues, and during the men-only meeting, the women, chaired by the commandant's wife, held sessions on the general welfare of coast guard members.

Jean attended the combined and wives-only sessions. It was very enlightening to her to observe, in person, how the leadership corps of the coast guard carried out its business. She enjoyed meeting the coast guard family and developed a fond relationship with the commandant's wife. Their friendly relationship continued for several years after the conference.

Developing Relationships with Counterparts in Department of Defense, 1984–2004

As one of the five armed forces, the coast guard collaborated with the Department of Defense (DOD) on several operational missions. Many of the coast guard's military personnel policies and procedures were fashioned after those practiced by the DOD. The coast guard considered adopting those DOD policies that the coast guard liked; the DOD policies the coast guard didn't like were not adopted for practical reasons. Keeping abreast of DOD policies and implications for the coast guard required continual collaboration and liaison with the DOD.

Not too long after I was appointed head of the coast guard's Civil Rights program, I reached out to my counterparts in the DOD. My interest in developing a collaborative relationship with DOD was communicated to the DOD assistant secretary for administration, who, among other responsibilities, was responsible for equal opportunity policy.

The Defense Equal Opportunity Council (DEOC) was responsible for developing policy for the DOD Equal Opportunity program. The DEOC was chaired by the DOD assistant secretary, who invited me to join the DEOC as a participating coast guard member, along with the other DOD armed forces. As an active member, I would discuss and comment on equal opportunity issues based on coast guard experiences, but I had no voting privilege on exclusive DOD policies. The DEOC was an excellent forum for introducing new ideas and evaluating established policies and practices, with a view toward improving the effectiveness and efficiency of equal-opportunity programs.

The Defense Equal Opportunity Management Institute (DEOMI) was the equal opportunity educational arm of the DOD Equal Opportunity program. Located in Melbourne, Florida, the mission of the DEOMI was to provide training for full-time military personnel working in equal opportunity programs. At its inception, the mission of the DEOMI was to provide training for military members, but it later saw the need to provide training for civilian equal employment opportunity specialists. The civilian element was eventually added later to the DEOMI mission.

The DEOMI was a state-of-the-art training facility. It offered training in human relations, equal opportunity concepts, principles, strategies, and other areas designed to address complex equal opportunity issues. The director of the institute invited me to speak to its members in full session. During the one-day session, I spoke about the coast guard's policies, practices, and processes. I also engaged the DEOMI members in a Q&A session to emphasize strategies and ideas of mutual interest. This was an excellent opportunity to begin a relationship with the institute, and this relationship continued. The DEOMI eventually became an excellent training resource for the coast guard.

Ultimately, the coast guard became an active client of the DEOMI. I issued a commandant instruction on training courses offered by the institute and how coast guard members could take such courses. Commanding officers showed great interest in courses sponsored by the DEOMI and frequently recommended their member for the available training opportunities.

The Office of Civil Rights made arrangements for our military and civilian members to attend one of the DEOMI's flagship courses—the sixteen-week Human Relations Awareness Training program, designed to review and understand the principles of equal opportunity and how such principles should be applied in military service, as well as in real life. The course was available to military and civilian civil rights service providers who served in full time positions. Upon completion of the course, those persons were strategically assigned to Coast Guard Headquarters and other major field facilities throughout the service. They comprised the elite corps of certified human-relations–awareness training facilitators. They were available to conduct this important training anywhere throughout the coast guard, upon request.

The DEOMI offered other useful services. I entered into a contract with the DEOMI to develop an equal opportunity assessment tool. The DEOMI did a fine job in designing the instrument, which was developed and tested by practicing psychologists at the institute. When certified as survey-ready, we used it to collect information that assisted in developing preliminary information, prior to conducting on-site equal opportunity reviews at Coast Guard Headquarters and field facilities. The tool improved the quality of our Equal Opportunity Onsite Review program.

The collaborative relationship with the DOD was a meaningful way of staying in touch with and learning from DOD policies and practices. Through the relationship, the coast guard was able to acquire some of its training needs in a cost-effective manner.

To compensate the DEOMI for the training and services it provided the coast guard, we designated two full-time resources to the institute— one officer and one enlisted member. Serving as liaison to the DEOMI, these coast guard members kept the civil rights office appraised of developments at the institution and facilitated cooperation between our respective organizations.

At the commandant's request, arrangements were made for the DEOMI to conduct a mandatory all-day session on sexual awareness and abuse-prevention training for the senior program directors at Coast Guard Headquarters. The one-day course was developed by the DEOMI and was administered in Coast Guard Headquarters by the director of DEOMI and select members of his staff. The commandant and all program directors attended the session. From all indications, the program was well planned and administered. Comments from participants confirmed this conclusion. The materials and techniques used to put on this program were studied and eventually created the basis for the coast guard's Sexual Awareness and Abuse Prevention training program. The coast guard's newly conceived program was made known to the secretary of transportation. As the word traveled throughout the department, interest developed among other elements of the department that wanted the program presented to their senior executives.

At the commandant's request, I briefed the secretary of transportation and his executives on the coast guard program. Afterward, the secretary asked the commandant to make the training available to his executives. I arranged for this training, which was provided by a select team of the coast guard's human-relations– awareness training facilitators.

Also, the administrator of the National Highway Traffic Safety Administration requested the training. We used the coast guard team to provide training to that organization. Feedback from all sessions was very positive, a tribute to not only the professionalism of the training facilitators but also the program's material.

Chapter 10

Studying Recruitment and Retention of Minorities in the Coast Guard, 1983–1985

THE ISSUE OF RECRUITMENT AND RETENTION OF MINORITIES IN THE coast guard came up at a commandant's staff briefing. It was the commandant's practice to hold a daily staff meeting with members of his senior leadership group (admirals and three civilians). The purpose of the meeting was to exchange information of mutual interest.

One day the commandant asked why the coast guard could not recruit and retain minorities, especially African Americans. Looking in my direction, he indicated that he had talked to members of the NAACP, the National Urban League (NUL), and other minority groups but had not been successful. He asked for my thoughts.

"If you don't mind," I said, "I'll take the question for action, as I have no answer off the top of my head at this time."

After the meeting, when I had returned to my office, I received a call from Rear Admiral Kenneth Wiman, chief of engineering, research and development. He said, "The commandant caught you off guard. Let's get him an answer. I have about fifty thousand dollars in my budget that I can make available to you if you can use it to conduct a study to get the commandant an answer."

"I can't thank you enough for the offer," I said. "I will take action to put the money to use."

Recalling my research-and-development assignment experiences during the three months in the FAA, I was eager to commission a contractor to investigate the commandant's question.

To that end, I led coast guard efforts to examine the issue of recruitment and retention of minorities in the coast guard. We entered into a contract with Morgan State University to study the problem. The study team surveyed civilian and military members of the service in headquarters and in certain field facilities. It conducted interviews with members of the coast guard, people outside of the service, and leaders in minority communities. Several meeting were held with coast guard–leadership members to provide status reports and collect information to supplement the final report.

Upon completion, which didn't take long, the study team presented its findings to the chief of staff, the assistant commandant for human resources, and me. Among the findings were that the coast guard was not well known in minority communities; some minorities considered the coast guard to be part of the navy; and recruitment practices for officers did not routinely consider minorities. The survey also revealed that a large number of minorities considered they were trapped in lower-level positions, with little hope of moving up in the organization. This was especially the case with minority officers in the military, as they were not offered career-enhancing assignments at the same rate as their nonminority peers. The study was limited to Coast Guard Headquarters and some of its major field units but did not include the coast guard academy.

The percentage of minorities in the civilian service was commendable, but the average grade for most of those employees was low, as many served in clerical, secretarial, and nonsupervisory positions.

The study team made several recommendations to address these findings. It was recommended that the coast guard develop an outreach program in minority communities to make local residents aware of its missions and the opportunities available for them to become part of the service, as civilian or military members.

It was recommended that the coast guard develop an affirmative-action plan for addressing civilian issues and that the goals and objectives of the plan be communicated throughout the service.

Finally, it was recommended that the coast guard appoint a minority-officer adviser to oversee coast guard efforts for recruitment and retention of minorities in the service and to monitor personnel practices to ensure minority officers were treated fairly in all personnel actions that affected their careers. The study recommendations were approved, in principle, by the commandant.

Headquarters program directors examined the recommendations to determine responsibility for implementing them. Developing an outreach program became the responsibility of the assistant commandant for civil rights, as I was already doing work in this area. The coast guard had relatively weak minority-community connections, and I volunteered to take on the assignment to expand efforts to reach out to minority communities, assuming that more money would be added to the budget of the Civil Rights program for this purpose.

Appointing an officer to oversee minority affairs was not as simple to implement as the outreach program. This was a new concept for the coast guard. What would be the billet's, or officer's, responsibilities? To whom should the officer report? What should be the grade level of the officer? These were some of the internal questions debated by coast guard leadership, including the chief of staff, the assistant commandant for human resources, and me, all important stakeholders in headquarters.

We reached a consensus along these lines. The assistant commandant for civil rights would set policy for the operation of the position, and the assistant commandant for human resources would implement policy, with the officer reporting to him. The rank of captain (0–6) was initially authorized for the position. A retired coast guard officer with the rank of captain (0-6) in the coast guard reserves was called up from inactive reserve duty to fill the position on a full-time basis. After the reserve officer went back into retirement, an active duty officer with the rank of commander (0–5) was placed in the position, effectively downgrading the status of the minority officer adviser.

In retrospect, I should not have agreed to this initial arrangement. The turnover of assistant commandants for human resources and chiefs of staff brought with it a different interpretation regarding how the officer should be utilized, thus causing organizational friction between the new assistant commandants for human resources and me. These new players were not there when the initial arrangement was worked out. Regretfully, the initial arrangement for utilization of the officer was not documented in writing. I was the only remaining program director available when the minority officer adviser was initially authorized, and I could not, in good conscience, agree with the arguments presented on changing how the position should be utilized. I strongly refused to yield to those arguments, which would nullify the original intent of the officer, as was recommended in the recruitment and retention study. Thus, tension arose between me and the other stakeholders in headquarters, which remained until I retired in 2004. The tension, however, was manageable.

Because of the study's revelations, this was a defining moment in the coast guard. Along with several other key developments, it laid the groundwork for the later formulation of a civil rights doctrine for the service.

It is unfortunate that when the Civil Rights program was established in the late 1960s, at the direction of the then-secretary of transportation, the secretary did not address issues of personnel and budget. These important issues were left to the coast guard to work out internally. Consequently, the coast guard authorized limited personnel for the office and no budget at all, requiring the Civil Rights program to rely on funding, as part of the discretionary money appropriated for the chief of staff, to manage. This became a problem.

At this time, however, money made available by the chiefs of staff for the Civil Rights program depended on their attitudes and commitments to the Civil Rights program activities.

When I first took office, money was not a problem. One chief of staff said he would treat the Civil Rights program as a "special privilege nation," a term of art he used to infer that he was fully committed to funding worthwhile civil rights activities with desirable outcomes in the interest of the coast guard. That chief of staff provided generous support. On the other hand, other chiefs of staff did not share the same funding philosophy, thus requiring me to make a case to the commandant for funding. I did not like to do that, but on some occasions I did it, especially when it was determined that money was needed to support external promotional activities, considered in the best interest of the coast guard.

Chapter *11*

Establishing the First JROTC Program in the Coast Guard, 1987–1989

THE COAST GUARD'S OUTREACH EFFORTS WERE INSTRUMENTAL IN establishing the first coast guard Junior Reserve Officers' Training Corps (JROTC). This JROTC is located at the Maritime and Science Technology Academy (MAST) in Dade County, Florida.

Ms. Linda Eades was principal at MAST in 1987 when it first enrolled students. She contacted an officer stationed at the Seventh Coast Guard District in Miami, Florida, to inquire if the coast guard would be interested in establishing a JROTC at her school. The officer suggested she contact me, as the Office of Civil Rights was responsible for developing outreach initiatives for the service.

When Ms. Eades called me, she said that MAST was a magnet high school, grades nine through twelve, with an enrollment at that time of approximately 850 students. Most of the students were minorities, with a high percentage of Hispanics and African Americans.

I said I was interested and would like to visit the school to explore the matter further.

I flew down to Dade County to meet with Ms. Eades. She introduced me to the Dade County then acting school superintendent and other school officials to discuss their interest, pointing out that the coast guard was the only service that did not have a JROTC program. The school wanted to give us an opportunity to use their school to establish one. Ms. Eades also introduced me to key officials in the local maritime community and to an elected official in the Florida state legislature. She assured me that she could get support from their representative in Congress to support the initiative, and their congressman would introduce an appropriate bill in Congress to establish the JROTC program. I was interested and assured her that I could get the commandant's approval.

I returned to DC and discussed the idea with Admiral Yost (the commandant) and all stakeholders in headquarters. The commandant approved the proposal. I returned to Dade County and discussed a plan of action to establish the JROTC in the coast guard. The MAST Academy and the local maritime community, working with the local state legislature, would get the support of their congressman to introduce the needed support in Congress. And I would work with the appropriate stakeholders in Coast Guard Headquarters to develop the legislative package necessary to submit to Congress.

During development of the proposal, I visited MAST Academy several times to assure the maritime community that the coast guard was aggressively pursuing its end of the agreement. During my visits, Ms. Eades arranged for me to appear on local radio talk shows to discuss the proposal. I answered questions and did my best to keep the community aware of what was happening. Admiral Yost also visited the school. He toured the facilities and the coast guard photographer took photos. The commandant met with school officials and the state legislator, reassuring them that the proposal had his full support.

Back in headquarters, working with the coast guard's chief council and the assistant commandant for human resources, we collaborated on the development of a legislative proposal to establish the JROTC. The proposal was vetted through several agencies of the federal government, including the DOT; the Departments of Defense, Commerce, Labor, and Education; and the Office of Management and Budget (OMB). The vetting process was successfully completed, and the OMB sent the proposal to Congress, where it was favorably approved, given the support of the local congressman from Florida. A JROTC at MAST Academy became a reality in December 1989. It was officially established as the Claude Pepper JROTC, in honor of its congressional sponsor.

Ms. Eades invited me to attend the first graduation of students at the academy in 1992. I arrived in Miami the night before the graduation and hosted a dinner to thank Ms. Eades and other officials who played a role in completing the JROTC project. The graduation was held on the "Carnival", multi-deck cruise ship.

We anticipated that the magnet school, with an ethnically diverse population of students, would become a fertile ground from which to recruit minority graduates for employment in the service in a civilian or military capacity. We were especially hopeful that some graduates would apply for admission to the Coast Guard Academy as cadets.

Because of its proximity to MAST Academy, the Seventh Coast Guard District became the sponsor of the JRORC. This was not a zero-sum project. It required the coast guard to establish a funding account to maintain the program, especially for military supplies and uniforms for the cadets. In addition, the coast guard assigned a full- time billet to the school for the purpose of introducing students to the military tradition and arranging formal reviews of school cadets before the commander of the local coast guard district.

Chapter 12

Developing Coast Guard
Outreach Program, 1987– 2004

THE CIVIL RIGHTS OFFICE LED COAST GUARD EFFORTS IN DEVELOPING and implementing a comprehensive outreach program for the service. The coast guard was perceived as having relatively weak minority connections. We worked hard to change this perception through development of a meaningful outreach program.

My vision for the program was to saturate minority communities with information about coast guard missions and opportunities for residents of those communities to become part of the organization. We knew this could not be accomplished in the short term. It would have to be an aggressive endeavor that spanned the terms of six different commandants, as the tenure of each commandant lasted only four years. Admiral James Gracey served from 1982 to 1986; Admiral Paul Yost from 1986 to 1990; Admiral William Kime from 1990 to 1994; Admiral Robert Kramek from 1994 to 1998; Admiral James Loy from 1998 to 2002; and Admiral Thomas Collins from 2002 to 2006. Admiral Gracey appointed me to the SES position in 1983, and Admiral Collins presided over my retirement in 2004. I worked under the direction of six commandants, so the coast guard's outreach initiatives had to be strategically planned as an ongoing and continual program. The program had to be fashioned with flexibility to meet unanticipated developments, should they arise, during the twenty-one years I served as assistant commandant for civil rights.

I reached out to the heads of all minority organizations that had a national headquarters in the Washington, DC, metropolitan area, as well as subordinate organizations located in communities outside that geographical area. I attempted to reach minority organizations that represented the interests of African Americans, Hispanics, Asian America Pacific Islanders, and Native Americans.

I sent personalized letters to the heads of all national minority organizations for whom I had an address. The letter requested a meeting— at any location they chose—to get acquainted and to introduce them to the coast guard and explore any interest they might have in establishing a relationship with the service.

I received positive responses from all the organizations I contacted, except the Asian American Pacific Islanders and the Native American groups. The Asian American Pacific Islanders organizations in the metropolitan area operated separately as independent entities in the various federal agencies and were primarily interested in civilian jobs in the federal civil service. They showed limited concern in expanding to include nationwide considerations. The coast guard accommodated the interests of this minority group by establishing a collateral duty position in Coast Guard Headquarters to sponsor activities on behalf of Asian America Pacific Islanders employees. Coast guard field installations were encouraged to do the same.

As for the Native American groups, I communicated with the president of a Native American college in North Carolina, who seemed interested in working with the coast guard on issues such as internships for Native American students but did not show much interest in establishing a nationwide relationship beyond that point.

The heads of African American and Hispanic organizations, with subordinate organizations located outside of the DC area, showed a great deal of interest in establishing relationships with the coast guard. We discussed their interests and reached a mutual agreement with certain parameters. These parameters became the basis for formulating memoranda of understanding.

As a result of comprehensive collaboration, the civil rights office drafted a memorandum of understanding (MoU) with heads of those minority organizations, which represented multiple chapters throughout the country. Those organizations included the National Association for Equal Opportunity in Higher Education (NAFEO), the National Urban

League (NUL), the Hispanic Association of College and Universities (HACU), and the National Association for the Advancement of Colored People (NAACP). The MoUs were signed by the heads of the respective organizations and the then commandant of the coast guard. The assistant commandant for civil rights was designated as the point of contact for the coast guard. The MoUs were distributed widely throughout the field organizations of the signatory parties and coast guard field facilities.

The content of the MoU was very explicit with regard to the values of the specific organizations and their mutual interest and expectations, as well as those of the coast guard. For example, the coast guard would exhibit and make speakers available at conferences sponsored by minority organizations, consider minority organizations for contract services for which they would qualify, and make employment opportunities available for their constituents. And the minority organizations would adhere to rules and regulations governing coast guard operations and widely distribute information, throughout their branches, on coast guard missions and opportunities for their members to join the service as military or civilian members.

To further demonstrate the coast guard's commitment to effectively honor requirements inherent in the MoU, The secretary of transportation, coast guard commandants, and other admirals got involved. They took the time to address various forums sponsored by minority organizations. They conveyed a persuasive message, supporting the memorandum, whenever they spoke to members of various organizations. They emphasized that the coast guard was interested in building a partnership for years to come in order to develop and successfully carry out projects of mutual interest. Their message was communicated not only to heads of minority organizations but also to members of their communities, resulting in meetings and discussions between lower-level coast guard officials and participants of minority organizations at the field level, looking for ways to work together. Thus, for the first time in the history of the coast guard, the organization commendably established a productive relationship with minority communities.

Chapter 13

Addressing Military Social-Climate Issues, 1990– 2004

OCCASIONALLY MILITARY MEMBERS EXPERIENCED UNPROVOKED challenging issues in local communities where they were stationed. Such issues could be characterized as social-climate issues that might create problems for military service members. A social-climate issue is defined as any unprovoked hostile act committed against a military member by a civilian resident of a local community where a coast guard unit is located.

Several military members of the coast guard expressed concerns they were not welcome in some local communities where they were assigned. Local residents did not welcome them in social settings, and the coast guard members were reluctant to participate in local community activities, fearing unprovoked problematic responses by local residents.

District commanders had threatened to move their units out of any location that did not welcome its members, as they were in those locations to serve the people who lived there. To lose coast guard services because of mistreatment of coast guard members would be an unfortunate loss of potentially helpful services to local residents. The coast guard considered hostile acts against any of its members as a social-climate issue that would not be tolerated.

Social-climate issues, by definition, did not pertain to civilian employees who might work or live in communities where military members were mistreated. Civilian employees were part of the community. They had other ways to address mistreatment issues, should they occur. And besides, they most likely were well known in their local communities and probably would not encounter social- climate issues, as a military member would. Furthermore, civilian employees could address such issues, if necessary, through local law enforcement systems and processes on their own time.

Military members could not address social-climate issues in the same practical way as civilian employees could. Military members were on duty twenty-four hours a day, and their schedules were determined by their commanding officers (COs); they were required to adhere to processes governed by the Uniform Code of Military Justice (UCMJ) and the military chain of command. So it was appropriate to develop special strategies that would effectively address social-climate issues encountered by military members. What could the coast guard do to effectively address such issues?

The Community Relations Service (CRS) division in the Department of Justice was established to work on problematic issues like those encountered by coast guard members. The CRS had field offices throughout the United States, primarily located in urban communities. Their people worked at solving difficult racial disputes in those communities.

I reached out to the CRS office to request a meeting with the Honorable Grace Flores Hughes, the head of the organization. The meeting was arranged. At the meeting, I briefed Ms. Hughes on the social-climate–issues problem that the coast guard was having in some local communities.

Ms. Hughes suggested the CRS might be able to help in some way. Her organization had regional offices throughout the United States with resources that could assist in addressing these issues. CRS employees, she said, were trained to defuse such issues through collaboration with mayors and community leaders with whom they worked on a regular basis.

The meeting offered great expectations. Ms. Hughes and I worked together to develop a MoU designed to assist the coast guard in solving social-climate issues whenever they arose.

I invited Ms. Hughes to meet with Admiral Bill Kime, the commandant. We had lunch together in the commandant's dining room. Afterward, the three of us signed the MoU together. The MoU was distributed to CRS regional offices and coast guard field facilities throughout the service.

The MoU laid the groundwork for representatives of the CRS to work as a team with commanding officers of the coast guard in the central and northwestern parts of the country in addressing social- climate issues. The knowledge and expertise of CRS representatives were valuable resources, as demonstrated through their adroit proficiency in solving social-climate issues on a number of occasions.

This speaks volumes about the importance of the MoU executed by the commandant and the director of the CRS and how the relationship between our two organizations added another device to the coast guard's toolbox for managing social-climate issues.

Chapter 14

Resulting Workforce Cultural Audit Roils Coast Guard Executives, 1991

THE COAST GUARD ENGAGED THE OFFICE OF PERSONNEL MANAGEMENT (OPM) to conduct a service-wide workforce cultural audit. When I first made the recommendation to have this done, there was resistance at high levels in the coast guard. I believe it was because the coast guard is primarily a military service, and it did not want the OPM, a civilian-chartered organization, delving into its business.

As the old saying goes, never wash your dirty linen in public. It was not my intention to do that. I just wanted to bring the coast guard into the twenty-first century by learning how members of the coast guard felt about what was happening in their work environment. This was something that any employer should want to know. My persistence eventually led to the coast guard's reconsidering and authorizing the cultural audit.

The survey was conducted throughout the service using a professionally designed random sampling process. Military and civilian members of the service voluntarily completed a questionnaire. Initially, some members were reluctant to take part in the survey, but eventually, more than two-thirds of the individuals contacted completed it. This was more than enough to validate the integrity of the random sampling.

An OPM representative briefed the Offices of Civil Rights and Human Resources on the survey findings. Among the significant findings were responses related to civilian and military personnel.

Civilian personnel had concerns regarding lack of career-development opportunities, upward mobility, and promotion, which may have been due to low turnover in the civilian workforce.

Military personnel showed concerns relating to the military detailing processes resulting from assignments, evaluations, and promotion practices. Further analyses of these concerns indicated that minorities were not treated the same as their white counterparts and, for this reason, could not advance to higher levels in the coast guard.

Officers' and enlisted women's responses showed a concern about being sexually harassed and that they were reluctant to report such behavior due to fear of retaliation by their superiors.

After further analysis of the survey results, the Office of Civil Rights prepared a briefing for coast guard executives that the deputy chief of civil rights presented to the coast guard's senior leadership corps at an admiral/SES (flag officer) conference. It was no surprise to me that the survey results were violently contested by several members at the conference. I sensed an attitude of denial that suggested the results of the audit were biased and did not accurately reflect the opinions of civilian and military members of the service.

I suggested that the workforce cultural audit had been done in a professional manner and that the survey had been scientifically designed to collect information. It had been tested and met generally acceptable standards for conducting cultural audits. I further offered that in my presenting the results of the audit, I was merely the messenger, with no interest in the results, other than to let everyone know the truth of how our men and women in the service responded to the various questions. I'd presented the results of these findings without any attempt to edit results, and they were what they were.

After a lively discussion regarding the survey and resulting recommendations, the commandant weighed in. He approved the audit in principle and provided guidance for implementation of the recommendations. He ordered a stand-down throughout the service. He directed that all members of the service, military and civilians, undergo eight hours of sexual awareness and abuse-prevention training if they had not participated in such training within the past year. The civil rights office was instructed to administer the training using the coast guard Certified Human Relations Awareness Training Facilitators.

The training accomplished was to be reported monthly to the civil rights office, to ensure compliance with the commandant's direction. The commandant directed eight hours of sexual awareness and abuse-prevention training for the senior leadership, all admirals, and SES officers in headquarters. I arranged for the director of the DEOMI and his professional staff to conduct the training. The training was successfully accomplished, with the commandant in attendance.

Decisions regarding the assignment, training, promotion, and other personnel actions that affected the careers of military officers were made by board deliberations, consisting of superior officers appointed by the human resources office. With respect to minority- officer concerns, the commandant added specific language to board charters that affected the careers of military officers to ensure minorities were treated fairly in the process. Assignment, training, and promotions boards were singled out and more closely monitored by the commandant to ensure his direction was applied during consideration of personnel actions that affected minorities. Final recommendations of board deliberations were reviewed and approved by the commandant.

The Offices of Civil Rights and Human Resources were directed to develop programs to address the concerns of minority civilian employees who were trapped in low-level positions. We were tasked to explore innovative ways to create training, upward mobility, and promotion opportunities. Finding ways to raise the level of minority civilians in low-level positions was a priority in the coast guard. Additional recommendations resulting from the survey findings were assigned to specific program directors in headquarters for implementation within their respective areas of responsibility.

Commanding officers throughout the service were charged with ensuring that all female members of the service were not subjected to any form of harassment or retaliation for reporting unlawful behavior.

A by-product of the survey was the introduction of the concept of diversity in the coast guard. How the term should be interpreted and translated in the coast guard's lexicon of personnel practices became a subject for discussion.

According to *Webster's Dictionary*, diversity means "a different kind." I too interpret the term to mean a *different kind*—a different kind of racial ethnicity (black, white, Hispanic, Native American, Asian American Pacific Islanders, etc.) in the context of hiring, selection for a seat in college, or representation in a civilian and military workforce. This was the intent of the Supreme Court's rulings when it rendered decisions on cases alleging discrimination based on the use of affirmative action to achieve diversity in a competitive selection process. The Supreme Court took the position that promoting diversity allows consideration of an individual's race.

Yet some learned colleagues in the coast guard tried to argue that diversity should be interpreted more broadly; for example, diversity of colleges where persons attended or regions of the country where persons were born. Such interpretations were absurd. I don't believe the Supreme Court had any of those interpretations in mind when it deliberated on cases alleging discrimination based on the use of affirmative action to achieve diversity. I believe my learned colleagues purposely complicated, for specious reasons, the problem the coast guard was attempting to address (that is, how to recruit and retain more minorities in the coast guard).

That kind obfuscation did more to harm efforts to recruit and retain a diverse military service that it did to help. Even coast guard members with good intentions were confused by this subtle misinterpretation of what diversity should mean in the service and how the term should be applied to personnel recruiting and retention practices.

To deny the Supreme Court's interpretation of lawful practices to achieve diversity in the workplace was absurd and unacceptable. Correcting this misinterpretation of diversity and explaining the value that racial diversity would add to coast guard excellence was a challenging issue that required intellectual attention by the civil rights office and all members of coast guard leadership.

Chapter 15

Collaborating with the National Urban League, 1987– 2004

THE OFFICE OF CIVIL RIGHTS NEGOTIATED A MOU WITH THE National Urban League (NUL). The MoU outlined the parameters that would govern how the NUL and the coast guard would strategically work together on matters of mutual interests. To effectuate the agreement, the NUL president and the coast guard commandant needed to get together to review and sign the document.

The civil rights office organized a meeting between Admiral Yost (USCG commandant) and Mr. John Jacob (NUL president/CEO). Mr. Jacob's calendar did not allow time for him to visit Admiral Yost in Washington, DC, any time soon. Since the commandant was eager to sign the document, he decided to travel to New York City to meet with Mr. Jacob and have a discussion with him before signing the MoU.

We boarded the commandant's jet and flew to the LaGuardia Airport in Queens, New York City. At the airport, we boarded a coast guard helicopter for the short flight to downtown New York City, where we landed on the East 34th Street Heliport pad in downtown Manhattan. We took an elevator down to the ground level where a coast guard vehicle was waiting for us, and the driver drove us to the office of the NUL president.

Admiral Yost met with Mr. Jacob for over an hour. The two of them chatted for a while before signing the MoU. A coast guard photographer was on hand to take photos during the celebrated meeting.

The commandant was extremely pleased with his meeting with the NUL president. He conveyed this to his coast guard leadership corps. He indicated that his meeting and chat with the NUL president was one of the best experiences he had had since becoming an officer in the coast guard—what an incredible revelation! It revealed the commandant's unqualified respect for the NUL president and a strong desire for members of the coast guard to work with members of the NUL on matters of mutual interest.

As an initial step to implement the MoU, the civil rights office organized a meeting with NUL branch presidents from all major US cities, and the response was great. We invited stakeholders in Coast Guard Headquarters, as well as representatives from the National Association for Equal Opportunity in Higher Education (NAFEO), as they had a potentially strategic role to play. The NAFEO was affiliated with the Black Executive Exchange Program (BEEP), which was an auxiliary of the NUL. BEEP was conceived to prepare students who attended historically black colleges and universities (HBCU) to enter the labor force upon graduation. BEEP consisted of successful business professionals who would volunteer to mentor HBCU students on their college and university campuses.

It was necessary for representatives from the NUL, NAFEO, and the stakeholders (human resources and contract personnel) from Coast Guard Headquarters to attend the meeting. The meeting was held in New Orleans, Louisiana. We met to discuss the MoU and develop an action plan for implementing the stipulated requirements of the MoU.

Mr. Jacob was invited as the keynote speaker for the forum. It was important for him to participate in the meeting to show his personal support and talk about what it would mean for the NUL and the coast guard to have a strategic partnership. During his remarks, Mr. Jacob raised curiosity and captured the group's attention with his persuasive articulation of how the partnership would benefit the NUL and the coast guard by producing results of mutual interest.

The conference lasted for several days and was very successful. The NUL branch presidents, NAFEO participants, and coast guard representatives shared a commitment to work toward making the MoU a successful enterprise.

To give recognition to the NUL and the coast guard in developing a partnership, the NUL president invited me to sit on the dais at the closing of the various NUL national conferences. The emcee always introduced me as the "coast guard assistant commandant for civil rights and liaison to the National Urban League."

We imagined that coast guard field facilities could support the MoU by establishing contact with urban league branches in their geographical areas. Appropriately, the civil rights office organized a meeting with Vice Admiral Clyde Robbins (Pacific Area commander) and the president of the Bay Area Urban League in Alameda, California. Staff members of both parties were present.

I chaired the meeting. The purpose of the meeting was to introduce the Bay Area Urban League president to the coast guard area commander and get the two of them talking about how they might work together, using their resources, to accomplish outcomes of mutual interest to their respective organizations.

Of specific interest was getting out a message to residents of the local minority communities serviced by the NUL that the coast guard was an organization worthy of consideration for employment in its military or civilian workforce.

It was known that some NUL branches held charters for some magnet schools. Magnet schools normally enrolled high-performing students. The coast guard was eager to establish relationships with organizations that chartered magnet schools. This was an excellent way to tap into the rich pool of magnet-school students whenever possible, and high school students would potentially be excellent candidates for coast guard recruiting programs. The coast guard was willing to offer its resources (speakers, mentors, tutors, or whatever was needed) to form a partnership with the NUL in that regard.

The meeting was well received by members of the NUL and the coast guard. An excellent exchange of ideas and personal information took place. They discussed suggestions for specific actions that could be taken and considered the need for additional high-level meetings. Also discussed were ways to get NUL units that operated in local communities to enter into dialogue with coast guard field facilities and how coast guard facilities could do the same in places where NUL activities took place.

Follow-up discussion with Vice Admiral Robbins revealed that the groundbreaking meeting went well. He recommended to his subordinate field-facility commanding officers that they should get involved with NUL branches in their geographical areas. In addition, Vice Admiral Robbins discussed his meeting with the NUL at a flag officer/SES conference and challenged other field commanders to reach out to the NUL, as he had done. Vice Admiral Robbins and the NUL branch president's meeting served as a precursor for more collaboration between the NUL and the coast guard, held at the field level.

Participating in National Urban League Black Executive Exchange Program, 1987–2000

The Black Executive Exchange Program (BEEP) was founded to assist students who attended historically black colleges and universities (HBCU). Many of the students were from families who had never attended a college before. They had limited knowledge of what to expect or how to deal with college life in general. The program assisted students in successfully navigating their way through problems they might encounter during their college matriculation and other related experiences.

BEEP, a voluntary partnership of the NUL, was created in 1969. Its mission was to "share the learning experience across generations, cultivate new leaders, and inspire achievements 'beyond the possible' through committed involvement and operational experience." The program was active at eighty-four HBCUs. It prepared students to become the sophisticated and knowledgeable employees that corporate America and its global competitors were seeking. African Americans executives, on loan from corporations and the federal government, participated in the program as "visiting professors." These dedicated individuals voluntarily participated in the program in order to give back to their communities and help credentialed African American college students to achieve their goals."

Visiting professors for the program were drawn from professionals in the private sector and managers and leaders in the federal government.

Participation in this program was an opportunity to interact with HBCU students, not only to share useful experiences with them but to present them with information on how to prepare themselves for opportunities in the coast guard—in the civilian workforce as well as the military service.

I was eager to join BEEP and support its mission; it provided an excellent opportunity to talk to college students about how they could become members of the coast guard. During my time with the program, I visited fourteen historically black colleges and universities, located in seven different states.

With the consent of the presidents of the institutions, I met with hundreds of students at all college levels and shared information with them on a variety of subjects. We talked about what it was like for me to attend college and the difficulties I had to overcome to graduate.

It was a particularly special opportunity to mentor students and talk to them about what it was like working in the coast guard and the federal government—the "real world," where college students were needed. It also was an opportunity to explain the missions of the coast guard and how students could prepare themselves to execute those missions as members of the service as civilian employees or members of the enlisted or officer corps. I emphasized joining the officer corps more than other options, as that was where the coast guard hoped to acquire more minorities after they graduated from college.

Some colleges seized the opportunity to consult with visiting professors on administrative matters. For example, the president of Paul Quinn College in Waco, Texas, asked me to join his management team as an unpaid member of its board of advisers, which met twice a year. Since serving in that capacity did not create any ethical problems, I accepted the position. It was an honor to serve as a member of the board for several years.

The coast guard message and compassion for minority college students resonated throughout the HBCU communities. HBCU presidents and their students were favorably impressed with the message. Jimmie Jenkins, PhD, president of Elizabeth City [North Carolina] State University, invited me to keynote his university's convocation assembly. Also, Ms. Kimberly Brown, a student at Virginia State University, asked me to speak to her classmates during their communications period. I accepted both invitations; I was honored that I was invited to speak at these institutions on such auspicious occasions, and it was a joy to share my thoughts with the students. At both forums, I emphasized why it was important for college graduates to develop an optimistic outlook for the future— they are the next generation of leaders. Minority college students, I said, should do their best to prepare themselves to become leaders of the future.

BEEP was an excellent platform for consultation with many interesting people—college presidents, faculty, and students—on HBCU campuses.

Chapter 16

Collaborating with the National Association for Equal Opportunity in Higher Education, 1987–2004

IMPLEMENTING THE OBJECTIVES OF THE MOU VARIED IN MANY WAYS. The coast guard had a MoU with the National Association for Equal Opportunity in Higher Education. Samuel Myers, PhD, was the founder and president/CEO of the organization. The civil rights office reached out to Dr. Myers. We wanted to inform him that the coast guard was interested in his organization and in the students attending HBCUs. It just so happened that around the time of this contact, Dr. Myers's organization was holding its annual conference in Washington, DC. It was there that Admiral Yost and Dr. Myers met for the first time.

I coordinated an arrangement for Admiral Yost and several other admirals in Coast Guard Headquarters to participate in the NAFEO annual conference. This was a good opportunity for admirals in the service to meet presidents of HBCUs, the educational leaders in the black community.

NAFEO invited the commandant and several coast guard admirals to attend its VIP annual conference reception. Several admirals in Coast Guard Headquarters accepted and became full participants in the conference. During their participation, they viewed exhibits and socialized with the HBCU presidents. Admiral Yost was invited to sit on the dais as a special guest during the closing conference proceedings.

Admiral Yost enjoyed the conference activities but commented afterward that the closing proceedings lasted longer than he had expected—it must have been around midnight when the conference ended. Admiral Yost was impressed during this first meeting with Dr. Myers and the HBCU presidents. He was intrigued by what the college students could potentially offer the coast guard.

Admiral Yost asked me to work with the HBCU presidents to possibly garner their support in developing a strategic program for attracting HBCU students to the coast guard, especially African Americans. Collaborating with Dr. Myers and HBCU presidents, the civil rights office led coast guard efforts in developing a proposal, referred to as the College Student Enlisted Program (CSEP). This proposal was conceived after several intense meetings of give-and- take between the civil rights office and the HBCU presidents, with Dr. Myers personally contributing as a sage adviser.

We considered the idea of authorizing grants to needy students who desired attending a historically black college or university; upon graduation, they would become candidates for officers in the coast guard, subject to passing a mental and physical examination. If the graduate could not pass the examination, the coast guard would consider the individual for enrollment as an enlisted member of the military service. We considered that concept as a starting point, subject to coast guard approval.

I vetted this concept with stakeholders in Coast Guard Headquarters and our parent organization, the Department of Transportation. There was reluctance throughout the vetting process, as some individuals thought giving grants to students in African American colleges without considering other groups might be a violation of the Supreme Court's decision regarding affirmative action.

Given this reluctance, Rear Admiral John Schor (coast guard chief counsel) and I discussed the pros and cons of the proposal and came up with an alternative suggestion. We recommended to Admiral Yost that the coast guard could use its authority to enlist African American college students into the service after completion of two years of college, at which time they would be required to pass an entrance examination for enlisted personnel.

After passing the examination, they would become members of the coast guard. At this point in their military careers, the coast guard would be free to grant them tuition assistance (including books and fees) to pay for their junior and senior years of college. Upon graduation, they would be subject to another mental and physical test. Those who passed the test would be enrolled in the coast guard's Officer Candidate School (OCS) and, subject to completion, would become officers in the coast guard. Those who did not meet the requirements for OCS would be obligated to serve at least two years in enlisted service.

I presented this idea to the HBCU presidents, and they agreed.

Admiral Yost approved the proposal for implementation.

The CSEP served as an important program for recruiting African American college students for the officer corps. Some of the students who signed up for the program but who did not meet all the requirements for the officer corps continued their relationship with the coast guard as enlisted members.

The CSEP was communicated throughout the HBCU community. Students at several of the colleges favorably considered it, and enrollment in the program was a notable success.

The CSEP was of special interest to Admiral Yost, and he delivered the keynote address to the first graduating class of HBCU students in the OCS program, after they completed their last two years of college as CSEP students. The graduation ceremony was held at the Yorktown, Virginia, training command, and the graduates were commissioned as officers in the coast guard.

The photographer on scene for this novel ceremony took photos and presented me a copy of two of the African Americans who were in the graduating class. This photo was placed on the wall in my office until one of those graduates visited me. He was so enamored of his picture with Admiral Yost that I let him have the photo as a keepsake.

The success of the CSEP may be attributed to collaboration between Dr. Myers, HBCU presidents, and coast guard officials, who worked together to find a way to attract minorities for the coast guard officer corps at the direction of Admiral Yost.

The coast guard's strategic involvement continued with the NAFEO.

Admiral Bill Kime (USCG commandant) was keynote speaker at an opening session of another NAFEO conference. He emphasized how important education was to effectively perform coast guard missions. He commended the NAFEO presidents on the importance of the work they were doing to educate leaders for the future. He indicated that the coast guard would like to attract some of their students for work in the coast guard. He emphasized that there were numerous opportunities available for graduates of HBCUs to join the service as civilians and military officers.

Another commandant, Admiral Bob Kramek, was invited to attend an HBCU summer retreat at Hilton Head, South Carolina. He accepted the invitation. This was his first opportunity to address the HBCU presidents and reassure them of the coast guard's continuing support for developing and implementing projects of mutual interest. Despite a weather forecast for stormy conditions, Admiral Kramek was determined to attend the forum. He arrived late because his aircraft had encountered a terrible rainstorm and had to land in Charleston, South Carolina, instead of flying directly to Hilton Head. Committed to fulfilling the engagement, Admiral Kramek boarded a coast guard helicopter in Charleston and flew to Hilton Head for the meeting.

The HBCU presidents were amazed by Admiral Kramek's determination to make the meeting. During his visit with them, he took photos and addressed the group. He talked about the coast guard's interest in working with the HBCU presidents on matters that would further the interests of their respective organizations. He expressed hopeful interest in welcoming their graduating students as members of the coast guard in various capacities, as military and civilian members.

Admiral Kramek made a significant impression on the HBCU presidents, as he reassured them that the coast guard was dedicated to developing a meaningful partnership with them.

Chapter 17

Executing Coast Guard Recruiting Initiatives for the Twenty -First Century, 1993–2000

ANOTHER CONCERN OF THE COAST GUARD WAS AN INADEQUATE EFFORT to attract African Americans to the coast guard academy. The academy's traditional recruiting practices were not doing enough to attract African Americans. The academy had relatively weak community connections with minority high schools and their counselors.

Rear Admiral Paul Versaw became superintendent of the Coast Guard Academy in 1993. He was aware of efforts the service was undertaking to develop a strategic relationship with minority organizations and what that could mean for attracting minorities to the academy.

We had talked about this issue on numerous occasions prior to his appointment as the academy superintendent. Rear Admiral Versaw was determined to get the academy involved in finding ways to attract minorities, and he realized the academy could not do this alone.

Rear Admiral Versaw recommended to the commandant that the coast guard establish a board of trustees at the academy to advise the superintendent on recruiting matters, as well as other issues that might improve the effective and efficient operation of the academy. His recommendation was vetted among stakeholders in Coast Guard Headquarters. The idea was referred to the chief counsel for legal review. And after legal review of the matter and concurrence of the coast guard's chief counsel, the commandant approved the board of trustees' concept, with the board to be headed by the assistant commandant for human resources.

After creation of the coast guard's board of trustees, Rear Admiral Versaw asked me to be a member. It was an honor and a privilege to serve on this prestigious board, and I thanked Rear Admiral Versaw for the opportunity. I told him I would be delighted to get involved in any way possible to find ways to attract minorities for consideration as cadets at the academy. He knew I was interested in the recruiting issue. And as a member of the board of trustees, this would be an official role—working with him and others to find ways to attract African Americans.

After establishing the board of trustees at the academy, remarkable strategic plans and activities improved the prospects for attracting minorities. At the outset, the military leadership and faculty members at the academy, except for an African American assistant athletic coach, were predominately white male individuals. Most of the faculty members had worked at the academy for a long time. Not too long after the board was established, the white male dean of academics at the academy retired. The dean was replaced by a white female dean. The superintendent also hired a female African American to serve as the equal employment opportunity officer for the academy. She was a very resourceful adviser to the superintendent, especially regarding diversity issues.

The board played a role in the search for and decision to hire the new dean. The search committee was led by an African American, Rear Admiral Erroll Brown, assistant commandant for engineering. Rear Admiral Brown also was a member of the board of trustees.

The board of trustees was made up of several program directors from Coast Guard Headquarters, a member of the Coast Guard Auxiliary, and a retired coast guard officer. We met quarterly at the academy. The agenda for meetings was drawn up by the academy superintendent and his staff. The superintendent arranged briefings on the status of the academy and presented recommendations on how the board could advance the vision of the institution, with emphasis on supporting activities to attract minorities to the organization. We normally met quarterly for two to three days during each meeting. After each meeting, the board briefed academy staff members on its deliberations and other pertinent information relative to the academy's strategic plans.

Rear Admiral Versaw asked me to speak at the academy to emphasize the commandant's commitment to developing an organization that valued diversity. This was one of the missions of the Civil Rights program. I visited the academy on several occasions and spoke to the academy military leadership corps, faculty members, and selected members of the cadet corps. I emphasized the importance of diversity in classroom deliberations and why diversity should be valued by our future leaders, especially the coast guard cadets.

Every year the superintendent sent me an invitation to attend the graduation ceremony. It was an honor and privilege to be there. On occasion, I ate lunch and attended formal dinners with the cadets. I listened to their stories about what life was like at the academy.

During candid conversations, some minority cadets talked about their personal experiences concerning social activities. The surrounding communities consisted primarily of white residents, they said, and did not offer amenities (such as barber shops) and social outlets for African Americans. This might seem a trivial matter, but it was very important to some minorities. Their stories motivated me to try to do more to attract minorities to the institution and to encourage the military leadership to understand the social concerns of minorities and to put forth efforts to address such matters, if possible.

In order to promote coast guard commitment to diversity, the superintendent sponsored a service-wide diversity summit. Academic scholars were invited to participate. The academic scholars spoke persuasively on the subject and aroused the attention and commitment of all in attendance. The summit was held at the time when the current commandant, Admiral Jim Loy, was retiring and was to be replaced by the new commandant, then Vice Admiral Tom Collins. Both of these leaders addressed the audience, reinforcing the coast guard's commitment to further efforts to develop a coast guard organization that valued diversity.

The academy seemed to be energized by these persuasive activities and was motivated to work harder to attract minorities to the institution. Their activities were recognized by organizations outside of the coast guard. Community organizations recognized certain members of the academy for their accomplishments. For example, the National Association for the Advancement of Colored People (NAACP) recognized a superintendent of the academy and a commandant of cadets. The NAACP awarded them the Roy Wilkins Renowned Service Award for their exceptional efforts in support of equal opportunity policies and dedication to improving recruiting efforts to successfully attract minorities to the Coast Guard Academy. Their commitment contributed to the overwhelming support for the Coast Guard Recruiting Initiative for the Twenty-First Century (CGRIT) and other decisions effectuated by coast guard.

The academy superintendent thought the institution could do more to attract minorities, especially African Americans. Traditional recruiting practices were not reaching potential minority candidates in high schools or in their communities. Why not explore the strategic relationship the coast guard was developing with historically black colleges and universities? Could collaborating with NAFEO help the academy to attract more minorities?

The civil rights office reached out to Dr. Samuel Myers to discuss this matter. Dr. Myers was a renowned educator. He was a graduate of Harvard University with a PhD in economics. He had served as president of several black colleges and founded the National Association for Equal Opportunity in Higher Education (NAFEO). As president and CEO of the organization, he championed the interest of the 117 historically black colleges and universities. He authored legislation to gain the president's support for HBCUs. Dr. Myers had a reputation as a visionary leader in the field of education.

Given his leadership role in NAFEO, he had influence among other HBCU presidents. By collaborating with this group of professional educators in minority communities, there was reason to be confident that with their knowledge and experience in academia, they would be able to offer alternative solutions to address the academy's recruiting problem. The presidents of HBCU were deeply rooted in black communities. They had built collaborative relationships with feeder high schools, from which they routinely attracted students to attend their institutions. If the academy could recruit a sufficient number of minorities—enough to create a critical mass of cadets at the academy—then this might encourage other minorities to think about the academy and what it had to offer.

This reminds me of how the number of females began to grow at the academy—an interesting story.

The Honorable William Coleman, then secretary of transportation, asked the commandant to consider admitting females to the Coast Guard Academy—all the other service academies were already doing that. The secretary advised the commandant that he could voluntarily do it and be viewed as a pioneer, or the secretary could direct the commandant to do it, but then he might suffer the embarrassment of the secretary's having to direct him to do it. The commandant chose the former option. The first group of female cadets entered the academy in 1976 and graduated with the class of 1980. Since then, females—mostly white females—have applied for admission to the academy in large numbers, so much so that in the mid-nineties, one-third of the entering class at the academy was females. The point is that great things can happen when there is the resolve to achieve a desirable goal. There is reason to believe that having a critical mass of females at the academy encouraged other females to become interested in attending the institution.

Recruiting more minorities for the Coast Guard Academy was a desirable goal. We had to lay everything on the table and accept that traditional recruiting practices were not good enough. We needed to think out of the box and explore new recruiting strategies, perhaps considering suggestions offered by Dr. Myers and HBCU presidents. The coast guard was open to this collaborative brainstorming.

In this collaboration, the civil rights office led coast guard efforts to develop and implement an initiative to recruit minorities for the officer corps. We considered three options as pathways to commissioning officers in the service. These possibilities included the College Student Pre-commissioning Initiative (CSPI), Officer Candidate School (OCS), and direct admission to the academy.

The College Student Pre-commissioning Initiative (formerly the College Student Enlisted Program, or CSEP) had already proved successful. It involved two phases for officer commissioning. Phase one: Upon successfully completion of two years at an HBCU, a student could enroll in the program as an enlisted member. Phase two: The student then would have to complete the remaining two years of college and would have to pass a coast guard mental and physical examination, prior to entering the coast guard's Officer Candidate School (OCS).

At any time during the student's four years of college, however, the student was free to leave the HBCU and apply directly for admission to the Coast Guard Academy. If admitted, the student would begin study as a freshman, as no provisions were authorized for transfer of credits from an HBCU to the academy.

During enrollment in the CSPI, the student was given a stipend. The coast guard would pay for tuition, books, and other fees. If the student completed the program and received a commission in the coast guard, the student would assume a three-year service obligation. If the student did not graduate from college, he or she would have the option of remaining in the coast guard as an enlisted member or walking away without any service obligation for not completing the program. The decision the student made, however, would depend upon approval of the coast guard.

The OCS was available to college graduates. Anyone completing a four-year college curriculum and graduating with a degree of any kind was eligible to apply for admission to the coast guard's Officer Candidate School. Upon acceptance and completion of the OCS— which consisted of military orientation, tradition, and physical fitness—the individual would be commissioned as an officer in the coast guard, with a three-year service obligation.

While the College Student Pre-commissioning Initiative and Officer Candidate School programs were options for commissioning officers in the coast guard, emphasis was placed on attracting minorities to the Coast Guard Academy. Graduation from the academy was a big deal. It was often perceived that graduation from the academy carried with it a more optimistic outlook for success as an officer in the coast guard.

To focus on the academy, the civil rights office led coast guard efforts to develop and implement CGRIT. This began by holding several meeting with Dr. Myers and a select group of HBCU presidents to explain the coast guard's problem—its inability to attract African Americans for the coast guard's OCS and academy programs. We solicited their ideas and suggestions. After several brainstorming sessions, we devised the concept referred to as the Coast Guard Recruiting Initiative for the Twenty-First Century (CGRIT). CGRIT was conceived as a visionary recruiting program to identify potential college students for consideration for enrollment as cadets at the Coast Guard Academy. The HBCUs would play a strategic role in working with the academy to implement the program.

CGRIT was an innovative idea that required much more discussion to formulate the process, procedures, and methodology to implement a successful plan of action. We were optimistic that with the HBCU presidents and Coast Guard Academy working together, it would produce results.

The HBCU presidents were willing to strategically work with the coast guard to develop a program that would attract African Americans to the academy. They envisioned mutually rewarding benefits, especially for any of their students who wanted to begin a public service career as a commissioned officer in the coast guard. They believed CGRIT would accomplish that goal. And if implemented successfully, CGRIT would offer the coast guard an alternative approach for attracting African Americans to the academy.

I presented the CGRIT concept to the body of HBCU presidents in attendance at their annual retreat held at Hilton Head, South Carolina. There was a consensus of agreement among the HBCU presidents. They suggested that the coast guard should move forward, taking the next step to make it happen.

With the HBCU community on board, I presented the concept to stakeholders in Coast Guard Headquarters and the superintendent of the Coast Guard Academy. They had no objections, so I briefed the commandant, who expressed agreement, in principle, with this pioneer program. He announced at an NAFEO annual conference in Washington, DC, that the coast guard planned to pursue the project. The next step, then, was to hire a contractor to facilitate the activities that might require expert handling.

In view of the commandant's guidance and nature of the work to be performed, the coast guard needed to commission the right organization to perform what it needed. The civil rights office held a discussion with the academy superintendent, headquarters stakeholders, and Dr. Myers to hash out the principal elements of the project. There was agreement that administration of the project should be handled by an outside contractor, with oversight under the direction of the Coast Guard Academy and the Office of Civil Rights.

The contractor would develop and administer a program to identify potential high school graduates who could possibly meet coast guard standards. And if the students desired to become officers in the coast guard, the contractor, following the guidance of the academy, would enter into an agreement with them, allowing one of two options for consideration. They could apply for immediate acceptance to the academy upon graduation from high school or elect to attend an HBCU for up to two years and then apply for enrollment in the CSPI. If they elected to apply directly to the academy and were accepted, they would enter the academy as freshman cadets in the incoming class of the year they applied.

If they elected to attend an HBCU for two years, they could sign up for the CSPI program. But they could not join the coast guard until after they had successfully completed two years of study at an HBCU. Then they could then enroll in the CSPI program. At this point the coast guard would pay all college expenses, including tuition, books, and other fees, while they attended the HBCU.

The essential elements of CGRIT were reviewed with the assistant commandant for human resources and the superintendent of the Coast Guard Academy. With their concurrences, I asked Dr. Myers to schedule a meeting with the full conference of HBCU presidents during their next summer retreat at Hilton Head so that I could present the initiative to them.

The meeting was scheduled with the HBCU presidents, and I chaired the meeting and presented the concept for discussion and evaluation. A primary concern the HBCU presidents expressed was that the coast guard would be taking some of their best students before they finished college. The HBCU presidents insisted on a plan that would provide grants to colleges that could be used to educate the students. I argued that was not acceptable, given the possibility that such an arrangement might not meet the Supreme Court's guidance on affirmative action. The coast guard did not want to open that can of worms.

Furthermore, instead of giving grants to institutions, the coast guard would, in effect, buy seats in the classrooms of the colleges. This would be another way of helping the colleges acquire monies to pay expenses. Also, there were two other things to take into consideration. If the students left college during their first two years of college at an HBCU to attend the academy, the individuals, upon completion of the academy program, would be assured of a challenging job as an officer in the coast guard. This could not be promised by merely graduating from college. Then, there might be a possibility of granting a dual degree, one from the HBCU and another from the academy, to a graduate of the academy, who had previously matriculated at both institutions.

Moreover, college students who enrolled as juniors in CGRIT would be given a stipend for two years, comparable to the salary of an enlisted member in the coast guard. These students would be among the "financially well-off" individuals on campus.

The conference of HBCU presidents offered no objection to CGRIT. The coast guard tentatively approved it for implementation.

The next step was to find the right contractor to do the job. Prior to issuing a request for proposal (RFP) to hire a contractor, the civil rights office scheduled an all-day meeting to be held at the Coast Guard Academy to finalize the details of CGRIT and to discuss the mechanics of implementing the project. In order to conserve time and for the potential participants to get to know each other, the superintendent and I hosted a meet-and-greet reception at a local hotel in New London, Connecticut, the night before. It was a great informal gathering that aroused anticipation.

Attending the meeting were the superintendent of the Coast Guard Academy, his key management officials, Dr. Myers and his staff, and the dean of academics from Morgan State University.

During the meeting the next day, no time was lost before the HBCU representatives commented on the typical backgrounds of African

American students graduating from feeder high schools, from which HBCU recruited their freshman students. They noted that many of the students grew up in predominately African American communities. The students were raised by their parents or grandparents, who might not have attended college. The potential students might not have ever traveled outside of their respective neighborhoods. The neighborhoods they grew up in and the world that they knew might be strikingly unlike the backgrounds of most nonminority students attending the Coast Guard Academy.

The HBCU representatives added that a successful blending of the two potentially different cultural backgrounds of minority and nonminority students who might attend the Coast Guard Academy together for the first time was a challenge that the academy should acknowledge and be prepared to deal with. The point of this message was that the academy should ensure that minority students would be welcomed into the academic environment at the academy.

We discussed the mechanics for CGRIT. This included including screening and recommending students, review of the students' backgrounds, acceptance for entering the program, testing, and the overall monitoring of the students throughout the process. The goals, expectations, and desired outcomes were hashed out. The meeting was very productive. Everyone in attendance was overwhelmed with an optimistic outlook for attracting minorities to the academy.

When the meeting ended, Rear Admiral Versaw directed a review of cadets to honor Dr. Myers for his outstanding accomplishments in education and public service. The cadets performed admirably. We were impressed with the passing of the cadets in their battalion formation.

After this formal ceremony, Dr. Myers spoke to a select group of cadets in an academy meeting room. He talked about the importance of education and what it meant for sustaining a high standard of living in our society.

I left the Coast Guard Academy with a bright outlook with respect to developing a strategic partnership between the academy and NAFEO and the mutual benefits that might be obtained with our respective organizations working together.

After returning to DC, the civil rights office requested the coast guard's contracting branch to issue a request for proposal (RFP) in the DC metropolitan area to obtain bidders on the impending CGRIT contract. The RFP was developed and released. One of the bidders was NAFEO. Given that NAFEO had the most relevant experience and appeared to be the best organization to perform what the coast guard wanted done, the contract was awarded to NAFEO in 1995 as a one-year year contract, valued at $500,000, with a four-year extension clause, to be exercised at the discretion of the coast guard, bringing the contract's potential total to $2.5 million for five years.

During performance of the contract, the contractual arm of NAFEO became Minority Access, Inc. Minority Access assumed responsibility for administering the contract and its performance for at least the last three years of the five years the contract was authorized. Dr. Myers served as chairman of the board of Minority Access. Ms. Andrea Mickle was appointed as president to run the nonprofit organization.

During performance of the contract, the academy superintendent, who strongly supported the contract, retired and was replaced by another superintendent with different ideas on how the coast guard should recruit minorities for the academy. This became an unforeseen problem that reverberated throughout the entire implementation process. Consequently, this undermined the original intent of CGRIT, and recruiting results were negatively affected.

An internal debate ensued within the coast guard about the value of the contract and whether it was producing the desired results. A junior officer was assigned as the project manager. I doubt if the project manager carried enough weight to sway the argument one way or the other, given that the argument to cancel the contract after three or four years came from individuals at much higher levels in the organization.

The contract had been strategically drawn up, requiring specific deliverables from year to year. For example, the contractor was required to recommend twenty minority high school students each year who met eligibility requirements of the Coast Guard Academy; to recruit ten students each year for the College Student Pre- commissioning Initiative program; and recruit ten graduates of HBCU and/or minority-serving institutions each year to enter Officer Candidate School. (Minority-serving institutions, or MSI, were added to include Hispanics who attended a college or university at which 25 percent of the students enrolled were Hispanic.) Although African Americans and Hispanics were the most sought-after students to potentially enrich diversity, anyone attending an HBCU or MSI was eligible to take advantage of CGRIT, including nonminority candidates.

A review of what the contractor did to meet the requirement of the specified deliverables varied between the contractor and the coast guard. This led to a coast guard proposal to cancel the contract.

According to the president of Minority Access, the first year of the contract performance was devoted to project planning, infrastructure building, recruitment of staff, and staff development. Meetings with stakeholders within and outside of the coast guard were also part of the first year's activities. Given this array of necessary activities, it should be assumed, if not specifically stipulated in the contract, that the first year of deliverables required by the contract should have been waived.

With regards to deliverables, Minority Access was required to deliver one hundred referrals to the Coast Guard Academy over a five-year period, but 108 referrals were delivered. The contractor was required to deliver fifty referrals for consideration for the CSPI program; the contractor delivered sixty-four. The contractor was required to recommend fifty referrals for OCS; the contractor delivered only nineteen.

Overall, however, the total number of referrals required by the contract over a five-year period totaled two hundred, as compared to the actual number of 191 referred by the contractor. In effect, the contractor submitted nine fewer referrals than the contract required.

The contractor's argument suggested if we looked at the performance over a four-year period—waiving the first year of the five years to account for planning and staffing requirements—the deliverables were acceptable. If this had been the case, the contractor would have been required to refer eighty candidates for the academy program but referred 108. The contractor would have been required to refer forty candidates for the CSPI program but referred sixty-four. The contractor would have been required to refer forty candidates for OCS but referred only nineteen. In effect, however, the contractor would have referred thirty-one more candidates than the contract required.

Whether we considered five years of the contractor's referrals or four years, we arrived at the same conclusion—191 candidates were referred to the coast guard for consideration for the academy, CSPI, and OCS. The question that needed to be answered was what disposition was made of the referrals. Were they accepted or rejected by the coast guard for any legitimate reason, or did the referred students voluntarily decline to become members of the coast guard? It seemed that Minority Access offered valid questions with regard to whether the contract should be terminated.

Throughout the debate over whether the contract should be extended or terminated, I did not see any convincing evidence that canceling the contract was warranted. The contractor indicated on a number of occasions that her company was meeting the requirements of the contract. She opined that, especially over the five years, she had submitted the required number of names of students to the academy for consideration, the primary goal of the coast guard. The CSPI and OCS goals were desirable but were not as important as the academy's referrals.

While trying to remain neutral, I looked for reasons to support either Minority Access's or the coast guard's point of view. Since there was not enough information to support either side, I took the position that the contract should be allowed to run for five years to see if any of the referred students graduated from the academy or OCS.

Granted, the CGRIT processes, procedures, and methodologies may not have achieved the desired results, but what were the reasons? I believed it was appropriate to analyze what had been done to develop an after-action report to determine if the relationship with Minority Access should be terminated. After all, CGRIT was a pioneering project, and some weaknesses in project planning should have been expected.

Other military academies must have gone through similar situations (and made adjustments) before determining what was best for them to recruit minorities. While my conversation with the dean of cadets at the USAF Academy did not offer an exact formula for recruiting minorities, it was optimistic. He indicated that the academy set goals for recruiting minorities, developed recruiting plans, and then appropriated enough money to reach their goals, year after year.

If the USAF Academy could spend money (much more than the coast guard) to recruit African Americans, then that was enough anecdotal information for me to argue keeping the coast guard contract for at least five years, and then analyze the results to determine if there were graduates from any of the three programs. This seemed a legitimate way to make a decision on whether or not to terminate the contract. After all, the coast guard was spending only $2.5 million dollars over a five-year "trial" period.

The coast guard contract was eventually terminated at the completion of five years, at the disappointment of the contractor.

I think CGRIT was a potentially good enterprise but not managed properly. The coast guard missed a great opportunity to grow an excellent program for recruiting minorities for the Coast Guard Academy. If we could do it all over again, I would suggest more closely monitoring the overall process and requiring the contractor to ensure that all high school students who signed up for CGRIT would take courses recommended by the Coast Guard Academy if they planned to apply to the academy, in order to better prepare themselves to handle a competitive admission process, as well the rigorous academic curriculum.

To get this message across, contact with high school counselors would be required prior to the students' graduation from high school. Counselors should know that students interested in CSPI should be required to take courses recommended by the coast guard in order to qualify for enrollment in CGRIT. According to the contractor's data, the referrals for candidates to the academy were not only met but exceeded, but the contractor provided no evidence of this to the civil rights office.

If this was the case, the coast guard should have provided feedback to the contractor on how many of those referred students were accepted and how many were rejected for not meeting academy standards. The contractor should have received this information following each submission of referrals, so that the contractor could make the necessary adjustments in the selection process.

Finally, the project manager should have been the dean of academics at the academy or someone chosen to represent the dean. I think this level of attention should have been required for a pioneering recruiting initiative such as CGRIT to ensure success.

As the coast guard's co-director for the project, a lot of personal and reputational capital had been invested in the initiative. The civil rights office was partially responsible for the outcome of CGRIT. It was no easy task to acquire the support of HBCU presidents and convince coast guard policy makers that the pioneer CGRIT was in the best interests of the service for recruiting African Americans and Hispanics to enhance diversity in the officer corps.

Briefings from my staff in headquarters who monitored the program and the academy superintendent's staff, during meetings held at the board of trustee sessions, were all favorable. The academy's commandant of cadets informed me that he reviewed the academy's admission process to ensure that the contractor's referrals were considered for acceptance, based on merit factors consistent with Supreme Court guidance. No one suggested to me, directly or indirectly, during any of those instances that the contract should be terminated for any reason. No information surfaced that would lead me to support termination of the contract. Perhaps in retrospect, the civil rights office should have exercised stronger oversight in order to detect any developing problems before they became so serious that cancellation of CGRIT was an option we had no choice but to exercise.

What the coast guard should take away from the CGRIT enterprise is that it added value to the coast guard's recruiting policies and practices. The coast guard's recruiting practices were enhanced. CGRIT introduced the coast guard to new relationships with historically black colleges and universities and to Hispanic-serving colleges and universities. Through effective collaboration with leaders in those organizations, contacts with African American and Hispanic communities were possible, thus exposing their constituents to employment opportunities available in the service. Collaborating with external organizations, such as HBCUs and MSIs, expanded the coast guard's outreach into minority communities and potentially enhanced opportunities to achieve recruiting goals in a cost-effective and efficient manner.

What's more, the outreach tactics employed to implement CGRIT may have unintentionally roiled the mind-set of coast guard executives. But the experience gained in working with minority organizations to recruit minorities for commissioning in the officer corps might be worth repeating if CGRIT-like programs are organized with specific outcomes and are managed better.

The CGRIT was conceived for recruiting purposes. But just as important, the CGRIT was about integrating civil rights policies and practices into coast guard policies, practices and operational missions. Civil rights policies, practices and missions were definitely in operation. They were necessary to ensure successful outcomes in the CGRIT project. A lot was riding on the CGRIT enterprise. In my opinion, CGRIT added immense value to the coast guard's policies and practices by enhancing coast guard outreach to minority communities and potentially improving recruiting results.

Chapter 18

Attending JFK Harvard University Program for Senior Managers in Government, 1992

IN 1992 I TOOK TIME OUT TO ATTEND THE PROGRAM FOR SENIOR Managers in Government, which was offered by the Harvard University, John F. Kennedy School of Government. The coast guard had been participating in this program for several years, sending rear admirals to study as part of their continuing education. I applied for the program, and the commandant approved my attendance, along with another rear admiral, for the three-week class, August 2–21.

I never envisioned attending Harvard University for any reason, but the three weeks spent there were great. Studying at the school turned out to be an excellent educational experience, something I'd never imagined. The program offered different perspectives on management and leadership theories for consideration by senior managers in government.

There were sixty four participants in the program. Program classmates included flag officers from the other military services, assistant secretaries in the federal government, congressional staff members, and other Senior Executive Service (SES) officials. The class of sixty-four was divided into smaller caucuses of eight. Members of each caucus met together to discuss topical issues and formulate its group's thoughts for presentation to the full class when we came together.

The program was intense. It consisted of lectures on leadership and management theory delivered by Harvard professors and visiting scholars

It included comprehensive reading, group discussions, and problem solving of case studies, many of which were actual situations that had occurred in the federal government and private industry.

When discussing case studies, the purpose was to examine various situations and formulate the best options for solving defined problems. In most instances, the rationale presented by each of the eight caucuses was enlightening and great teachable experiences.

In addition, there were several days of lectures and discussions on negotiating principles, strategies, and techniques. This part of the program was led by some of Harvard University's outstanding negotiators, who had represented United States interests on the international scene.

The expert negotiators designed simulated exercises to challenge our negotiating skills. They facilitated discussions and evaluated our performance. The feedback from evaluation of our simulated exercises was an excellent teaching experience and provided insight into how to master negotiating skills, which is so important in the decision-making process. This part of the program stood out as one of the most significant educational experiences of the program.

Individual caucus groups were tasked to develop a project. The eight caucuses were challenged to compete against each other for the Best Project Award. To choose a project for the competition, each member of a caucus group was requested to develop a project and present it to its small group. After observing the eight presentations from its members, the small group decided on which one of their group's eight presentations should represent its caucus before the full class of sixty-four members. Separately, each of the eight caucuses presented its project to the judges, who were Harvard university professors. The judges selected the best project from among the eight caucus presentations.

I took this opportunity to get an objective evaluation on the model we had used in the coast guard to develop affirmative-action plans. It was a model designed to correct civilian workforce imbalances throughout the service. The total number of minorities in the civilian workforce was commendable, but the majority of them occupied low- level positions. Moving them out of low-level positions and placing them in higher-level positions was the difficult problem we tried to solve through affirmative-action planning and effective execution. The model contained a multifaceted approach. We projected the number of new available positions for the year based on retirements, volunteer separations, creation of new positions, and any other vacancies that occurred.

Given these projections, along with statistical data on percentages of minority representation in the nation's labor force, we used this substantive collection of data to put together the coast guard affirmative-action plans. The desired outcome was to create a civilian workforce in which the percentages of minorities in the coast guard would match their respective percentages in the national labor force. The action plans were distributed to potential hiring officials. We anticipated they would make the right decisions to train, promote, and/or hire employees during the year to achieve the desired outcome. This would potentially correct civilian imbalances in their respective organizations.

The model was not a scientifically developed instrument, but it was better than not having anything at all. When I presented it to my group, their feedback was candid and very encouraging. The general consensus was that probably no other federal agency was doing as much as the coast guard, so we should keep using the model.

My small group, however, selected another member's project to compete against the other seven small groups—and our group project won over the seven other group projects. As winners of the Best Project Award from Harvard University, each member of my group received a four-inch silver platter, engraved with the university's logo and the words "First Prize, Best Case Award, Small Group." The program director stated that our project was very important because winning projects might be used as possible case studies to be examined by other participants in future classes.

This three-week program was very useful. It gave me a different perspective on leadership and management theories. The negotiation section was great. The Harvard University staff referred to the intensive three-week program as a "comprehensive teaching experience," comparable to getting an MBA in three weeks.

There was some downtime during the three-week program. We were free to use this time at our own discretion, especially on the weekends.

I toured the campus and the city of Cambridge. There was an ice cream store in the city that offered the most delicious ice cream in the area. I visited this ice cream parlor after dinner on several occasions.

Also, I discovered the Charles River, with two bridge crossings situated about one-half the distance of a football field apart. This was an excellent place to jog on either side of the river. My jogging route entailed running across the first bridge, running the distance to the second bridge, crossing it, and running back to the first bridge; I repeated this trip several times, for a distance of about three miles in total. I spent many days jogging there, especially on weekends and at times when there were no classes.

The Friday after the program ended, my wife joined me in Cambridge for the weekend. She came up from Washington, DC, on the train. We spent the weekend touring the Harvard campus and visiting the surrounding cities. Jean had memories of Harvard because our daughter had graduated from the university with a master's degree in education and counseling psychology in June 1986. When she graduated, we were there for a short time to witness the celebration. I was delighted that Jean came up after the program ended. It was an opportunity to tell her all about the program as we drove back to Washington.

I returned to the coast guard, refreshed and enthusiastically motivated to tackle the complex issue that involved integrating civil rights policy and practices into the coast guard's operational policy and practices. The Harvard program offered a useful perspective on leadership, management, and negotiating skills. Furthermore, the objective feedback from my program colleagues on the coast guard model used to correct civilian workforce imbalance was encouraging. The three-week program was useful in strengthening leadership knowledge, skills, and abilities.

Chapter 19

Collaborating with the National Association for the Advancement of Colored People, 1993–2004

THE CIVIL RIGHTS OFFICE COLLABORATED WITH NAACP OFFICIALS to publicize the coast guard's missions in African American communities. This was an outreach initiative strategically organized to expose African Americans to career opportunities in the service.

We arranged for the coast guard to exhibit at annual NAACP conferences. Initially, our exhibits portrayed a limited message. But after signing the MoU with the NAACP, we expanded our exhibits for annual conferences. The chief of staff made this possible by providing more money for exhibiting at conferences. Sponsoring exhibits was considered a worthwhile expenditure because it enhanced the outreach program and recruiting efforts in minority communities.

We believed exhibiting was a strategically wise investment. The NAACP had more than two thousand chapters located throughout urban cities in the United States. The coast guard wanted to develop a relationship with those chapters and its members. In an effort to reach those members, the coast guard expanded its exhibits at annual NAACP conferences. We started posting civilian and military recruiters (officer and enlisted) at exhibit booths to pass out memorabilia and answer questions from conferees. The recruiters interacted with conferees of all age groups.

One year we purchased an enclosed exhibit pavilion at an NAACP conference to highlight our missions and initiate meaningful conversations with conferees. The exhibits consisted of memorabilia, lifelike cardboard poster images of successful people in the service, and simulated tasks available for conferees to act upon. The exhibits caught the attention of everyone who stopped at the pavilion. The activities were well received and served to establish a model for marketing at NAACP and other minority-sponsored conferences.

The civil rights office collaborated with the NAACP military program director and the DOD equal opportunity director to arrange for coast guard personnel to receive awards at annual NAACP conferences. Before this development, the awards were available only to members of the Department of Defense.

In addition to the exhibits, the coast guard became active in the NAACP Military Affairs program. Coast guard commandants Admirals Yost, Kime, and Loy addressed the Military Affairs dinner at NAACP conferences on different occasions.

The commandants presented inspiring messages on the status of African Americans in the coast guard, especially military officers and enlisted personnel. They reviewed the history of military members in the service and coast guard plans and vision for the future. The commandants articulated their commitment to the vision of the NAACP and equal opportunity in the military service.

Admirals Kime, Kramek, and Loy were presented the NAACP Meritorious Service Award for championing equal opportunity and civil rights–policy initiatives. This award, as a matter of NAACP practice, was presented only once every six years to a deserving military member in one of the five military services and also the National Guard. As the coast guard assistant commandant for civil rights, I was a member of the panel that evaluated recommendations presented by the coast guard to receive the prestigious award.

I coordinated the participation of Rodney Slater (the honorable secretary of transportation) in an NAACP conference. Secretary Slater was chosen as the keynote speaker to address the Military Affairs banquet. I was honored to have the opportunity to introduce him to the audience. The secretary roused the audience with his strong support for the military services and his commitment to ensuring the coast guard played a leading role in practicing diversity and equal opportunity in the military services. The secretary was awarded the Benjamin L. Hooks Distinguished Service Award on the evening he addressed the Military Affairs banquet on behalf of the coast guard.

The Roy Wilkins Renowned Service Award was presented annually to a military or civilian member for outstanding achievements during the year. All military and civilian members of the coast guard, regardless of grade, rank, or status, were eligible for nomination. The award was based on contributions made during the year to promote civil rights and equal opportunity initiatives. Individuals selected for this award were chosen annually by a service-wide nomination and selection system administered by the civil rights office.

I took care to appoint a rear admiral or SES official to chair the nomination panel for the selection of individuals to receive the award. The involvement of rear admirals and SES officials in the nomination process expanded their knowledge of the contributions made by individuals working in the Civil Rights program throughout the service. Nominees selected and recommended to receive the award were approved by the assistant commandant for civil rights.

Each year the successful nominee was presented the award at the NAACP Military Affairs banquet, attended by thousands of people. Two rear admirals (Richard Cueroni and James Card) received the award. Rear Admiral Cueroni was presented the award for his visionary work in recruiting minorities at the Coast Guard Academy. Rear Admiral Card received the award for outstanding work in supporting equal opportunity initiatives as a program director in Coast Guard Headquarters. And Admiral Paul Yost was presented the award the year he retired from the service for his equal opportunity accomplishments throughout his tenure as commandant, 1986 to 1990. Admiral Yost also keynoted one of the NAACP Military Affairs banquets during that time.

I was honored to receive two NAACP awards. The DOD nominated me for the NAACP Benjamin L. Hooks Distinguished Service Award and the Roy Wilkins Renowned Service Award for developing and implementing progressive civil rights and equal opportunity initiatives and programs in the coast guard. The NAACP Roy Wilkins Award was presented in 1987 and the Benjamin L. Hooks Award in 1993.

In 2001 the NAACP annual conference was held in New Orleans, Louisiana. At that time, the district commander in New Orleans, Rear Admiral Roy Casto, was interested in doing something to develop a pilot program to attract minorities to the coast guard. He had an idea that a pilot program, if successful, would stimulate other district commanders to consider doing the same. There was agreement. We discussed his idea several times. Eventually we decided to approach the NAACP to see if the Eighth District could plan an exercise of some sort with the assistance of the NAACP.

Following up on his idea, I introduced Rear Admiral Casto to NAACP leadership and arranged for him to participate in the opening session of the conference. He was invited to sit on the dais. He gave brief remarks and led the recitation of the Pledge of Allegiance during the presentation of the colors. This recognition enabled him to interact in a meaningful way with the NAACP branch presidents later on during the conference.

Prior to convening the conference, the civil rights office urged all field civil rights officers to make an effort to attend the convention for an important meeting with NAACP officials. The response to the request was great. Civil rights officers from all the major field commands showed up.

Rear Admiral Casto, the field civil rights officers, the coast guard chaplain, and I met with the NAACP branch presidents. Captain Leroy Gilbert, the coast guard chaplain, offered a prayer to begin the meeting in a solemn manner. This put everyone at ease.

Rear Admiral Casto and I facilitated discussions with those in attendance. We explained why the meeting was called and that we would like to partner with the NAACP to develop a pilot project to talk about opportunities available in the coast guard for constituents in their communities. We discussed coast guard missions and the kinds of occupations available in the service, with emphasis on encouraging students to sign up. Everyone offered comments and suggestions. A consensus was reached to focus on high school students.

We discussed various options for planning an exercise that could be held somewhere within the jurisdiction of the Eighth Coast Guard District but not too far from a local high school. The Louisville, Kentucky, NAACP branch president offered to host an activity in Louisville. We talked about several events that would make for an interesting and exciting day for students in that city.

Rear Admiral Casto said his district would arrange the transportation for students to and from the location where the exercises would be held. He would set up simulated exercises for the students and provide a wholesome lunch for all participants. The Louisville branch president agreed to arrange for participation of students from a magnet school located in his city. He also would coordinate student participation with the school's principal. He would ensure all-day attendance by students. Rear Admiral Casto agreed to hold the event on the banks of the Ohio River in Louisville.

On the day of the event, students showed up with glowing enthusiasm and anticipation, ready to participate in the project. The event took place on an excellent day with perfect weather conditions. Simulated exercises for the project were educational. They were designed by military personnel from the district to provide an appreciation for some of the work performed in the service. Military members facilitated participation of students in the activities. It was apparent that the students enjoyed themselves.

The overall goal of the project was to encourage high school seniors to consider applying to the Coast Guard Academy upon graduation. If not the academy, other options to consider were enlisting in the military service or signing up as a civilian civil service employee.

Rear Admiral Casto anticipated that such a pilot project could serve as a best practice and be emulated by other district commands. From all indications, he accomplished what he set out to do. Student participation was great. They were overwhelmed by everything that was planned for them.

Feedback from the head of the NAACP, Louisville branch, indicated that the event was successful. The students enjoyed the event, and they talked about their experiences with their peers in school and in their local communities.

Rear Admiral Casto talked about the details of this event to commanders of his subordinate field units He described the event as a best practice worth emulating. He suggested to his commanders that they should reach out to NAACP branch presidents in their geographical areas and organize similar events.

Displaying Coast Guard Assets at the NAACP Convention, 2000

The 2000 NAACP convention was held in Baltimore, Maryland. This was the year in which the coast guard was honored as one of the five military services. This provided the coast guard an opportunity to do some unusual things. Admiral Loy and I discussed a plan of action for participation in the conference. I addressed the conferees and gave them a preview of what to expect from the coast guard this year and invited them to visit our exhibits and some of the ships, helicopter, motor boats, etc. that would be on display during the conference

Admiral Loy was the keynote speaker at the Military Affairs banquet during this conference. It was an honor for me to introduce him at this prestigious dinner. Prior to delivering his remarks, Admiral Loy was presented the NAACP Distinguished Service Award by the president/ CEO of the NAACP for his outstanding support of equal opportunity policies and initiatives.

The civil rights office worked hard to ensure that coast guard participation in this conference was at an exceptionally high level. Exhaustive planning was part of the preparation for this conference. Admiral Loy and I agreed that we wanted to make this conference a memorable event executed by the coast guard. We wanted to do something special to make the service stand out among the other services by inspiring the conferees with an awesome display of coast guard assets.

At Admiral Loy's suggestion, I called Vice Admiral Vivian Crea, the Atlantic area commander, to discuss what we wanted to do. She indicated her support and suggested calling the director of operations to inquire what could be done. I phoned the director of operations and asked if it was possible to make some Atlantic-area assets available for display at the NAACP convention as a recruiting initiative. He said he would check his operations plan for assets scheduled to be in the Baltimore area during the time of the convention and get back to me.

The Atlanta area operations officer called back. He discussed a proposal that included a 210-foot medium-endurance cutter and the Coast Guard Academy's training vessel, the tall ship *Eagle*. The endurance cutter was available for only three or four days, but the tall ship *Eagle* could be available longer. A helicopter also was available, if desired, to simulate a rescue exercise. I said, "That would be great. Let's do it."

The tall ship *Eagle*, a 295-foot vessel, had some historic significance. The United States captured it from the Germans during the Second World War. It was later turned over to the United States Coast Guard Academy for use as a training vessel for cadets and other officers.

On the way to the convention, the *Eagle* sailed with a crew from New London, Connecticut, to the Baltimore harbor, where it docked not far from where the convention's activities were taking place.

The academy superintendent and I held a VIP reception aboard the *Eagle* for NAACP members and guests from the other military services and the National Guard. The superintendent welcomed guests, and we exchanged pleasantries during the reception. We engaged our guests in discussions with regard to the coast guard's interest in recruiting African Americans. All of our guests were given a tour of the *Eagle*. The reception served as an excellent approach to engage the audience in talking about coast guard missions and what the coast guard had to offer the general public at large.

The 210-foot coast guard cutter sailed from Portsmouth, Virginia, and also docked in the Baltimore harbor. Prior to arrival, the cutter stopped in Annapolis, Maryland, to participate in a ceremony honoring history relevant to the coast guard and the NAACP. My deputy, Captain Ronald Hoffman, met the ship and delivered comments to celebrate the event. After the historical event, the vessel sailed on for display at the NAACP convention in Baltimore.

Following its docking in the Baltimore harbor, conferees were invited to board the cutter. The ship's crew explained everything about the vessel and offered tours to all who boarded the ship. The crew explained its mission and where the ship normally sailed with a crew to perform their seagoing duties. The crew struck up conversations on how coast guard members spent their time aboard the vessel and provided any additional information in response to questions.

In addition to the *Eagle* and the cutter, a forty-four-foot motor boat was included among the assets on display. The boat coxswains explained the purpose of the boat and how they were trained to navigate it.

Coast guard coxswains received their training at the coast guard's motor boat school, located offshore of the Columbia River in Oregon. The Columbia River has the reputation of being the most difficult river in the world to navigate. Coxswains from all over the world would come to the United States to attend the coast guard's motor boat training school.

From pedestrian traffic, the motor boat seemed to get the most attention as it drew the greatest number of people. We tried to accommodate all of them. Boat rides were available for everyone who wanted them throughout the day. Since the boat could accommodate a certain number of people at one time, anyone desiring a short boat ride around the harbor was asked to sign up for a ride, as the boat would drop off and pick up people continuously during the daylight hours.

As a special surprise for the conferees, the coast guard put on a simulated search-and-rescue exercise. The motor boat sailed out into the harbor with a crew member, who jumped overboard to stage a person in distress. The helicopter flew in at a propitious time to make the rescue. A rescue basket was lowered with a rescue swimmer, who plucked the seaman out of the water and safely placed him in the basket. The rescued seaman was flown to the 210- foot cutter, where he was dropped off and lowered on to the vessel, which happened to be anchored nearby in the harbor. The helicopter crew waved at the throngs of people watching and then hovered above on its way. This likely was the most exciting event ever witnessed by a crowd who may not have been familiar with the coast guard and the important rescue services provided daily to the public.

This simulated search-and-rescue exercise was definitely the highlight of the day.

Feedback from conferees was positive; the coast guard's display of assets was very successful and met all of the coast guard's expectations. Conferees wanted to know when the coast guard would have another display of assets like the one enjoyed during the NAACP convention. Even members from the other services commended the coast guard for its creative planning and execution of such an outstanding display of coast guard assets and the memorable impact the display had on NAACP conferees.

After the convention, when things returned to normal, I contacted the service members responsible for putting on the show. I thanked them for their contributions to such a successful display and suggested that the substance of their NAACP participation should be provided to their superiors for evaluation and fitness-reporting purposes, as such information would validate the outstanding support of civil rights initiatives.

Chapter 20

Collaborating with Hispanic Association of Colleges and Universities (HACU), 1999–2004

THE COAST GUARD PARTICIPATED IN SEVERAL ANNUAL CONFERENCES sponsored by the Hispanic Association of College and University (HACU). We contracted with the organization to set up exhibits and promote career opportunities for Hispanics to join the service as military and/or civilian members.

To demonstrate coast guard support for the organization, I coordinated a speaking engagement for Vice Admiral Thomas Barrett (USCG vice commandant) to address one of the closing sessions of a HACU conference. It was an honor to introduce Vice Admiral Barrett to the audience, and he was well received. He delivered a stimulating message on the importance of the developing partnership between the coast guard and the HACU organization. Not too long ago, the commandant had signed a MoU with the HACU president. Vice Admiral Barrett encouraged HACU to work with the coast guard in looking for strategic opportunities to develop and implement projects of mutual interest to our respective organizations. He emphasized that the coast guard wanted to attract more Hispanics to hire for employment in our military and civilian workforce. He encouraged the HACU organization to offer suggestions on how the coast guard could contribute to their academic mission.

During his remarks, the vice commandant told an interesting story that a member of a foreign country had passed on to him. It was about the character of the coast guard and the way other countries valued coast guard services. The essence of the tale described the way other countries viewed the work of our organization. The audience gave Vice Admiral Barrett a standing ovation as a tribute to the coast guard and its positive reputation throughout the world.

During the conference, Vice Admiral Barrett met with the board of directors of the institution and gave his commitment to working with Hispanic colleges and universities on projects of mutual interest.

One thing the board was interested in was finding ways to get internships for Hispanic college students during the summer. This was one of the provisions in the MoU between the coast guard and HACU. The vice commandant assured the board that he would communicate their concern to coast guard facilities in geographic areas throughout the country where HACU institutions were located. Also, the board was interested in being considered for projects the coast guard advertised for contract consideration. The vice commandant indicated this was a matter to which the coast guard would pay special attention whenever contracts were under consideration.

To follow up on the vice commandant's pledges to members of the HACU board, I requested a meeting with the board members, to be held in Dallas, Texas, to discuss some of the promises made during the conference.

At the meeting, I reiterated the coast guard's commitment to working with HACU to identify and pursue projects of mutual interest. We had a lively discussion regarding the MoU and what could be done to employ Hispanic interns during the summer and to look for ways to get HACU involved in coast guard contractual activities. It was suggested that having a coast guard liaison officer to assist in this regard would be an excellent resource to HACU.

Dr. Antonio Flores, HACU president, suggested that it would be helpful to them if a military officer were authorized to assist his organization in addressing various issues pertaining to the MoU. We discussed the potential role of an officer assigned to the organization and what it would mean to have such a person working with the HACU president. I told the board that I would see what we could do about the suggestion.

Upon return to the office, I presented the suggestion to the chief of staff in headquarters. The chief of staff approved the suggestion for implementation. He authorized the assignment of an officer to serve as liaison to the HACU organization, reporting directly to the HACU president. We screened and interviewed several coast guard officers for this new assignment. Captain Alfonso Ramirez, a Hispanic, was selected for the position.

I informed Dr. Flores of the coast guard's decision. I issued a Coast Guard COMMUNICATION (COMMONLY REFERRED TO AS

ALCOAST) to highlight the partnership between the coast guard and the Hispanic Association of Colleges and Universities. The ALCOAST was distributed throughout the service and to colleges and universities where more than 25 percent of their students were Hispanic.

The position (billet) was allocated to the Office of Civil Rights for coast guard oversight and management. This was the first time the coast guard had demonstrated such a commitment to a minority organization by making such an assignment. It was evident that the coast guard was dedicated to accomplishing measurable results in working with HACU, consistent with the terms of the MoU.

Captain Ramirez traveled to various states where HACU institutions were located. He spoke to students in high schools and to those attending colleges or universities. The captain was very aggressive in recruiting students who eventually entered the coast guard as enlisted members or potential candidates for coast guard officer programs. I provided remarks in his annual performance appraisal about his outstanding work. Captain Ramirez was a valuable asset to the overall coast guard recruiting efforts and an excellent resource to the president of the Hispanic Association of Colleges and Universities.

Chapter *21*

Partnering with Public Elementary, Middle, and High Schools, 1991–2004

IN 1991 THE COMMANDANT, ADMIRAL BILL KIME, ASKED ME TO DEvelop a Partnership in Education program for implementation service-wide. The Office of Civil Rights immediately began to consider the issue and started developing concepts for formulating a program that was acceptable to the commandant. After several iterations, we developed a draft document that consisted of policy, responsibilities, processes, and desired outcomes. As a matter of policy, Coast Guard Headquarters and all major field facilities would have a role to play in implementing the concept.

The proposal was coordinated with stakeholders in headquarters and Atlantic and Pacific area commanders, requesting their comments. We received valuable input for consideration, which was carefully evaluated. And all that added value to the program was incorporated into the proposal before submitting it to the commandant for his consideration and approval. Upon approval, the program was finalized and promulgated as a coast guard instruction bearing the commandant's signature.

The program was widely received throughout the service. Headquarters and field facilities reached out to schools in their local areas, including elementary, middle, and high schools. More than 250 partnership agreements were formed in less than two years.

The Partnership in Education (PIE) program was very popular throughout the service. Even the chief of staff, Vice Admiral Thad Allen, found a way to get involved. One year he visited an elementary school in the DC area, took photos with students, and addressed the assembled audience. He was excited to have played a part in the PIE program, which was obvious from the way he offered comments about the elementary students at the school he visited. This was typical of the support that Coast Guard Headquarters and field commands demonstrated for the PIE program.

Coast guard units dedicated all kinds of resources to assist local schools in their education process. For example, civilian and military members served as tutors and mentors, which were the primary resources that schools requested. Some members assisted the schools by performing tasks, such as painting at schools, moving furniture, and doing other things asked of them. Coast guard members were allowed free time away from their normal jobs to support PIE activities.

To add an incentive to the important work members of the coast guard performed, I established an awards program, Commandant's Award for Excellence. The award was a simply designed plaque with the field unit and school name embossed on it, along with a short citation commemorating their accomplishment. Every year headquarters and field units that had PIE programs were invited to compete for the annual award. The award program was widely received throughout headquarters and coast guard field facilities. Numerous nominations were received each year. After consideration and selection of a winner, we made arrangements to visit the unit to make the onsite presentation to the winners, including the school and the coast guard unit.

It was a pleasure to visit the winning coast guard unit and its partnering school to present the award. Making the presentation validated the importance of the program, as you could observe the celebratory atmosphere at the school. Some schools not only allowed their students and faculty to attend the award ceremony, but they invited parents, school superintendents, local politicians, and members of Congress representing their local community to attend as well.

Of the many awards made over the years, there was nothing I would rather do than recognize the winner of the Commandant's Award for Excellence for having the best PIE of the year. I made awards to many coast guard units and schools throughout the country, including those located in Alaska and Hawaii. There was no limit to how far I would travel to support this important program; after all, it was designed to enhance the quality of education for our students.

One year a presentation was scheduled for a coast guard unit and school in Honolulu, Hawaii. On my way there, the airplane landed in San Francisco to refuel. It experienced a mechanical problem that could not get fixed until the next day. We were stranded in the city for a day and a half, two days before Thanksgiving. The airplane didn't get to Honolulu as scheduled; it arrived two days late. During the time I waited at the airport, there was no chance to get a good night's sleep. I was exhausted when we got to Honolulu. After checking into a hotel for a couple of hours, it was then time to get up and prepare to leave for the presentation.

I made the presentation to the coast guard unit and the school on the day before Thanksgiving. It was a celebratory occasion, witnessed by a large turnout of students, faculty, parents, and coast guard members.

Despite the unfortunate delay and not being home for the traditional Thanksgiving dinner, the trip was definitely worthwhile. Presentation of the Commandant's Award was accomplished in grand form.

The PIE was a very popular program in the coast guard. Even the commandant, Admiral Bill Kime, presented one award to a school and coast guard unit located in Seattle, Washington.

At the time of my retirement in 2004, coast guard units had contacted over two million students through the PIE program. The Honorable Rodney Slater, secretary of transportation, commended the coast guard for its accomplishments. He presented me with the secretary of transportation's Garrett A. Morgan Gold Medal Award on behalf of the coast guard for excellence in administering the Partnership in Education program in the department.

Chapter 22

Leading Coast Guard Efforts to Create a Model EEO Program for the Service, 2003–2004

IN OCTOBER 2003, THE EQUAL EMPLOYMENT OPPORTUNITY Commission (EEOC) issued Management Directive MD 715. The directive provided new guidance for developing equal employment opportunity (EEO) affirmative-action plans. It required agencies to analyze organizational data to identify barriers to employment, training, and promotion of minorities and women in its workforce. Furthermore, the new guidance directed that the civilian EEO program be integrated into the policies and practices of agencies.

This new guidance was much different from the guidance that federal agencies had been operating under until this time. The EEOC theorized that if strategies were developed to remove workforce barriers, then this would result in a positive workforce, free of discrimination and unfair practices in the hiring and retention of employees in the workforce.

Previously, regulations required agencies to develop civilian EEO affirmative-action plans, generally, to correct workforce imbalances. Plans were formulated to address the difference between the percentage of each of the ethnic minority group members and white females in the workforce and their respective percentages of representation in the national labor force.

This was an unachievable measure of success, in my opinion, because the anticipated results could never be reached, especially when you consider the types of positions and/or average grade levels held by employees in any given agency's workforce. All agencies would be competing for the same available workers in the national workforce. Even if one agency was fortunate enough to reach parity between the percentage of onboard employees and their respective percentage in the national labor force, inequality might still exist in other agencies that competed for the same available workers. So from this point of view, the previous regulations were inadequately conceived to effectively correct civilian workforce imbalances throughout the entire federal government—an impossible proposition.

Moreover, the former regulations did not offer guidance to deal with discrimination complaints resulting from unfair personnel practices that might have occurred when taking actions such as hiring, training, promotions, dismissals, etc. Those are the kinds of personnel practices that, if not handled properly, formed the basis for allegations of discrimination. Guidance related to causes for filing discrimination complaints was omitted in the former EEOC regulations.

After thoroughly studying the new MD 715 guidance, I was encouraged by its potential to address the full range of issues concerning workforce imbalances and causes for filing complaints of discrimination. This new guidance required agencies to analyze their personnel practices and procedures to identify barriers that existed to developing and maintaining a positive workforce environment.

The key here was *positive workforce environment*. By analyzing data and decisions leading to hiring, training, promotion, dismissal, and other personnel practices, it was more likely than not that an agency might discover unintended or undesirable actions taken that could have been handled differently in some instances in order to ensure equal employment opportunity. Findings from such an analysis would constitute the basis for identifying barriers to an effective merit decision-making process. The analytical findings would also validate the basis for formulating factually based recommendations for removing barriers to equal employment opportunity to ensure a model EEO program, free of discrimination.

The new guidance required a significant change in the way we had formerly developed affirmative-action plans. I directed my civilian

EEO directorate to develop a program for implementing the new EEOC guidance coast guard–wide. The EEO directorate transmitted the guidance to all units that employed civilians throughout the coast guard, along with instructions to get familiar with it and prepare for a follow-up seminar to discuss plans and strategies for implementation. In addition, the directorate scheduled one-day seminars for meetings, to be held in headquarters and at the Atlantic and Pacific area commands. Seminars at those commands were to encompass participation by all coast guard facilities that employed civilians. The seminars were to include participation by our human resources counterpart, as they would play an important role if the coast guard were to successfully implement the new guidance.

The EEO directorate, in collaboration with the human resources counterparts, drafted a substantive plan of action for a seminar to implement the new EEOC guidance at Coast Guard Headquarters and all the field commands. The plan of action allowed for a comprehensive discussion of the guidance material, strategies for performing an analysis of personnel actions, mandatory elements for preparing affirmative-action plans, and internal coordination within the unit in order to acquire approval by the commanding officer.

Meetings were scheduled through representatives with EEO responsibilities for developing affirmative-action plans in Coast Guard Headquarters and the two area commands. The EEO directorate held preliminary discussions with those EEO representatives to ensure the adequate logistical arrangements were made and that the desired attendees would be available to attend the seminar.

The seminar was planned to discuss the EEOC guidance and address any problems that might have developed at the unit level. It was structured to discuss strategies for examining hiring, training, and promotion procedures, step by step, to potentially identify barriers to a positive work environment. It was designed to review strategies for examining procedures for identifying and selecting positions and candidates for upward-mobility positions. It offered suggestions for identifying potential retirees and new positions resulting from voluntary retirements and organizational growth and/or retrenchment. It discussed strategies for examining closed cases of allegations of discrimination and remedies offered for solutions. It offered suggestions for examining EEO procedures and processes to identify potential barriers. Any barriers identified at the unit level were to undergo internal scrutiny within the organization. And finally, an effective internal process for review and approval by commanding officers was to be part of the considerations studied.

Our first one-day seminar was held in Coast Guard Headquarters with members of the civilian EEO directorate and representatives from headquarters, EEO, and human resources staffs. We discussed the purpose of the meeting and suggestions for desired outcomes. We emphasized how important it was for the coast guard to implement the new guidance, as it would give the coast guard an opportunity to lead enactment efforts of the new guidance in the Department of Homeland Security, our parent organization. I stayed long enough to address any policy questions that were raised. The meeting was then turned over to the EEO directorate staff members, who facilitated discussions during the seminar. They did an excellent job engaging the participants in dialogue throughout the seminar. Feedback from all in attendance was very favorable.

The EEO directorate developed an after-action report on the meeting and made suggestions for improving the seminar prior to implementation at the area commands. Of significance was a recommendation that the conferees from the area commands come prepared to introduce new material based on "best practices" employed in their respective organizations. The substance of the after-action report was considered as a basis for refining the plans for the seminars held at the area commands.

The seminar was held with representatives of the Atlantic area command in Norfolk, Virginia and with the Pacific area command representatives in Oakland, California. The modified format of the seminar held in headquarters served as the basis for discussion, and it was well received with highly favorable results.

The civil rights office was commended by the head of the Civil Rights program in the Department of Homeland Security (DHS) for taking the leadership in addressing the new EEOC guidance. The DHS civil rights director asked the coast guard to take the lead in advising other organizations in the Department of Homeland Security, regarding how to effectively implement the model EEO concept.

Moreover, when I was out on the West Coast introducing the seminar for the model EEO program, I met with Vice Admiral Harvey Johnson, Pacific area commander. I briefed him on plans to update the Equal Opportunity Manual and develop an organizational structure for the Civil Rights program. The plans included integrating the Civil Rights policies, practices and missions into the coast guard's operational missions, policies, and practices. When completed and issued, the manual would become the civil rights doctrine for the coast guard. Vice Admiral Johnson thought it was a good idea and commented that he would support plans for issuing a coast guard civil rights doctrine.

An important by-product emerged during the seminar sessions. It just so happened that among the participants at our sponsored seminars in headquarters and the two area commands were EEO counselors from each of the respective commands. EEO counselors are considered part-time or collateral duty personnel in the EEO program. They are the first contacts an aggrieved person must approach to begin the process of formally alleging discrimination. The counselors suggested that there should be some type of award for the services that counselors perform, given that their work is very important and often overlooked in the process of adjudicating difficult workforce issues.

I agreed with these counselors. Their recommendation was favorably considered for action. The civil rights office raised the suggestion with stakeholders in Coast Guard Headquarters. There was no objection. In fact, the idea was widely accepted. The Civil Rights program already allowed awards for outstanding performance in the Equal Opportunity and Partnership in Education programs. Why not celebrate outstanding performance by EEO counselors by developing an award program for excellence in the EEO counseling area?

With overwhelming support for the idea, I established an annual award for EEO counselors who exhibited outstanding performance in the handling and resolution of allegations of discrimination raised by civilian and military personnel. The award was referred to as the Commandant's EEO Counselor Award for Excellence.

This award program was open to all EEO counselors in the coast guard who demonstrated outstanding performance in processing civilian and/or military complaints during the year. The award program was

administered by the civil rights office. Nominations were solicited annually for consideration. A panel was commissioned to review nominations and make the recommendation for the award. The person selected annually as the winner was invited to meet with the commandant, who would present the award. Travel expenses and lodging, if required, were borne by the Civil Rights program.

I issued a commandant instruction to promulgate the EEO Counselor Award program. The program was favorably received throughout headquarters and in field facilities. Competition for the original award was exceedingly heavy.

Admiral Thomas Collins presented the first award to the winner from the Coast Guard Academy in 2003. It was a simple plaque engraved with the recipient's name and an inscription of accomplishments.

Chapter 23

Codifying and Promulgating the Coast Guard Civil Rights Doctrine, 2000–2004

INTEGRATING THE COAST GUARD'S CIVIL RIGHTS POLICY AND PRACtices into the coast guard's operational policies and practices was a goal that the civil rights office had been working toward for some time. With the new EEOC guidance, there was renewed optimism that this eventually would be accomplished.

Why was there optimism? The coast guard is a military organization. Military organizations have a reputation of following orders from superiors. The EEOC had just issued a government- wide mandate that required agencies of the government to integrate EEO policies and practices into the agencies' overall policies and practices. This was a chance to press ahead to complete refinement of missions for the Civil Rights program and develop an appropriate organizational structure for seamless integration into the coast guard's operational policies and practices.

The civil rights office had already begun to do this on a limited basis. We had developed civil rights missions and promulgated this information throughout the coast guard for implementation in headquarters and in our field facilities. We had begun reviewing the effectiveness of this guidance during regularly scheduled reviews of Civil Rights programs implemented at headquarters and in the field.

Also, I visited several field units, headed by admirals, for the purpose of discussing the guidance and to get their opinions on whether the civil rights guidance was understood and being implemented within their respective commands. I learned that the guidance was understood mainly at the command levels but was not well implemented at levels below. Their findings were mixed but very informative.

I discerned that the desired outcomes of the civil rights missions needed to be explained in such a way as to ensure a better understanding of the outcomes and the value they added to the coast guard operational mission performance. I believed it was imperative to formulate a civil rights doctrine, integrating the civil rights policies and practices into the coast guard's operational missions, policies, and practices.

The civil rights office aggressively stepped up field reviews to collect more information on how civil rights missions were being implemented in the field. Civil rights office review teams sent out a survey instrument in advance of their visits to targeted units. The instrument was designed to collect information on how field units were responding to the civil rights missions and what needed to be done to ensure the units were working effectively and efficiently to achieve the desired outcomes of the civil rights missions.

The civil rights office continued to look for other ways to highlight the civil rights missions by soliciting high-ranking coast guard officials (e.g., commandant, chief of staff, and district commanders) to participate in annual civil rights conferences. Talking points were provided in advance for them to speak specifically about the civil rights missions. This proved to be an excellent way to communicate the value that civil rights providers added to coast guard mission accomplishments.

Additionally, I visited the Pacific area command, headed by Vice Admiral Thomas Collins, to further promote the civil rights missions. Vice Admiral Collins arranged for me to address his leadership corps and some other members of his command. A large number of civilian and military members were invited to attend the gathering. I talked about the civil rights missions and the value they added to coast guard personnel readiness and mission performance.

After the presentation, I offered to take questions. The exchange progressed very well.

Vice Admiral Collins commented to the audience that it was "good information." Because of his intelligent response, there was reason to believe that the civil rights missions would be accepted throughout other commands in the coast guard.

This conclusion was reached because Vice Admiral Collins was known to be a "cerebral" individual. He knew what he liked and what he didn't like, but seldom did he respond emotionally to anything. When he stated that the presentation was "good information," that was his way of showing approval. You could bet that he meant what he said. His endorsement of anything meant a great deal throughout the coast guard. He was a highly respected individual in the service.

After meeting with Vice Admiral Collins, I decided it was time to draft a civil rights doctrine to integrate the civil rights missions into the coast guard's operational missions, policies, and practices.

I briefed my civil rights team on my discussions with the coast guard vice admirals about integrating civil rights policies and practices into coast guard operational policies and practices. I relayed the substance of my get-together with the Pacific area commander, the telephone conversation with the Atlantic area commander, and various consultations with the chief of staff regarding plans to develop a coast guard civil rights doctrine. Their responses were favorable and indicated support for the project. The chief of staff, while supporting the project, delayed making an immediate decision on one position I proposed, but he later authorized it.

After several meetings with my team, hashing out the complexities of the project that led to an ultimate plan of action, there was unanimous agreement that we should move ahead to complete the project. The scope of this endeavor was awesome. Successful completion would require a total team effort. Everyone was on board and determined to treat promulgation of a civil rights doctrine as the number-one priority of the Civil Rights program.

Captain Mark Blace, my deputy, was selected to oversee the work of drafting the coast guard's civil rights doctrine. Having served as deputy, civil rights, for three years, he had extensive knowledge of the program. Captain Blace was a graduate of the Coast Guard Academy. He had a reputation of being a very professional and competent officer. He understood the culture, traditions, and practices of the coast guard.

He was exceptionally good at drafting documents, such as revisions to the coast guard's Equal Opportunity Manual.

I reviewed the project with him. After extensively conferring with the civil rights staff, we created an outline of the potentially essential provisions that should comprise the civil rights doctrine. Captain Blace was asked to work with the civil rights staff and other appropriate headquarters and field members of the service to draft a comprehensive revision to the Equal Opportunity Manual to integrate the civil rights policies, practices and missions with coast guard policies, practices, and operational missions.

Captain Blace was directed that the civil rights doctrine should also include an organizational structure that would integrate civil rights policies, practices, and staffing into the coast guard's policies, practices, and organizational structure. The roles and responsibilities for the Civil Rights program should be clarified throughout the coast guard so that accountability for decision making was explained for all civilian and military members of the service, regardless of their grade, rank, or status in the organization.

He was instructed that, as a service-wide program in the coast guard, the civil rights office had responsibility for policy, budget, resources acquisition, and support to the field commands. And the civil rights office was responsible for ensuring that a field civil rights organizational structure was established and maintained. This was to guarantee that the necessary work of the program was performed in an effective and efficient manner. These obligations were to be made clear, without equivocation.

Captain Blace was advised that responsibilities for civil rights were vague in field organizations, Coast Guard Headquarters units under the chief of staff, the Atlantic area command, and the Pacific area command. The roles and responsibilities of persons heading those commands should be made clear in the Equal Opportunity Manual.

He was counseled that in the coast guard, three chains of command reported to the commandant and that each of these commands should integrate civil rights policies, practices, and an appropriate staffing structure into their spheres of command. For example, the chief of staff in headquarters should assume responsibility for integrating civil rights policies, practices, and staffing structure into the policies and practices of all headquarters units, including the Coast Guard Academy. The Atlantic area commander should do the same for all area commands employing civilians in the Atlantic area. And the Pacific area commander should integrate civil rights policies, practices, and staffing structure into all area commands employing civilians in the Pacific area.

Captain Blace was instructed that, as a minimum, staffing for the civil rights functions at the chief-of-staff level and each of the area command headquarters should include a senior civilian EEO policy adviser (preferably a GS-14 EEO manager) with leadership and management experience and an additional civilian EEO specialist with knowledge, skills, and abilities required to manage a civil rights program, including civilian and military complaints. Additional resources might be recommended by the senior civilian EEO policy adviser, with the concurrence of the chief of staff and/or the area commanders.

Captain Blace was instructed that, as a minimum, a civilian EEO adviser should be authorized at each of the field units employing civilians, reporting to the chief of staff, as well as each of the field units, reporting to the respective area commanders. EEO advisers, with the concurrence of their commands, might request additional staffing as warranted.

As directed, Captain Blace took care to ensure all of the guidance was considered and made part of the draft document of the manual.

In the draft document, the civil rights missions and organizational structure with staffing and roles and responsibilities were explained in the Coast Guard Equal Opportunity Manual.

It was stipulated in the EO Manual that the chain of command was the basic organizing concept, under which lines of authority, supervisory relationships, and accountability were established and implemented for all coast guard military and civilian employees. A fundamental part of the coast guard's military organization was the responsibility and authority inherent in the chain of command, both in terms of a commander's obligation to establish and enforce policies and standards and the responsibility of all personnel to adhere to those policies and standards.

Also, the commanding officers (COs) or officers in charge (OICs) throughout the Atlantic area, Pacific area, and chief of staff (headquarters offices and field units) should support the policies, regulations, and laws of the Civil Rights program.

Five guiding principles comprised the coast guard's civil rights missions. These missions, along with the civil rights organizational staffing structure, comprised the coast guard civil rights doctrine. They included the following: demonstrate command leadership, develop an organizational culture that values diversity, correct civilian workforce imbalances, resolve discrimination complaints at the lowest level, and promote affirmative outreach.

These missions were formulated based on laws, statues, rules and regulations, management directives, and several memoranda negotiated with external organizations. In addition, countless sources of data collected through studies, a cultural audit, and onsite reviews and surveys contributed to the fine-tuning of the missions. The objectives and activities of the missions (partially extracted from the Coast Guard EO Manual) were elucidated in the manual to ensure clarity and understanding for all members of the coast guard.

1. Demonstrate command leadership. Objectives were to promote the policies, regulations, and laws of the Civil Rights and Equal Employment Opportunity programs. Activities might include setting clear expectations; establishing goals and standards; promoting openness, inclusiveness, and tolerance; creating a positive work environment; being aware and involved; and enforcing accountability.
2. Develop an organizational culture that values diversity. Objectives were to work toward eliminating discrimination in the workforce; and celebrate and fully draw on the diverse talents and perspectives within the workforce. Activities might include conducting cultural observances; holding human- relations council meetings; mentoring subordinates; raising awareness through sexual-harassment prevention and human- relations training; communicating standards and expectations; and conducting climate surveys

3. Correct civilian workforce imbalances. Objectives were to recruit, promote, and retain people from groups that are underrepresented in the workforce, such as women, minorities, and people with disabilities. Coast guard workforce reflects the relevant local civilian labor force. Activities might include conducting annual self-assessments to identify barriers to equal employment opportunity (EEO) for civilian employees (including applicants for employment); developing and implementing strategic plans to eliminate identified barriers to equal employment opportunity; orienting and training supervisors and managers on plans to eliminate barriers and achieve a model EEO program; and monitoring progress in meeting objectives.

4. Resolve complaints at the lowest level. Objectives were to optimize productivity and improve morale; promote organizational harmony; repair workforce relationships; and save time and money associated with prolonged complaint processing and litigation. Activities might include informally resolving complaints at the unit level; ensuring process integrity and timely action; using open communication and feedback; respecting personal privacy; and employing mediation to resolve disputes (including those that do not involve allegations of discrimination).

5. Promote affirmative outreach in the community. Objectives were to foster positive the public image of the coast guard; raise awareness of the coast guard's missions in the community; and to be viewed as a good neighbor and an employer of choice. Activities might include partnering with civic and community entities to resolve social-climate issues; partnering with civil rights, equal opportunity, educational, and community organizations; and serving as mentors and volunteers in local schools as part of the Partnership in Education program.

The civil rights doctrine integrated the civil rights missions, policies, and practices with the coast guard's operational missions, policies, and practices. It set forth standards for performance and accountability for actions and behavior in the execution of the integrated coast guard missions. These fundamental principles were embodied in the current version of the coast guard's Equal Opportunity Manual.

The Equal Opportunity Manual was updated with the relevant information and readied for internal coordination. As is customary when developing or modifying coast guard policies, I sent the document to all headquarters program directors (chief of staff, judge advocate general, and all assistant commandants) for review and comment. The Equal Opportunity Manual was a lengthy and comprehensive document. I allowed three weeks for responses, with the proviso that failure to respond on the part of any program director would constitute concurrence for the record.

The civil rights office received responses from all who were asked to comment on the draft. We reviewed and carefully considered all the comments received. We meticulously made all adjustments that added value to the manual. After making those changes, the EO Manual was readied for publication and distribution as policy guidance for implementation throughout the coast guard.

I notified the commandant of this significant milestone. In my letter to him on September 27, 2004, I wrote,

> As program director and subject-matter expert for the Civil Rights, Equal Opportunity, and Equal Employment Opportunity programs for the coast guard, I have approved and signed the enclosed Equal Opportunity Manual and would welcome your cursory review before release. I would offer that this is the most comprehensive documentation of civil rights doctrine ever written in the history of the coast guard. What's more, it establishes the Civil Rights program within the chain of command, thus offering the best opportunity to achieve optimum effectiveness and efficiency in program operations. The manual is formatted with a table of contents that makes it easy to review any or all parts of the document, depending upon your interest.

The commandant did not offer any comments for consideration. I released the Equal Opportunity Manual for printing and distribution on September 28, 2004.

Chapter 24

Participating in Retirement Ceremony Officiated by the Coast Guard Commandant, 2004

I RETIRED FROM THE COAST GUARD ON SEPTEMBER 30, 2004, WITH nearly fifty-four years of public service. Thirty-four of those years were with the United States Coast Guard, twenty-one of which were as the assistant commandant for civil rights.

When admirals and Senior Executive Service (SES) officials retired from the coast guard, it was customary to hold their retirement celebrations at the close of a coast guard flag officer and SES conference, normally held in the spring or the fall of the year in which they retired. It would take place during a special dinner following the close of the conference. Wives were in attendance. The retiree was roasted by his or her peers and then given the last word to respond in any way deemed appropriate in a grateful manner.

I recalled how such retirements had taken place in the past and was sure this would be an enjoyable evening. When word of my retirement circulated throughout the coast guard, several admirals and SES officials called me to congratulate me on my service to the coast guard and said how much they enjoyed working with me. Some of them said they were looking forward to giving me a great send-off at the next flag officer and SES conference. I was sure such a send-off would be a memorable occasion.

But I did not want the traditional coast guard retirement ceremony; I wanted something different. I wanted to have a public retirement ceremony outside of the coast guard so that I could invite friends and associates with whom I had worked in the Department of Defense and civil rights and educational organizations. I wanted to thank those special people (especially heads of national organizations) who contributed tremendously to the success of many of the projects on which they voluntarily worked with the coast guard in executing the coast guard's outreach initiatives and the Partnership in Education program.

My headquarters staff and I had planned a dinner to be held at Fort McNair on a date and time mutually acceptable to the commandant. We had developed a guest list and had invitations printed, ready to mail. And to ensure a good turnout of special guests, I was prepared to finance the entire cost of the dinner myself.

But because the commandant and I could not agree on scheduling, we were unable to settle on a mutually convenient date for holding the retirement dinner at a facility outside of Coast Guard Headquarters. Unfortunately, I had to change my ambitious plans.

The commandant, Admiral Thomas Collins, presided over my brief retirement ceremony. The ceremony was held in the anteroom at the Coast Guard Headquarters building, with mostly my headquarters staff and other interested civilian and military officers in attendance. Some retired admirals apparently were informed of my retirement plans and showed up for the event. Appropriately twenty-five to thirty people (maybe more) attended my retirement celebration.

The commandant made brief remarks that highlighted the significance of my service to the coast guard. He presented me with the United States Coast Guard's Distinguished Career Service Award. He also presented me the Department of Homeland Security's Certificate of Service—"On the Occasion of Retirement after Fifty-Four Years of Service to the People of the United States of America."

In my response to the commandant's remarks, I said that the Office of Civil Rights had promulgated a civil rights doctrine that integrated the Civil Rights policies, practices, missions and staffing structure into the coast guard policies, practices, operational missions and command structure. And I hoped that the doctrine would seamlessly transform and improve the effective and efficient way in which the coast guard executed its operations. I reminded everyone that individuals who worked in civil rights programs did not always get the recognition they deserved and that the coast guard's leadership corps should be cognizant of this fact. Coast guard leaders should take care to recognize the value that members of the civil rights community added to the coast guard's excellent mission performance on a daily basis.

To offer a parable and bit of levity to this serious assertion, I left the audience with the following witticism: "There was a governor who never received any positive write-ups from a local newspaper about his performance; every write-up was negative. He wanted to do something to change this. He took a high-ranking dignitary out on his boat. He invited the press to cover the occasion, hoping he would get a positive write-up in the next day's daily newspaper about something that happened that day. It was a windy day, and the dignitary's hat blew off his head and into the water.

"The governor dived off the boat to retrieve the hat. He walked on the water to where the hat was floating, picked it up, re-boarded the boat, and handed the hat back to the dignitary. The governor had walked the water. And the newspaper writers were in awe and inspired by what they had seen—the governor had walked the water. The governor knew the newspaper writers had seen him walking on water. He thought they would write about it in the next day's newspaper. The next day, the governor purchased several newspapers and opened one of them to the front page. And to his disbelief, the newspaper's headline read, THE GOVERNOR CAN'T SWIM.

"The moral of this story is that members of the civil rights community are always doing something worth praising. What civil rights workers do, in metaphorical terms, is 'walk on water' without being noticed. They 'walk on water' when they do praiseworthy things, but seldom does anyone acknowledge or praise them for the value they've added to mission accomplishments. This should be noted because it is good. As the late retired chief petty officer Alex Haley always reminded us, we should 'find the good and praise it.' I implore the leaders of the coast guard to find the good in what their civil rights workers do and praise it—and the workers—whenever it occurs."

As I stood in a receiving line to speak with and receive congratulations from the guests in attendance, the chief of staff, Vice Admiral Thad Allen, approached me to shake my hand. As he did, he whispered in my ear, "I'm going to approve the last civilian position you requested to complete the civil rights staffing for the civil rights organizational structure."

This was a great message. This decision would structurally improve the civil rights doctrine, and it was the best going-away present I could have received. I had been aggressively pressing the chief of staff for a decision on this one issue for the past three months. I was delighted to learn that the United States Coast Guard's civil rights doctrine would be effectively indoctrinated into the coast guard's historical documents, with a fully staffed organizational structure.

Sending Farewell Emails to All Coast Guard Admirals and Senior Executive Service Officials

I am forever grateful to all the coast guard admirals and Senior Executive Service officials. Their friendship, cooperation, and participation in the outcomes of the civil rights and outreach initiatives we achieved together meant so much to me. I sent each of them an email that expressed my thoughts about working with them over the twenty-one years I served as assistant commandant for civil rights. The original message follows:

> From: Somerville, Walter
> Sent: Thursday, September 23, 2004 10:26 a.m. To: 1st-CCS-Flags
> Subject: Thanks for the Memories
>
> Colleagues: This is to let you know that I plan to retire on 30 September 2004. I have enjoyed our camaraderie. Permit me to take this opportunity to share my "sea stories" and thank you for the memories.
> It has been nearly thirty-four years since I came to work as a GS-15 employee at the coast guard. Now I plan to leave after serving in the Senior Executive Service (SES) from 1983 to 2004. These thirty-four years have

been exciting times to be part of the coast guard. In 1967, three years before I started to work at the coast guard, the organization was transferred to the Department of Transportation (DOT), and now the service has moved to the Department of Homeland Security (DHS). I recall that in 1969, it was Secretary John Volpe who first established the Departmental Office of Civil Rights and the Office of Civil Rights in the coast guard. During his tenure, the DOT made great strides in increasing the representation of minorities in the department, as well as in the other agencies of the department. In my opinion, Secretary Volpe showed more dedication and commitment to changing the composition of the workforce than any of his successors. These were exciting times. As a matter of fact, working in civil rights during Secretary Volpe's tenure was a desirable place to be. That is one of the reasons I elected to become part of the civil rights community in the Department of Transportation and the United States Coast Guard.

I have seen many changes since Secretary Volpe's tenure. Despite the laws, statutes, and regulations that govern civil rights, the program's emphasis is largely determined by persons in responsible leadership positions, ranging from the president to department and agency heads. Civil rights can sometimes take on the character of the political influence in vogue. But as a nonpolitical agency, the coast guard has remained true to its values of honor, respect, and devotion to duty. These values have guided the coast guard's transformation from a somewhat insular organization (my opinion) to a world-class organization in the international maritime community, with a focus on internal positioning as well as external social, political, economic, and demographic factors that matter. The Civil Rights program has been an advocate for change. For example, the coast guard opened its doors to women at the Coast Guard Academy. The coast guard performed a study on the recruiting and retention of minorities in the service. The coast guard established its first JROTC program. The coast guard conducted a cultural audit. The coast guard established special recruiting programs to attract candidates to the Coast Guard Academy and the officer corps programs. The coast guard developed partnerships with civil rights and minority organizations and educational institutions. The coast guard is leading a prominent effort in DHS to implement MD 715 and integrate elements of the model EEO program into coast guard policies and practices. The coast guard is establishing a field civil rights infrastructure to support execution of robust Civil Rights and Equal Employment Opportunity programs. Several of these innovative developments have been the envy of the other military services as well as other agencies of government. I think Secretary Volpe would have been pleased to hear about these developments, as they reflect the vision of a forward-looking organization with a desire to acquire and sustain a reputation of world-class status.

I guess you can tell by now that Secretary Volpe had a great influence on my career as a civil rights professional. It is from this perspective that I have tried to lead the civil rights effort in the coast guard over the past twenty-one years. While there is more to be done, I am reminded of what Vice Admiral Terry Cross said when I discussed my plans to retire with him. In essence, he said, "You have to let go and move on at some point." I think I have reached a point in my career when it is time to move on. As is said in the military, I have stood my watch and now stand ready to be relieved. This assumes, however, that the watch will continue in good hands. There is a message somewhere in this affirmation, and that is that what is left behind is a visionary and vigilant Civil Rights program. I hope it will be strongly endorsed by all members of the senior leadership corps because the outcome of the Civil Rights program adds value to coast guard missions and exemplifies the excellence inherited in mission performance. I would opine that this qualitative measure of effectiveness is best applied by members of the senior leadership corps. You are the leaders of the coast guard and you direct operations and oversee mission performance.

I would like to offer my special thanks for the memories. All of you have been my strength and inspiration. To know that you are still standing the watch gives me confidence that the coast guard is in good hands and the service will continue to meet the demanding yet sometimes unpredictable needs of the American people. Good luck, and God bless.

Thanks for your camaraderie and all the fond memories.

Walt

Several members of the coast guard's leadership corps phoned and sent me emails expressing best wishes on the occasion of my retirement. And following the Flag and SES conference held in the spring of 2005, the commandant sent me a 20"x14" picturesque painting of the USCG Barque Eagle Flag Ship and a Sand Hourglass Set as a memento of an everlasting relationship with the coast guard and its leadership corps. The inscription on the painting read as follows,

Fair Winds and Following Seas Mr. Walter R. Somerville From the Flag and SES Corps Spring 2005 USCG Barque Eagle

Sending Farewell Emails to My Civil Rights Staff Members

My office civil rights staff members were my daily inspiration and motivation throughout the twenty-one years I served as assistant commandant for civil rights. I am indebted to all of them for what we accomplished together as a team during this period. That is why it was so hard to say goodbye to my team. The email I wrote to each of them is a reminder of what we accomplished together. The original message follows:

From: Somerville, Walter
Sent: Monday, September 27, 2004 12:01 p.m. To:
1st-GH
Subject: Hard to Say Goodbye

Sometimes you wonder why it is so hard to say goodbye. With this on my mind, I am aware that the next three and a half workdays will be my last days in the office. This is difficult to imagine, knowing that I have been coming to this very same office for the past twenty-one years. Much has happened in those twenty-one years. From my perspective, it has been good, not because of me but because of what we have done together. I can truly say that the coast guard has prospered from the work you have done as advocates for civil rights in the service.

Let's just ponder for a moment and reflect on the many things that have happened because of the direct influence of the Civil Rights program. For example, the coast guard opened its doors to women at the Coast Guard Academy. The coast guard performed a study on the recruitment and retention of minorities in the service, thus focusing attention on issues relating to ethnic minorities. The coast guard conducted a study on women in the service. The coast guard established its first JROTC program. The coast guard conducted a workforce cultural audit, the forerunner of the diversity dialogue in the service. The coast guard established special recruiting programs to attract minorities to the Coast Guard Academy and other officer procurement programs. The coast guard developed partnerships with civil rights and minority organizations and educational institutions, creating awareness that created sources of recruiting in minority communities. The coast guard authorized a captain's billet to operate out of the office of the HACU president/CEO, for the purpose of opening up and enhancing recruiting opportunities in Hispanic communities. The coast guard is leading a prominent initiative on behalf of the DHS to implement MD 715 and integrate elements of the model EEO program into coast guard policies and practices. The coast guard is establishing a field infrastructure within the military chain of command to support execution of robust Civil Rights and Equal Employment Opportunity programs, thus improving the effectiveness, efficiency, and quality of program operations. The coast guard is about to promulgate the most comprehensive civil rights doctrine ever written in the history of the coast guard, thus institutionalizing a visionary and vigilant Civil Rights program, arguably the best in government.

I could go on and on. All I would need to do is talk to you about your personal accomplishments. I know there are many stories you can tell that would exemplify the contributions the Civil Rights program has made to the coast guard and its people. Take it from me; there are many stories just waiting to be told. They are similar to some of those unimaginable achievements cited above. I opine that most of this would not have been possible without the advocacy and influence of the Civil Rights program. Each of you can take great pride in the fact that many of your civil rights accomplishments have been the envy of our sister services, as well as other agencies of government.

Seldom does the Civil Rights program receive public recognition for the contributions you make on a daily basis. This is understandable in a sense (maybe) because we provide important segments of inputs to other coast guard missions that are more visible than specific civil rights contributions. But our contributions are part of the history of the coast guard. As you know, history is not always the flavor of the day. Nonetheless, it is always a good idea to remember your history, as it can serve as lessons learned, as well as a precursor for the future. Knowing civil rights history in the coast guard can bring back memories of what it was like to be part of a visionary enterprise. It is something important to all of us; civil rights history is an important part of the coast guard's history.

This is the context in which I would define my professional relationship with each of you. I submit that the numerous accomplishments we realized over the years are a tribute to the camaraderie and team spirit we enjoyed together, coupled with your dedication and commitment to make life better for the coast guard and its people. When I look back over the twenty-one years of working in the same office (sharing memorable experiences with you), I am blessed. I would not trade those memories for anything of value. And this is what makes it so hard to say goodbye. Good luck, and God bless.

I will certainly miss all of you,
W. R. Somerville
Assistant Commandant for Civil Rights United States Coast Guard

During the retirement ceremony, Ms. Tina Calvert (Director of Civil Rights External Programs) gave me an attractively engraved "14" VASE on behalf of the coast guard civilian civil rights providers. And Senior Chief Petty Officer (SCPO) Kurt Nance (Civil Rights Budget and Resources Manager) presented me an American Flag that had flown over the Capitol on behalf of the coast guard military civil rights providers. I will cherish these mementos. And they will serve as a reminder such a wonderful group of people I worked with, all dedicated to achieving and sustaining a positive workforce in the coast guard.

Recognizing Exemplary Deputy Assistant Commandant for Civil Rights

It would be a careless blunder if I did not commend my deputy, Captain Mark Blace, for the outstanding work he performed during the three years he served in the Office of Civil Rights, 2001 to 2004. When Captain Blace joined the Civil Rights program, he had limited knowledge of its vision and direction, but he was a quick study. He quickly mastered the civil rights profession and began making noteworthy contributions. He became a resourceful liaison for the Civil Rights program, working on and solving complex issues with military and civilian members at all levels throughout the coast guard. He was an ingenious policy adviser. He made remarkable changes to the Civil Rights Onsite Review program, focusing on examining how well the five civil rights missions were being implemented in headquarters and at field locations. He developed and put in place a rating system for how well the civil rights missions were being performed. This inspired units that were being evaluated to work harder at competing to achieve a rating higher than their counterparts. The chief of staff showed interest in the rating systems and requested a briefing on it from Captain Blace. After Captain Blace explained the rating system to him and what it was designed to achieve throughout the coast guard, the chief of staff commended him for introducing such an innovative best practice for managing the onsite review program. Captain Blace was responsible for supervising members of the Coast Guard Headquarters Office of Civil Rights, whom he nurtured, instructed, and motivated in an exceptional manner. He led the important task of drafting the civil rights doctrine. For his exemplary, superior performance and incredible contributions to the Civil Rights program, I recommended him for the US Coast Guard Legion of Merit Award, the highest award that can be granted to a military member during peace time. The recommendation was approved by the coast guard's awards and recognitions board.

Chapter 25

Musing on Rise from impoverishment to make a Difference in Lives of Others, 1930–2004

I TRAVELED AN UNIMAGINED JOURNEY FROM 1930 TO 2004. MY JOURney may be described as a rise from an impoverished environment to make a positive difference in the lives of other ordinary people.

I had hopes of becoming a professional baseball player, but in 1951 I realized that this dream would not be fulfilled. Then what was next? I gave up my dreams of a baseball career in favor of a mission of public service in the federal government.

After nine years of active duty in the United States Air Force, I accepted an entry-level position as a civilian employee in the federal government. With hard work and determination to make a difference, I was able to rise from the entry-level position to an enviable position in the Senior Executive Service (SES), the highest level attainable for a nonpolitical civil service employee.

This position carried with it an incredible level of influence in the coast guard. I used this newly acquired influence to develop new policies and innovative strategies to change the way the coast guard carried out its business, especially with minority organizations. But more than that, I advocated for creating an environment of cultural awareness in the coast guard. The coast guard was noted for its exemplary work in the maritime community. This was fine, but the maritime community consisted of mostly white players. The coast guard was perceived as an insular organization (my opinion). Its traditional practices were relatively limited in minority communities.

To open up the coast guard to a broader community, I led coast guard outreach efforts to do a number of things that heretofore were not part of coast guard's traditional way of doing business with external organizations. I fostered relationships with minority organizations and educational institutions for the purpose of developing strategic partnerships and collaborating on matters of mutual interest. I established the coast guard's first JROTC program. I developed and implemented a wide-ranging Partnership in Education program throughout the coast guard, and members of headquarters and field facilities made over two million contacts with students before my retirement. I developed and implemented new strategies for recruiting minority candidates for the coast guard's Officer Acquisition program. I initiated implementation of MD 715, the EEOC guidance for developing a model EEO program in order to create and sustain a positive workforce environment, free of discrimination.

An African American male was promoted to rear admiral in 1998, the first in the history of the coast guard. He wrote me a letter on his personal stationery, praising my work that led to his promotion, owing it to my successfully advocating a cultural-awareness environment in the coast guard. Rear Admiral Erroll Brown wrote in his letter dated September 30, 2004:

> I want to thank you for all you have done for our organization throughout your career. Thank you for caring, your passion, and your commitment. And I especially wanted to thank you for all you have done for me and countless others who may never realize the profound influence you have had on shaping and changing this organization for the better.
>
> For more than you know, you have been a role model to me as a driving force and shining example of what it means to be dedicated to a right cause. You have been selfless and unwavering in living your strong beliefs in the face of countless and difficult challenges. I believe

that your relentless pursuit of better and fair, to the benefit of all, will stand forever as your legacy to the Coast Guard; and in the end, I am certain our history will record that among the pioneering change agents, Mr. Walt Somerville stands as a giant.

I believe that no one makes it alone, and we all had help along the way. I genuinely believe that you were one of the single most influential individuals in shaping and guiding my success; and for that, I can never thank you enough.

For all you have done for me and for so many others, I want to thank you so very much. Unquestionably, I stand here today because of you! Thank you so much for guiding and lifting me to these heights.

In addition to Rear Admiral Brown, when I retired from the coast guard, two additional African Americans were promoted to rear admiral. There was none when I was appointed to the SES position in 1983.

Furthermore, I was thrilled to receive a personal letter from Norman Mineta, secretary of transportation (DOT), after my retirement. The coast guard was transferred from DOT to the Department of Homeland Security in 2002. Secretary Mineta wrote to commend me for outstanding achievements while leading the coast guard's Civil Rights program. I had developed a relationship with him during the time the coast guard was part of DOT, and I had the privilege of working on projects under the direction of his immediate office. He was pleased with the outcome of those projects and wanted to let me know that he considered the coast guard's program a leading enterprise in the federal government. It was an honor to receive Secretary Mineta's warm and friendly comments.

The Honorable Secretary of Transportation Norman Y. Mineta wrote on September 30, 2004:

Congratulations on your retirement from government service. You have distinguished yourself as a public servant, especially during your twenty-one years as the Coast Guard's Assistant Commandant for Civil Rights. Under your leadership, the Civil Rights program can boast direct influence on the Coast Guard opening its doors to women; developing a Junior Reserve Officer Training Program; enhancing awareness among minorities about the service through strategic partnerships and special recruiting programs; and establishing a field civil rights infrastructure. These are just a few of the milestones that reflect the visionary leadership you have shown in the Coast Guard over the past two decades.

One of the advantages of being around for a long time is seeing the fruits of your labor. Fortunately for the Coast Guard, those fruits are a civil rights program that is the envy of other federal agencies. Your vision will carry on not only in the comprehensive civil rights doctrine that will be published shortly but in the hearts and minds of the men and women of the Coast Guard who have benefited so much from your vigilance. ...

I am exceedingly grateful for the compliments from Rear Admiral Brown and Secretary Mineta. I always will cherish their writings as thoughtful reminders of their praise for the coast guard's civil rights program and for an incredible job well done.

Additionally, it was an honor for me to develop personal relationships with presidents of historically black colleges and universities (HBCU). Those relationships began to evolve during the times I spoke at their conferences and when some of them invited me to speak on their campuses at special student forums. I invited some of the presidents to Coast Guard Headquarters to dine in the commandant's dining room and to meet and chat with some of the admirals. From my observation, the admirals enjoyed chatting with the presidents, especially during times when they were exchanging "sea stories" and ideas on how to develop proposals of mutual interest. I always will cherish my personal relationship with the HBCU presidents, who often addressed me endearingly as "Mr. Coast Guard."

In addition, I am grateful for the camaraderie shared with the president of the Association of Hispanic College and Universities (HACU). We collaborated on many issues, including the appointment of a senior officer in the coast guard to serve on his immediate staff as the liaison to Hispanic colleges and universities. What's important is that this was the first time the coast guard had approved assignment of a military officer to a nonprofit organization in order to open doors of opportunity for Hispanics to become members of the service. This was a pioneering initiative that proved valuable to the coast guard.

Developing a civil rights doctrine for the coast guard was one of my most important achievements. This doctrine set forth the manner in which the Civil Rights program was organized, its missions, organizational structure, and staffing. It outlined roles and responsibilities for all members of the service, regardless of status, rank, or grade level. It integrated the civil rights policies and practices into the overall coast guard operational policies and practices.

This civil rights doctrine constituted very important policy for the effective and efficient operation of the coast guard. It resolved the long-standing issue regarding the role of military leaders and commanders in dealing with personnel issues, especially complaints. Heretofore, military members had indicated that it was not their responsibility to play a role in resolving discrimination complaints. They opined that those matters should be handled by the civil rights office. This civil rights doctrine dispelled that notion and clarified the roles and responsibilities of all member of the coast guard, including military and civilian members, regardless of their status, rank, or grade level. The civil rights doctrine required all military and civilian members to be held accountable for their actions or inactions, under penalties imposed by coast guard policy. This policy was long in coming but now has been indoctrinated into the culture of the coast guard.

Despite the new initiatives and strategies advocated by the Civil Rights program, most outcomes may be perceived as qualitative, not quantitative, and therefore cannot be measured in statistical terms until later. Some of these issues will take a while before measurable results can be tabulated.

It is suggested that thousands, if not millions, of contacts were made with minorities through the partnerships the coast guard formed with minority organizations and education institutions. Arguably, the law of probability would indicate that if an appreciable number of minority males and females were among those persons contacted, many of them would have decided to join the coast guard in some capacity. It is unfortunate that the coast guard's intake recruiting systems were not equipped to keep records of candidates who were reached though the civil rights outreach initiatives, prior to 2004.

There is reason to be optimistic, however, that with full implementation of the civil rights doctrine, including the model EEO program, the coast guard will show significant positive statistical results in its military and civilian workforce. The important thing to take away, in my opinion, is that the coast guard is better off now than it was before I accepted the position of assistant commandant for civil rights in 1983.

Serving as assistant commandant for civil rights afforded me an opportunity to meet dignitaries in the United States and from abroad. For example, I met President Bill Clinton in 1996, when he spoke at a coast guard graduation. Before we took our seats on the dais, we chatted for about five minutes, and I found him to be a very warm and down-to-earth individual.

I was invited to the White House in 1988 for a briefing by President Ronald Reagan and members of his cabinet. Although it was a promotional initiative to get African Americans to support his reelection, I enjoyed the event. The president provided a luncheon meal and shook hands and took photos with all in attendance. I chatted with him for about thirty seconds, and I found him to be a very personable man. The White House sent me a copy of the photo with his inscribed comments. I had the photo framed and placed it on my "ego wall" in my den.

I met the prime minister from New Zealand. We sat together on the commandant's plane during the flight from Washington National Airport to the Coast Guard Academy to attend the graduation ceremony. One of his country's students was graduating.

I had lunch with the president of Burundi, Melchior Ndadaye, and his wife at a local restaurant at the invitation of the Dr. Samuel Myers, president/CEO of NAFEO. President Ndadaye was from East Africa, visiting the United States to study our education systems. I also have a photo of him and his wife among my collection, hanging on my ego wall in my den. Unfortunately, President Ndadaye was assassinated in October 1993; his wife was lucky to escape to France.

I met the head of the Russian coast guard when he had lunch in the commandant's dining room. I also ate lunch in the dining room that day.

These were interesting times for me, and I enjoyed them all. They would have never occurred, had I not been the assistant commandant for civil rights and having had the protocol status of the position.

Serving as assistant commandant for civil rights was a challenging opportunity and a difficult undertaking, but it presented unlimited opportunities. It offered a unique opening to use my influence to make a difference throughout the coast guard by advocating a cultural-awareness environment in the service, changing the character of the coast guard's culture, developing an organization that values diversity, and creating a better workforce environment for everyone.

Only history will tell the degree to which my work achieved these sought-after outcomes. Nevertheless, I believe I stood my watch with the utmost dignity. The coast guard is better in 2004 than it was in 1983, when I was appointed assistant commandant for civil rights.

With the civil rights doctrine in place, the Civil Rights program will continue to add value to personnel readiness and the effective and efficient performance of coast guard operational missions.

Chapter 26

Gratifying Experiences in Retirement, 2004–2017

Keeping in Shape

WHEN YOU RETIRE, PEOPLE USUALLY WANT TO KNOW WHAT YOU ARE doing in retirement. Do you have another job? How do you stay busy? These questions come all the time. I would like to offer answers to some of those questions.

My wife and I retired in sequential years. She retired in 2003, and I stopped working in 2004. We wanted to stay active but did not want to get another job, working from eight to five.

We try to eat healthily and exercise every day. My wife uses DVDs to guide her daily exercise workouts. I like to jog and walk outside the house every day.

After getting up in the morning, I routinely stretch my leg muscles, especially around my knees and hip joints, for about thirty minutes. This starts my blood circulating. Then I go out to walk. For the past thirteen years, I have been walking an average of five miles a days on most days, year-round in all kinds of weather, unless it is less than twenty-five degrees outside. This exercise program was recommended especially for me by a doctor as the best workout to stay in shape.

Jean and I have tried to maintain a healthy diet and exercise program for years. And it has paid off for us. I believe it's the main reason we have enjoyed relatively healthy lives, especially for two senior citizens.

Purchasing Timeshare Home from Washington, DC

Occasionally, we took a trip to Las Vegas, Nevada. We visited the historic sites in and surrounding Las Vegas, Eisenhower Dam, Reno, Carson City, Lake Tahoe, and the Four Corners, where the states of Utah, Colorado, Arizona, and New Mexico come together at one point.

We normally stayed at the casinos on the Las Vegas Strip. The musical entertainment and plays sponsored at the casinos on the Strip were excellent. All of the casinos we visited offered buffet dining. The casinos may have competed with each other, offering different kinds of foods to attract the most people. We liked visiting Las Vegas so much that we thought it would be a good city in which to purchase a timeshare as a second home away from Washington, DC.

There were many opportunities to purchase timeshares in Las Vegas in 2007. A salesman lured us into purchasing a timeshare at the Marriott Grand Chateau. It was a 1,200-square-foot, two- bedroom timeshare that could accommodate eight people. We paid $27,200 for the timeshare.

It was well supplied with furniture, appliances, TVs in every room, and everything else you would expect to have in an upscale furnished home. At the time, we thought we were doing something great that would benefit us in future years. The entire 1,200-square- foot timeshare was available to us for one seven-day stay during the year, or we could use only half the space twice a year for seven days each time.

The Marriott Grand Chateau was located in close proximity to most of the casinos we normally frequented on the Strip. Its location was ideal for us. It provided shuttle service to shopping centers and grocery stores, and we took advantage of the shuttle service to purchase food items to cook for breakfast. On most days, we cooked and ate breakfast in our timeshare. We then purchased lunch and dinner at the casinos. Jean would take the shuttle to shopping centers when they were not within walking dance. We often spent casual hours at the chateau, just watching TV and talking about things we never took the time to talk about at home.

I applied to serve on the board of directors for the chateau. I wanted to know more about the timeshare industry and how decisions were made regarding various aspects of administration. Serving on the board would afford that opportunity. Apparently, my application was not competitive enough to be selected the year I applied, and I didn't make any further attempts to serve on the board.

There were some things the salesman did not explain to us when we purchased the timeshare. Marriott charged processing fees for almost everything except for making one reservation for an annual stay at the chateau. Because of the potentially large number of people making reservations through other organizations to stay at the chateau, it was advisable to make reservations to use the property a year in advance if we wanted to get our preferred dates. And if we wanted to change our reservations, we had to pay a processing fee to change the dates. We even had to pay a processing fee the year we requested use of only half of the timeshare space so we could use the other half for a second stay in the same year.

Getting our preferred dates became problematic, especially during the summer months. During summer, the temperatures could rise to over one hundred degrees. We gave up requesting reservations during the summer and opted to get them in the early fall. Reservations were handled by an agent working out of a Marriott office in Orlando, Florida.

To have another option for making reservations, I joined Interval International. The Interval International vacation network took requests for reservations from all over the world. The Marriot Grand Chateau was part of this network. I used Interval International once to get reservations at our timeshare. I also tried to use the organization to get reservations at a hotel in China when we traveled there, but the only place it could book us was too far from the hotel where the people we were traveling with were staying.

After several years, we realized that the maintenance fees for the timeshare increased year after year, to a point where it might have been less expensive to stay at a casino on the Strip, especially when we were not so excited about visiting Las Vegas every year. When we considered the problematic reservations process and increasing annual maintenance fees, the novelty of owning a timeshare began to dissipate.

All attempts to sell the timeshare on the open market were unsuccessful. Realtors were eager to advertise the timeshare for sale on the commercial market for a fee but would not guarantee they would find a buyer for the property. Realtors would advertise the timeshare year after year, as long as the advertising fee was paid.

I reached out to Marriott to see if they would buy back the timeshare. Marriott agreed to repurchase it in 2014 for $5,200. Since this was the best offer we could get on the commercial market, we sold it back to Marriott, taking nearly an 85 percent loss.

Chapter 27

Vowing to Aid Access to College

DURING THE MANY YEARS I WORKED THROUGHOUT MY CAREER, I acquired an appreciation for the importance of education. Education is an enabling factor. I did not have a college degree when I joined the United States Air Force. I wanted to become an officer in the service but was reluctant to apply because of my limited education.

My first job in the federal service was as an Air Force Reserve technician. This job did not require a college degree, nor did many other entry-level civil service jobs at that time. But in order to move up in the federal civil service, work experience and/or education beyond high school was required in order to compete successfully with other candidates who were seeking promotion to most technical and middle-management positions.

I acquired an appreciation for having an education beyond high school while working at the Federal Aviation Agency (FAA). My initial job there entailed handling the personnel records of FAA employees at all grade levels. I observed that most of the employees who worked in technical jobs had college degrees, and this motivated me to return to college. The time I served in the air force entitled me to benefits under the GI Bill, which made me eligible to get financial funding for college from the government. I enrolled in evening college courses in 1957 and ultimately completed the requirements for a bachelor's degree in business and economics from the University of Maryland University College, just before taking a civilian job in the United States Coast Guard.

Having a college degree was a contributing factor to my success in the federal civil service. I developed an appreciation for the value of education. This is what inspired me to help others get an education.

Creating a Living Legacy

Graduating from the University of Maryland University College was not easy. Earning my degree took money I did not have—and also limited my time away from personal pleasures. Nevertheless, I possessed an unyielding determination to succeed in getting a college degree. The manner in which I attained my college education inspired me to think of others who might be experiencing similar situations to get a college education.

As a living legacy and to establish a college scholarship fund, I created the University of Maryland University College (UMUC) Walter R. Somerville Jr. School of Undergraduate Studies Business Students Endowed Scholarship Fund. It offers scholarships for undergraduate students majoring in business administration. The scholarships are available for community college transfer students who maintained an annual GPA of 3.0 or higher when transferring from a community college and who demonstrate financial need. I signed a memorandum of understanding with Ms. Susan Aldridge, PhD, president of the University of Maryland University College, to establish this scholarship fund in 2007.

Creation of the scholarship fund was given wide publicity at UMUC campuses in this country as well as UMUC locations in Europe and Asia. The college arranged for my photo to be taken along the Anacostia Walkway overlooking the Potomac River in southwest Washington, DC. And the photo images were used on posters and distributed to college campuses in the States and overseas where UMUC students studied. Additionally, I granted an interview to a writer hired by the college to develop a profile highlighting my professional career. The profile was published in the UMUC magazine, the *Achiever*. The magazine has wide distribution within and outside of the USA.

UMUC selected me as the Distinguished Alumnus for 2008. Dr. Aldridge presented the award to me at the University of Maryland University College graduation exercises that year. The award was inscribed thusly: "In recognition of your loyal and dedicated services to the University of Maryland University College. Your exceptional leadership, continued support, dedication, and commitment to UMUC."

UMUC gave me an annual scholarship report from the college, for the academic year 2015. Four students received scholarship support from the fund that year. Each prepared an application for scholarship assistance.

One student wrote, as part of her application for financial assistance, "During my two-year attendance I used my personal funds to pay for college tuition. Since then, I have given birth to a baby boy and have limited funds to survive ..." This student made the point that she wanted to continue her education but was in dire need of financial assistant. Money from the fund was authorized for her support, and she is continuing her education.

A second student wrote, in part, "For as long as I can remember, I wanted to attend and graduate college. I found it to be very difficult, as the cost to attend has been more than my finances allow. Initially, I attended community college and paid for the 60-plus credits that I earned. The great thing was that upon completion, I was debt-free. The downside was that I wanted to continue my education to pursue a bachelor's degree in business administration. Tuition and the cost of books are much greater this time around and with the general cost of living, I find that it is not an easy load to bear without financial assistance ..."

A third student wrote, in part, "I was recently laid off from my job due to the company's financial struggles and am currently unemployed. I had been regularly employed for the past twelve years and also attended college during that time. Fortunately, my parents allowed me to move back home, which helped me reduce my living expenses. Previously I had been able to avoid incurring debt for my education by using savings from my job and from a Pell Grant. However, my savings have drastically decreased, and I do not have enough to fund the remainder of college expenses ..."

Finally, a fourth student wrote, in part, "With a degree, I would expect my salary to increase significantly, affording us the ability to pay for after-school care for our daughter, which is simply not cost- effective at my current pay rate. Once I complete my degree, I plan to pursue full-time employment in the human resources field ..."

These stories from needy students are moving commentaries. Providing them financial assistance is testament to the usefulness of the scholarship fund. I am delighted to play a small role in their lives by sponsoring a scholarship fund that is available to them in a time of need.

I received a scholarship report for 2016 that indicated five students received financial assistance from the fund. As the fund continues to increase, more students will be accommodated. The scholarship report for 2017 revealed that seven students received scholarship assistance from the fund.

I established a second Walter Raleigh Somerville Jr. Endowed Scholarship Fund at Morgan State University on July 22, 2022. The purpose of this fund was to provide financial assistance to the Foundation in awarding scholarships based on demonstrated financial need. Potential students must have a 2.75 or greater GPA, majoring in Business or Economics. Financial funding may be used for university related expenses such as tuition, fees, textbooks, and emergency funds needed to cover current semester balances. This fund reinforced my commitment to help needy students realize their dreams of becoming college graduates.

Chapter 28

Enjoying Professional Sports

Attending Professional Baseball Games

THE DISTRICT OF COLUMBIA HAD BEEN WITHOUT A PROFESSIONAL baseball team for many years. The Montreal Expos moved from Montreal to the District in 2006. A group led by Ted Lerner purchased the team in May of that year. The name of the team was changed from Montreal Expos to the Washington Nationals, better known as the "Nats." The Nats play their home games at Nationals Park, which opened for business in 2008.

Because of my love of baseball, I was overwhelmed to have a professional baseball team in the District. The baseball park is located six city blocks from where I live. It is convenient for me to walk to the park. I purchased a partial season ticket in 2008, which allowed me to attend twenty games during the baseball season.

In 2010, my son-in-law also purchased a partial season ticket. We had great seats, located in the mezzanine section on the third-base side of the park, but most of the seats in the ball park are good for viewing the game. Jean attended some games when the temperature for being outdoors was perfect, and my son-in-law was unable to attend. My son-in-law also brought his daughter to the ball park several times when she was on recess from college. Unfortunately, he moved to Connecticut, and now I attend the games without him.

Baseball is not Jean's favorite sport. She opines that the game is too slow. She said that watching baseball is like looking at paint dry. Nevertheless, she is learning the game. She has her favorite players and will defend them with all her might during any baseball conversation. We enjoy talking about baseball and sharing our different perspectives on the game.

In 2016 the Nats won the Eastern Division championship in the National League. This was not the first time they won the division title, but it was the first time I had purchased postseason tickets. I thought the Nats had a good chance of winning the first round of the postseason and moving on to the next round. They didn't make it through the first round, though, which was a disappointment.

In 2017 the Nats won the Eastern Division for the second year in a row, with more wins than they had the previous year. I did not buy postseason tickets, however, because I had a gut feeling that the Nats would not survive the first round. I was right, even though they played five games, losing in the fifth game at home, a game that many thought they should have won.

It was great for the DC metropolitan area when Ted Lerner and his partners purchased the franchise for the Nats to play in the District. I was invited to watch a game during the 2016 season with one of Ted's partners, Rodney Slater. Rodney was a former secretary of the federal Department of Transportation. During the game, we talked about the Nats—their past, present, and future.

The Nats drew large crowds—baseball fans of all ages—to the ball park, often playing to a full house for their home games. To ensure continuing support for the Nats, though, they will have to win not only the postseason games but also a national World Series.

I remain optimistically hopeful that the Nats will win postseason playoff games in the National League and will go on to win the World Series. I can envision an electrifying parade along Pennsylvania Avenue— that's how great I think the Nats are.

Attending Professional Basketball Games

Professional basketball is Jean's game. Sometimes I think she has more love for basketball than I do for baseball, if that is possible. One of Jean's college classmates encouraged us to attend basketball games. She lived in the next block on the same street where we live. Her husband had been a basketball player in college and continued to follow professional games throughout his career with the federal government. He had purchased four season ticket packages of forty-one Wizard games for many years. He purchased some of the best seats in the arena, located at center court. This is an indication of how much he loved basketball. He had several friends he would invite to attend games with him and his wife.

Jean's friend invited us to a game with them. I was very impressed with the location of the seats and the view we had while sitting at center court. The invitations to the basketball games kept coming, and we would always accept them. Attending the games was such an enjoyable experience for Jean. To add to the enjoyment, we would have dinner at a restaurant before the games. I paid for the dinners on a couple of occasions, and then the husband of Jean's friend insisted that we should alternate paying for the dinners. So that is what we did. This experience became enjoyable and at the same time caused Jean and me to develop a love for professional basketball.

Eventually, Jean and I talked about getting our own basketball tickets. We did not think a full season ticket plan was appropriate for us, so I asked a ticket agent what other options were available. The agent advised me to consider a fourteen-game plan, and that was just what we were hoping to get.

I purchased our first fourteen games for the 2016–2017 season of basketball. It was advertised as a star-studded ticket with some of the best teams on the schedule. Our seats were located at center court. The seats were a little expensive, but because of Jean's new love of the game, I thought it was worthwhile. Besides, I had become accustomed to watching the games from center court and didn't want to change; I had enjoyed it so much when we were at the arena with Jean's classmate and her husband. Jean and I got another partial plan the following year for thirteen games in the 2017–18 season. It was an all-star plan.

We enjoy basketball more than you might ever imagine. Before the game, we routinely dine at a nice restaurant. We eat and chat about the game and any other thing that comes to mind. The games normally start at seven, and we plan to be in our seats by that time. Getting to the game is very convenient. We live directly across the street from the subway. We take the subway to and from the game. Jean and I look forward to the games as well as dinner before the game starts.

Jean has her favorite players and shares her observations about the opposing teams the Wizards play. She is becoming an expert basketball analyst. She understands the basketball jargon, such as *flagrant foul, walking, pawning the ball, three points from downtown, three-second violation, pick and roll,* etc. We enjoy talking about the players and their strengths and weaknesses as demonstrated during the game and sharing our different perspectives on various developments in the game.

The Wizards have played in postseason games but have not played well enough to compete for the national basketball crown. I believe they have the talent, but they seem to freeze when they compete in postseason games. Jean once asked what would happen if the Wizards won all of their games. I said they unquestionably would be the best team in basketball. According to the law of probability, that is possible, but I don't think it will happen. I just want to see the Wizards win a national basketball championship.

Chapter 29

Enjoying Tourism

JEAN AND I DID NOT DO MUCH TRAVELING ABROAD TOGETHER DURING the years we were working full-time jobs. We did, however, take summer trips to nearby places in the Caribbean Islands, such as the Bahamas, Puerto Rico, Nassau, the Virgin Islands, and Aruba. It was not until 2008 that we decided to visit farther-away countries: France, Costa Rica, Dubai, and China.

Touring Nice, France

Jean was a member of the Washington DC Oasis social club, which planned a tour to Nice, France, in 2008. We decided to go on the tour, which was sponsored by Collette Vacations from March 5 to March 12.

Collette Vacations provided transportation from the Oasis Club headquartered in Prince George's County, Maryland, to Dulles International Airport, where we flew on United Airlines to the Frankfort airport in Germany. From there we flew on Lufthansa Airlines to Nice, France.

Our flight was overnight, departing Dulles International Airport at 5:27 p.m. on March 5 and arriving at the Nice International Airport at 10:15 a.m. on March 6, about a ten-hour flight. During the flight from Frankfort to Nice, we had a gorgeous view of the Alps mountain range, and I took as many photos of this magnificent mountain range as I could. We were met at the Nice airport by a Collette representative with a bus, which took us to Hotel Splendid Nice, where we stayed during the six nights we were on the tour.

Our tour began with meeting other Collette tourists at a welcome dinner that first evening at the hotel, about thirty-five more people Before beginning the tour the next day, most of us went to a nearby bank and transferred our dollars to euros. This was advisable. The tour director opined that French merchants preferred their money to US currency.

After exchanging our dollars for euros, we were eager to begin the tour and learn more about the beautiful city of Nice and its surroundings.

Nice is the fifth most populated city in France and the capital of the Alpes-Maritimes department. The metropolitan area of Nice extends beyond the administrative city limits. Located in the French Riviera on the southeast coast on the Mediterranean Sea and at the foot of the Alps, Nice is the second largest French city on the Mediterranean coast. It's about eight miles from the principality of Monaco and is one of the most visited cities, drawing more than four million tourists every year. Nice is nicknamed *Nice la Bella*, which means "Nice the Beautiful."

The tour began with a visit to a charming town in Ventimiglia, Italy. Ventimiglia is a popular summer destination for tourists on the French Riviera. It is located eighty-one miles southwest of Genoa, Italy and four miles from the French–Italian border. Particularly popular is the weekly street market, held on Fridays along the town's seafront, which causes major traffic congestion. We explored the outdoor market, which offered all types of merchandise, local crafts, and fresh produce. The time spent there afforded us tourists an opportunity to examine the various items on display and make purchases.

No public restroom facilities were available in walking distant of the market. At this location, in order to use restroom facilities, we had to pay a small fee or purchase something at a place of business. So we stopped at a small eatery a short walking distance from the outdoor market. Two members of the tour group with us ordered a pizza and sat at a table, talked, and used the restroom facilities.

Continuing on the tour, our next stop was San Remo, the luxurious capital of the Italian Riviera, on the Mediterranean coast of Liguria in northwestern Italy. It was founded during Roman times and is known as a tourist destination. It hosts numerous cultural events, such as musical festivals and cycling classics. We had lunch in this city, popular for its cuisine.

We visited the perfume capital of the world in Grasse. Grasse has had a prospering perfume industry since the end of the eighteenth century. It has three perfume factories that offer tours and demonstrations for visitors. At the perfume factory, we got to meet some of the people whose noses are trained to distinguish over two thousand kinds of scents. Grasse produces over two-thirds of Frances's natural aromas for perfume and food flavorings. It was interesting to observe the operation of the perfume industry. Various kinds of perfume were on display and available for purchase.

Continuing on our tour, we observed the marvelous scenery along the Loup River to Saint Paul, which is situated on a hill overlooking the countryside. This medieval walled town was filled with historic buildings, hidden alleyways, restaurants, and specialty shops. It is well known as one of the oldest medieval towns on the French Riviera. It is noted for its modern and contemporary art museums and galleries.

Jean, leaning on huge stone in a narrow street in Nice, France

At the tour guide's direction, the bus driver took us to a local resident's home on a mountain side overlooking the town, where the family treated us to a barbecue- style steak and wine dinner. The dining atmosphere was stimulatingly relaxing, with two wood-burning fireplaces with crackling fires in the background.

We walked on the promenade along the Mediterranean seafront at Nice. The promenade extends from the airport on the west to a distance on the east approximately 4.35 miles. This was an interesting outing that included a stop to observe a flower market and fabulous fruit stands. The flower market and fruit stands displayed some of the most impressive products imaginable. I took photos to help memorialize these magnificent products because it was hard to explain their lusciousness in words only.

We toured the Chagall Museum and scrutinized its collection of celebrated paintings. The museum was dedicated to the work of painter Marc Chagall. His work was inspired by religion. The museum houses the series of seventeen Chagall paintings that illustrate a biblical message, which were offered to the French state in 1966. The series illustrates the books of Genesis, Exodus, and the Song of Songs.

While touring the spectacular coastline, we passed a town where we stopped and surveyed the impressive Rothschild Villa and Gardens. The villa was designed by a French architect and constructed between 1905 and 1912. It is surrounded by nine gardens, each with a different theme: Florentine, Spanish, Garden a la "francais," exotic, stone, Japanese, roses, Provencal, and *garden de Sevres*. The garden was conceived in the form of a ship, to be viewed from the loggia (a gallery or room with one or more open sides) of the house, which was like the bridge of a vessel, with the sea visible on all sides. It was inspired by a voyage Baroness Béatrice de Rothschild made on the ocean liner *Ile de France*, and the villa was given that name.

We visited Saint-Tropez on the French Riviera, about sixty-two miles west of Nice. It is known for being a fashionable seaside town frequented by movie stars, artists, and writers. We enjoyed the sights while observing the surroundings of the yacht-filled bay, overlooking the picturesque seaside.

Afterward, we headed to the popular resort of Cannes on the French Riviera. It hosts the annual Cannes Film Festival, Midem (the leading industry event for the music ecosystem), and Cannes Lions International Festival of Creativity. The city is known for its association with the rich and famous, its luxury hotels and restaurants, and for special conferences held at the French Rivera resort.

We explored *Le Suquet*, which is the old quarter of Cannes, best known to tourists for the climbing, winding, cobble-stone lane with local restaurants. A clock tower and a church sit high, facing east, overlooking the Bay of Cannes and the city itself.

We walked along the elegant Boulevard of de la Croisette, a prominent road in Cannes. It stretches along the shore of the Mediterranean Sea and is nearly two miles long. It is listed in the cultural heritage general inventory of France.

We visited Monaco, which features the casino of Monte Carlo and other attractive tourist sights. Some of the tourists went inside the casino, but Jean and I did not because visitors and gamblers had to pay an entrance fee. We didn't think it was worth that.

Monaco also featured the Palace des Armes, Prince's Palace, Avenue des Beaus Artes, and Saint Nicholas Cathedral, where Prince Rainier III and Princess Grace are buried. This cathedral was a significantly historical edifice we definitely wanted to visit.

Another highlight of our visit to Monaco was the captivating Oceanographic Museum. This museum ostensibly has all the creatures in the Mediterranean Sea on display. This includes starfish, seahorses, turtles, jellyfish, crabs, lobsters, rays, sharks, sea urchins, sea cucumbers, eels, and cuttlefish, to name a few. The museum also has a great variety of sea-related objects, including model ships, sea animal skeletons, tools, and weapons. It also contains a collection of material culture and ritual objects made from the integration of substances such as pearls, mollusca (a phylum of invertebrate animals) and nacre (inorganic composite—mother of pearl).

On March 11, the final day of the tour, all members of our group gathered together for a photo. The tour director arranged to have the picture taken at a scenic spot on the seafront promenade overlooking the Mediterranean Sea. Later that day, we all assembled for a farewell dinner to celebrate our unforgettable trip.

The next day we departed for the Nice International Airport and returned home safely to Dulles International Airport. After arriving, we were met by a Collette-sponsored limousine and driven home. This was a tour we thoroughly enjoyed, and Collette contributed to our pleasure by providing transportation to and from the airport.

I took hundreds of photos on this trip, and Jean later edited them. She displayed the ones she kept in an album to commemorate our remarkable trip to Nice.

Touring Costa Rica

Costa Rica was our next tour sponsored by Collette Vacations. We enjoyed the Collette logistics so much during our tour to Nice that we decided to take another Collette tour, this time to Costa Rica. Jean's cousin accompanied us on this trip. Costa Rica is located in Central America. It is noted for its lush forests and stunning waterfalls. It has rumbling volcanoes and endless coastlines. Some describe Costa Rica as a "sliver of paradise." So, we wanted to see and enjoy what this Central American country had to offer.

Our nine-day tour began on March 4, 2009. Collette sent a limousine to pick us up and take us to Dulles International Airport. We left at 7:05 a.m. on Delta Airlines and flew to Hartsfield Jackson International Airport in Atlanta, Georgia where we landed at 8:59 a.m. From there we boarded another Delta flight at 9:45 a.m. and flew to the San Jose airport in Costa Rica, where we landed at 12:47 p.m. The flying time from Dulles to San Jose was approximately five hours and forty-two minutes, including the short layover at the Hartsfield International Airport. After we cleared customs, we were met by a Collette representative and taken to the Ramada Plaza Herradura San Jose Ciudad "Cariari" Hotel. San Jose is the colorful capital of Costa Rica.

Upon arrival at the hotel, we were joined by other members on the tour. And for the rest of the day, we relaxed and toured the sights and surroundings of the city.

Sightseeing began the next morning when we traveled by bus through the luxuriant countryside of the Central Valley. We explored the charming town of La Fortuna and spent two nights at a typical lodge, within breathtaking view of the majestic Arenal volcano.

The Arenal volcano is located in northwestern Costa Rica, around fifty-six miles northwest of San Jose. It measures at least 5,358 feet high. It is conically shaped with a crater that is about 450 feet in diameter. Geologically, the Arenal is considered a young volcano, as it is estimated to be nearly 7,500 years old.

The volcano was dormant for hundreds of years and exhibited a single crater at its summit with minor fumaroles (steam vents in the volcano from which steam and hot gases such as sulfur dioxide are released). The volcano was covered with dense vegetation. In 1968 it erupted unexpectedly, destroying the small town of Tabacon. Due to eruption three more craters were created on the western flank, but of the three only one of them still exists today. Since 2010, Arenal has been dormant.

When we arrived, the volcano had been generating constant lava for the past thirty days. We were scheduled to view the volcano close up, but because of the sounds coming from the volcano over the past few days, it was too dangerous to get to close to it. We had to view the volcano from a safe distance.

We visited Cano Negro Wildlife Refuge, located near the border of Nicaragua. It is a natural wildlife refuge, full of biodiversity, and is considered the third most important wetland in the world. It is the home of the largest viewable selection of indigenous wildlife. The Cano Negro Wildlife Refuge spans nearly twenty-five thousand acres of grassland, rainforest, marshes, rivers, and lakes near Costa Rica's northern border. Our tour took us on a guided riverboat ride down the Frio River in a *panga* (covered canoe), and we made frequent stops to watch and photograph the wildlife around us. Crocodiles, river otters, sloths, river turtles, exotic birds, and rare butterflies live in the area. The Raphia palms that line the banks of the Frio River drop fruit that turn the water black, giving the wetlands its name, *Cano Negro*.

Our tour took us to the Monteverde Cloud Forest, where we observed the trees. Tour guides briefed us on the evolution of the trees that grew to heights of over one hundred feet. We encountered various species of vegetation in this spectacular ecosystem.

We visited Selvatura Park, a cloud forest preserve. We explored the insect museum and saw an astonishing exhibition of beautiful live specimens of lizards, snakes, frogs, geckos, and many other species rescued and gathered from all over Costa Rica. They were in terrariums with controlled climates, which provided these creatures with environments similar to their natural habitats. We learned about the habits of tree frogs, terrestrial frogs, and toads, as well as the differences between each of these families. We also were told about snake behaviors, their eating habits, and their role within each ecosystem. This part of the tour was an amazing educational experience.

Our visit to the park included an exciting opportunity to fly through the cloud forest on a zip line canopy tour or take a guided walk among the treetops on a series of hanging bridges. Jean and her cousin chose the guided walk on the hanging bridges. The treetop walkway was a 1.9-mile trail that crosses through the cloud forest. You can walk across eight different bridges of various lengths, ranging from 150 feet to 510 feet and at altitudes ranging from thirty- six feet up to 180 feet. Each of the bridges is five feet wide and has a capacity of up to eighty people per bridge, making them both the longest and strongest bridges in Costa Rica.

Jean and her cousin walked part of the way to see what it felt like to navigate this awesome experience. They were overwhelmed with their experience from the distance they walked.

I chose the zip line canopy tour for an adrenaline-packed ride through the remarkable cloud forest ecosystem. It appeared to be a dangerous experience, but this did not discourage me. The tour guide prepared me for the trip. Before taking off, he provided a comprehensive safety orientation and told me everything to do. This relieved some of my fear. The orientation was very helpful in understanding what to expect throughout the zip lie flight across the forest, soaring above the treetops.

With the guide's help, I slipped on a safety harness, helmet, and other essential equipment, and then trekked across the forest floor to reach the first of eighteen treetop platforms. Also with the guide's assistance, I clipped on to each zip line and then let go to fly from one platform to the next, traveling to only fifteen of the eighteen platform stops along the way through the mist-shrouded rain forest canopy. The zip line course in Selvatura Park, consisting of eighteen different cables reaching fantastic heights, is among the longest in Costa Rica. This was a excitingly breathtaking experience that I thoroughly enjoyed. I have a photo that was taken during my journey through the clouds—a treasured image.

Walter on zip line, soaring above treetops in rainforest in Costa Rica

Before leaving the Monteverde Cloud Forest, we planted a tree in this spectacular nature reserve. And we visited one of the world's largest butterfly gardens. The gardens also contained more than fourteen species of hummingbirds.

We also visited a local coffee-production plant in the city and observed how a Costa Rican bean is transformed into a cup of coffee. Guides explained the details of picking, peeling, roasting, and all the processing that coffee needs before you can drink it. Coffee is one of the most important products produced in Costa Rica, which is considered to have some of the best coffee in the world.

We traveled to the spectacular Guanacaste region. On the way there, we stopped at a small cooperative, where locals showcased their handmade merchandise. Guanacaste is a province of Costa Rica, located in the northwestern region of the country along the Pacific Ocean. It borders Nicaragua to the north, Alajuela Province to the east, and Puntarenas to the southeast. It is one of the smallest provinces in Costa Rica, covering an area of about 3,915 square miles. The Guanacaste Province is home to the bulk of Costa Rica's all-inclusive resorts. This, along with its proximity to both beaches and the Arenal volcano, has made it one of the more popular tourist destinations in the country.

Our next stop was at Playa Tamarindo. This town is known for its breathtaking beauty and fine-sand beaches. Tamarindo is a town and district of Santa Cruz canton, located on the Nicoya Peninsula of the northern Pacific coast of Costa Rica in Guanacaste. Its main attractions are surfing and eco-tourism.

During our tour there, we relaxed on the beach, observing the mesmerizing ocean views and lush tropical greenery. We walked in the sand along the side of the ocean. For dinner that evening, Jean and I each had a fully headed red snapper as our entree. We spend a night at the Tamarindo Diria Beach and Golf Resort and explored the nearby town, taking advantage of the amenities offered by the resort hotel.

The next morning, we were given a leisurely ride through the countryside to Sarchi. This town is known as the cradle of Costa Rican artisans because of its fine workshops. Sarchi is Costa Rica's most famous crafts center. The town offers more than two hundred stores and small family-operated woodworking factories. These factories produce wooden bowls and tableware, fold-up rocking chairs of wood and leather, and a wide variety of kitschy items.

We observed the artistic work of the local artisans as they created the famous oxcarts. As part of Costa Rican history, the oxcart was used in the mid-nineteenth century to transport coffee and other goods from the Central Valley to the ports of Puntarenas and Limon. Oxcarts were locally known as *carretas* and served as the only means of transportation for many rural families in those early days. The town is also known for its many furniture shops that feature both modern and rustic pieces.

We continued on to San Jose, where we enjoyed a wonderful farewell dinner and prepared to leave the next day for home. We were driven to the San Jose airport on March 12, 2009. We boarded Delta Airlines at

8:00 a.m. and flew to Hartsfield-Jackson International Airport, landing at 2:06 p.m. From there we boarded Delta Airlines at 3:55 p.m. and flew to Dulles International Airport, where we landed at 5:41 p.m. We were met by a limousine driver provided by Collette Vacations and driven home.

During our tour, we stayed at five different hotels, lodges, and resorts. Everywhere we went we traveled by bus, from one town to the next. This required starting out early most mornings in order to accommodate our timetable for the tour.

Nevertheless, we enjoyed the tour very much, as this was our first visit to a Central American country. What we learned on this trip could only be known through personal knowledge, experience, and observations acquired from being in the country. In addition, I snapped many photos of the diverse things we observed. These hundreds of photos will enhance our memorabilia that Jean put together to elucidate our knowledge of Costa Rica and its people.

Touring Dubai

In April 2012, Jean and I decided to take a trip to Dubai, United Arab Emirates. We learned about this trip from Bettye Bouey-Yates, PhD, a member of our Christ United Methodist Church.

Dr. Yates founded the Bettye Bouey-Yates Education Foundation to provide financial assistance to support educational activities for dissident young girls in South Africa. She invited us to attend a meeting that she organized to explain the trip. Many members from other churches were also invited. The trip was planned as a tour to raise money for the foundation. The discussion of the trip was so appealing that we decided to sign up for the six-day tour, from April 15 through April 21, 2010.

We boarded Delta Airlines at the Baltimore–Washington International Airport on April 14, 2010, in the early morning, and we landed at Atlanta International Airport, where we had a two-hour layover—enough time to eat breakfast.

Then we boarded another Delta flight for Dubai. The flight was smooth and uneventful. On board, the crew was friendly and accommodating. We were given all the food and drinks we wanted. There was a large selection of movies available to watch. I watched several of them. After flying for about fifteen hours, mostly across the North Atlantic Ocean and over Middle Eastern countries, we landed at the Dubai International Airport on the evening of April 15, 2010.

After we cleared customs, we were met by a local Dubai representative. Our representative assisted us with our luggage and transfer by bus to the Royal Ascot Hotel. This is where we would stay throughout the time we were in Dubai.

We were filled with curiosity and anticipation. We checked into the hotel and then went outside the building to walk around and observe the environment. This didn't last long because we wanted to get a fresh start the next morning. We went inside, purchased a snack, ate it, and then went to our room to retire for the night.

The next morning we were eager to get started on the tour. After breakfast, we met in a conference room with our host, where he briefed the tourists on the activities that were planned during the tour over the next five days.

The tour began with a stop at the Jumeirah Mosque. The Jumeirah Mosque is noted as the most photographed mosque in Dubai. It was built around 1976 in the traditional Fatimid architecture style in North Africa. Modest dress was preferred, but traditional Muslim attire was available from the mosque, upon request. Most of our tour group requested Muslim attire and put it on. I took photos to commemorate the occasion.

The mosque had become renowned as the focal point of Dubai's "Open doors". (A mosque with "Open Doors" invites the community in). This mosque is the only one in Dubai that is open to the public and dedicated to receiving non-Muslin guests. Guests could join a unique opportunity to learn about Emirati culture and religion in a relaxed, casual, and open atmosphere at this magnificent mosque. Visitors could ask any question and get answers about the mosque and Muslin culture, without reservations.

We stopped at the Mercato Shopping Mall, located in one of the most prestigious Dubai residential areas. Mercato epitomizes the very best Italian architecture, which takes you back to the Renaissance period. It has over 140 shops and service outlets, offering a wide variety of international brands, and it caters to the needs of Dubai residents and international tourist alike. Mercato gives you a hand- picked selection of the most popular yet accessible brands, from fashions and beauty to houseware, jewelry, electronics, and confectionery. It has a large skiing facility, offering snowboarding and ski lessons. It has a "Fun City" for kids, supermarkets, cinemas, and eateries as well.

We stopped for photos of the luxurious Burg Al Arab Hotel. This hotel, the Tower of the Arabs, is a lavish establishment located in Dubai. It is the third tallest hotel in the world at about 920 feet high. It is located on an artificial island from a beach and is connected to the mainland by a private curving bridge. The shape of the structure is designed to resemble the sail of a ship. It has a helipad close to the roof at nearly 689 feet above the ground.

Our tour took us along the Sheikh Zayed Road, where we passed the Emirates Towers and the Dubai World Trade Center. This is the longest road in the Emirates. It stretches from the Al-Silah in the Emirates of Abu Dhabi to Ras al-Khaimah emirate, running roughly parallel to the UAE coastline along the Persian Gulf.

The Emirates Towers is a building in Dubai that contains the Emirates Office Tower and the Jumeriah Towers Hotel. It represents the symbol of the city of Dubai. The Emirates Tower complex is set in over forty-two acres of gardens, with lakes, waterfalls, and public seating areas, with parking for up to 1,800 cars. The Dubai World Trade Center was built in 1979. It is an all-purpose building for exhibits and exhibitions. It consists of 1.3 million square feet of exhibition and event space, with twenty-one halls and over forty meeting rooms on three levels. The Trade Center hosts over five hundred events annually and attracted over 2.74 million visitors in 2015.

We traveled along the Zabeel Road and viewed the exquisite palace of the royal family. We were not allowed to take photos of these magnificent buildings. We could only view the establishments and imagine what wonderful photos we could have had.

We stopped at the Dubai Mall and walked across the street to the Burj Khalifa, a mega-tall skyscraper in Dubai. It towers upward to a height of nearly 2,722 feet, with a roof height of 2,717 feet, the tallest structure in the world.

The building opened in 2010 as part of a new development called Downtown Dubai. The building is reportedly based on the government's decision to diversity from an oil-based economy to gaining international recognition. The building broke numerous height records, including its designation as the tallest tower in the world. Its design is derived from the Islamic architecture of the region, such as the Great Mosque of Samarra. Its Y-shaped tripartite floor geometry is designed to optimize residential and hotel space. Its top floor, level 156, is 1,918 feet high. Its observation floor, level 148, is 1,823 feet high. It has two below-ground parking levels. It contains fifty-seven elevators and eight escalators.

Our tour group took elevators to the observation level on the eighty-second floor. Looking out the windows of the observation tower, we got a magnificent view of Dubai. I likened it to looking out of an airplane on a clear day. I took photos from every angle possible of a view I never imagined existed.

From there, we stopped at the Dubai Creek Park and observed some of the most famous tourist attractions, such as an aquarium of dolphins, cable cars, camel rides, horse-drawn carriages, and exotic bird shows. Dubai Creek played a vital role in sustaining the life of the community in the city. Many boutiques and jewelry stores are in the city. Dubai is referred to as "the City of Gold" and the Gold Souk in Deira; it houses nearly 250 gold retail shops.

After this visit, we returned to the hotel, ending our first exciting day touring Dubai. We had a welcome dinner at the hotel, and most of us retired for the evening.

The next morning, we had breakfast and then were off for a full-day tour of Abu Dhabi. Abu Dhabi is one of the richest and most modern cities in the world. It is the capital of the United Arab Emirates. It is the center of the oil business and the administration of the country. Abu Dhabi is located about one hundred miles from Dubai.

Build on a natural sand island, the emirate includes a number of offshore islands and vast expanses of desert. The city is noted for its lush greenery, planned development, and beautiful cornices. Abu Dhabi also offers spectacular desert scenery.

When arriving at the Sheikh Zayed Mosque, the women were asked to cover their heads and dress in the Muslims tradition. These garments were provided as a tradition with the visit. Everyone was asked to remove their shoes, which we did.

The Sheikh Zayed Mosque is the largest mosque in the country. It is the key place of worship for Friday gatherings and *Eid* prayer. The Eid prayer takes place on two Islamic holidays when Muslims come to pray on these holidays honoring the willingness of Abraham to sacrifice his son as an act of obedience to God's command. During Eid, the mosque may be visited by more than forty-one thousand people. It was built between 1996 and 2007, reportedly at a cost of $6 billion.

The building complex measures about 960 feet by 1,380 feet, covering an area of more than thirty acres, excluding landscaping and vehicle parking. The project was launched by a late president of the United Arab Emirates, who wanted to establish a structure that would unite the cultural diversity of the Islamic world with the historical and modern values of architecture and art. The operation of the mosque is managed on a day-to-day basis.

Sheikh Zayed Mosque in Abu Dhabi, United Arab Emirates

The mosque serves as a center of learning and discovery through its educational and cultural activities and visitor programs. Its library serves the community with classic books and publications that address a range of Islamic subjects, such as sciences, civilization, calligraphy, the arts, and coins, including some rare publications dating back more than two hundred years. These materials are available in a range of languages, including Arabic, English, French, Italian, Spanish, German, and Korean.

Our tour group spent several hours exploring the facility. I took hundreds of photos and a video of our group touring this magnificently elegant mosque. These few words do not adequately describe the beauty of this incomparably stunning white marble structure and its interior floors, panels, walls, clocks, ceilings, chandeliers, and other fixtures. This visit was one of the highlights of our trip to Dubai.

When we left the mosque, we visited the Heritage Village. The Heritage Village displays live images of the old traditional life in the United Arab Emirates. It symbolizes elements of wildlife, marine life, and mountain life, where visitors can identify closely with the traditional customs of the country and the special characteristics of old houses, handicrafts, and other forms of living. It is owned and managed by the Culture and Arts Authority. We stopped here to explore displays and to seize the opportunity to do some attention- grabbing shopping.

From there we traveled past the homes of the wealthy sheiks who run the country. And we also were driven along the Corniche Road. The road forms a sweeping curve on the western side of the main Abu Dhabi Island and consists of cycle paths, fountains, and park areas. Certain parts of the road have significant deposition of sand, with people using the area as a public beach. We did not stop during this travel but observed as much as we could from the widows of our bus.

Our local tour guide was well informed on the customs, traditions, evolutionary progress, and development, as well as future plans of the United Arab Emirates. He shared a great deal of information during the trip regarding the history, culture, and other important aspects of life in the United Arab Emirates, including commentary on the sheiks and the past and present history associated with the Corniche Road.

On the third day, in the afternoon, we headed out for a desert safari extravaganza, an exciting and memorable evening. We were taken out to the sand dunes in the desert for what is called a "dune bashing." As we approached the dunes, the specialist desert driver stopped the SUV we were riding in to let some of the air out of the tires before we began the breathtaking ride throughout the sand dunes.

We were taken on a roller -coaster ride, dune after dune, before coming to a stop at the top of one high dune to see a magnificent sunset. I took photos from the vantage point. During the ride to this point, the driver increased and cut back on the speed of the SUV, with the vehicle leaning, at times, about 30–45 degrees toward the sand. As we sped around some elevated sand dunes, the sand brushed powerfully up against the side of the window where I was sitting, across from the driver. At times, I thought the vehicle would flip over, but the driver's expert maneuvering of the vehicle prevented that from happening.

After this unforgettable experience, we were taken to a Bedouin camp, where we were welcomed in the traditional Arabic style—with dates (a dark oval single-stoned fruit) and Arabic coffee. We settled in for an exciting evening. Music was playing in the background. Men were offered the *sheesha* (pipe) to smoke. Body tattooing was offered, and some took advantage of this. In fact, Jean got a tattoo, but I did not. Dubai belly dancers were there on a stage, dancing to the Arabic music. The belly dancers enticed some of our members to join in and dance with them.

We had an opportunity to ride camels. Jean and I rode a camel separately and then rode one together. I took a video of Jean's ride on the camel and a member of our group used my camera to video Jean and me when we rode the camel together. Dubai men were there to help us get on and off the camels.

I took lots of photos, and I also purchased an eight-by-ten photo of Jean and me with two other members of our group, taken by a photographer on the scene. In the background of this photo, all you could see, was an endless mass of desert sand, surrounding us.

Standing in the sand, all we could see in any direction was desert sand. It reminded me of a ship sailing across the Pacific Ocean, when all you can see is water that appears to meet the blue sky. The vast amount of sand we saw in the Dubai desert looked as though it was meeting the sky.

We ended the evening with a sumptuous Bedouin dinner before returning to the hotel for the evening.

The next day we visited the Wafi City Mall. This mall was the home of more than 350 shops, a family entertainment center, and a selection of eating places. It is one of the most expensive malls in the world, with numerous upscale shops. It contains a series of pyramid- shaped buildings with fantastic Egyptian architecture and art.

We visited the Dubai Mall, the largest shopping mall in the world in terms of total area. It is the twenty-first largest mall in the world. It is part of a $20 billion downtown complex in Dubai, with 1,200 shops. It is the size of more than fifty football fields, with over thirteen million square feet of space. It has a 250-room luxury hotel, twenty-two cinema screens, and 120 restaurants and cafes.

The Dubai Aquarium and Underwater Zoo is located in the mall, with over three hundred species of marine animals, including sharks and rays, on display. The mall has a 76,000-square-foot indoor theme park, with over 150 amusement games, including motion simulators, classic games, skill games, and an array of redemption games. The mall is the home of a Rainforest Café, made to emulate tropical ruins, with moving ruins and light shows. KidZania, located in the mall, is an interactive entertainment theme park for children. It offers kids an opportunity to experience adult life through role play in a child-sized city.

Our next stop was at the Mall of the Emirates. This mall showcases more than 630 retail outlets, 7,900 parking spaces, over one hundred restaurants and cafes, eighty luxury stores, and 250 flagship stores. It also includes a ski resort and snow park, five-hundred–seat community theater arts center, and Magic Planet, which is one of the largest indoor family entertainment centers in Dubai. The architecture in the three-story complex combines Arabic and Mediterranean designs, each connected to a car park. This mall was built at an estimated cost of $218 million. It was one of our must-see malls on our tour.

We visited the Lost Chambers, a themed aquarium with over sixty-five thousand marine animals. It presented a safe environment to try snorkeling, diving, and swimming with a number of different creatures, from the big and scary to the small and colorful. Lost Chambers featured an underwater world of avenues and passageways where the ruins and relics of the Atlantic Ocean life intertwined with the various sea creatures.

Our day ended with a Dhow Cruise of Dubai Marina. This was a sea trip with dinner on an Arabic wooden boat known as a dhow. The dhow is built according to Dubai modern safety standards. We spent our evening aboard this vessel, where we enjoyed a romantic-like dinner, gliding down the creek of Dubai under a starry sky. Dinner was served and dancing music was played throughout the cruise, which added another dimension of joy and happiness. The cruise offered an intriguing, different view of this amazing city.

We saw many other wooden vessels that still sail the seas to deliver goods to faraway places. We also saw some super-modern yachts and ships. We enjoyed the scenery by night within its beautifully lit city, which was mesmerizing to observe. We also admired the architecture of the places we passed during the cruise.

After the dinner cruise aboard the dhow, we returned to the hotel for the night.

On the next and last day of our tour, there was no scheduled event. Jean and I, along with some other members of our tour, decided to take a shuttle to have lunch at the Burj Al Arab Hotel. We had observed it from a distance a couple of days before and heard that this hotel had the only seven-star rating in the world.

Reservations were made for us to have brunch at the hotel. The Burj Al Arab is described as the most luxurious hotel in the world.. We wanted to explore more of the Burj Al Arab Hotel to see if it warranted a seven-star rating, even though we knew of no other seven-star hotels to compare with it.

The hotel was built on a man-made island. It is structured in the shape of a billowing Arabian dhow (a Dubai wooden ship) sail in a nod to the country's seafaring heritage. It has become a symbol of Dubai, just as the Statue of Liberty in New York and the Eiffel Tower in Paris.

The Burj Al Arab was founded on sand, not rock. It stands 920 feet tall on 250 concrete columns, each about five feet in diameter and goes

148 feet under the sea. Its lavish interior is marble, adorning over 258,000 square feet of walls, with flooring that is the rarest (and most precious) found in Italy. Real 24-carat gold leaf covers approximately twenty-two thousand square feet of interior, including the TV screens. The 202 rooms are duplex suites boasting spectacular views of the Arabian Gulf. The smallest room is 1,830 square feet. One of the two royal suites measures 8,400 square feet, with revolving beds surrounded by mirrors, slowly spinning around at the push of a button.

The hotel has nine restaurants and bars with fine ocean views. We had lunch in the Al Muntaha ("The Highest") restaurant, located on the twenty-seventh floor.

The food was served in a buffet-style, consisting of European and Middle Eastern foods. The chef was very courteous and accommodating. We must have arrived at the restaurant around the time the chef was preparing to close down the buffet, as he had to bring out more food for us to complete our meals. The cost of the lunch buffet was sixty-five dollars per person.

I don't know if this was the regular price you would normally pay for dining in such a fancy restaurant or if the price was discounted for us being visitors from the USA. The food was good but not discernably different from what we would normally expect from a buffet-style luncheon costing thirty dollars at the Bellagio Casino in Las Vegas.

This restaurant was an ideal location for taking photos and viewing the spectacular surroundings. We took the elevator down to the lobby and I took photos of the opulent surroundings adorned with luxurious fixtures, leopard upholstery, embroidered silk wallpaper, and other precious pieces.

Afterward, we returned to the hotel, where everyone on our tour was meeting for a farewell dinner. This was a very informative and enjoyable occasion. Everyone took turns sharing their experiences and exciting moments during the trip. I took photos and videos of everyone during the farewell dinner.

The next morning, breakfast was served. And then everyone went back to their rooms to finish their packing, check out from the hotel, and get ready to depart for the airport to board a flight back home.

We left for the airport at 6:30 p.m. to catch a Delta flight to Atlanta at 10:30 p.m. There was a several-hour layover at the airport, and after we quickly cleared customs, there was nothing else to do but sit around until it was time for the flight to leave.

The flight left on time, and we arrived at the Atlanta International Airport on schedule, where we transferred to another Delta flight to the Baltimore International Airport, landing about fifteen hours later in the late evening.

Jean and I rode the airport shuttle service to our house. The shuttle driver made so many stops dropping off other riders that it took more time than we thought it should have to get home. The ride home was a disappointing way to end our fascinating tour to Dubai.

I took over four hundred photos and several videos during our trip to Dubai. I transferred the photos and the videos to DVDs. Jean organized a reception and invited all the travelers who lived in the DC metropolitan area and some of our neighbors to join with us in watching the photos and videos. She prepared a delicious assortment of hors d'oeuvres, along with serving a variety of wines. Our guests enjoyed the evening, watching the DVDs and chatting about their experiences and the good times they had during the tour. In addition to the DVDs, Jean placed all the photos in an album to memorialize our trip to Dubai.

Touring China

Collette Vacations routinely send out material on the trips they sponsor throughout the world. We have been getting this material since we took our trip with them to Nice, France. In looking at some of their tours planned for 2011, the trip to China caught our eyes, so we signed up for the tour—May 11 to 22, an eleven-day adventure.

At the beginning of the trip, a driver in a sedan transported us to the Dulles International Airport. We boarded United Airlines Flight 897 at 12:39 p.m. and departed for China. We landed at the Beijing airport at 2:40 p.m. on May 12, after a flying time of approximately fourteen hours.

We cleared customs and collected our luggage. Outside the baggage claim area was a Collette representative, who introduced herself and arranged for our transfer to the JW Marriott Hotel in the city of Beijing, the capital of China.

On May 13, we had breakfast at the hotel and were joined by about twenty other travelers, who were from a variety of cities in the United States—Boston, Chicago, Miami, San Francisco, Los Angeles, and Silver Spring, Maryland. Also, a couple from London, England, was part of the tour group.

Our Collette tour director was a lawyer from Seattle, Washington. She gave us a short lesson on the local language, especially how to say good morning in the Chinese language. Also, she talked briefly about herself and what we could expect on the tour. This was an informative session, intended to prepare everyone to begin the tour in Beijing.

Beijing, located in northern China, is the world's third most populous city and most populous capital city. It is governed as a direct-controlled municipality under the national government, with sixteen urban, suburban, and rural districts. Combining both modern and traditional architecture, Beijing is one of the oldest cities in the world and is rich in history.

We were escorted by an astute Collette Vacations tour director with the assistance of a local guide who spoke Chinese.

Throughout the tour, our director was very creative. She made us feel as if we were one big family. She used a clever technique that was intended for us to get to know something about each other on the tour. Most of our travel from one site to another was by bus, sometimes taking more than an hour or more to reach our designated location. There was plenty time for conversation while traveling. During the travel time, she asked us to write down three things about ourselves, two being false and one truthful. Members on the bus were asked to guess the truthful thing. Everyone took part in this exercise, resulting in each of us telling everyone things about ourselves that would reveal some of our life experiences. This was a fun thing to do. Everyone enjoyed it, and we got to know each other much better during the tour.

Our tour began with a visit to Tiananmen Square, a landmark

widely referred to as a national symbol of China. It was built during the Ming dynasty in 1420. It covers an area of one hundred acres. It is the entrance to the Imperial City, within which the Forbidden City was located. Nationally televised protests took place here in 1989. A portrait of Mao Zedong was displayed above the Tiananmen gate when we were there in 2011.

The Chinese name of the gate is made up of the Chinese characters for *heaven*, *peace*, and *gate*, which is conventionally translated as Gate of Heavenly Peace. Other historical names for the gate also exist. For example, the Gate of Heavenly Peacemaking and the Gate of Earthly Peacemaking are each significantly important influences in the history of the Chinese culture.

Chinese soldiers were strategically located on the grounds of Tiananmen Square. And they made it known, by giving hand signs, that they did not want their photos taken.

We visited the Forbidden City, which is a palace complex in central Beijing. It took over fourteen years and a million workers to build the Forbidden City. It is a rectangle with 3,153 feet from north to south and 2,470 feet from east to west. The complex contains 980 buildings that spread over 180 acres. The Forgotten City is surrounded by a twenty-six-foot–high wall at the base, tapering to 21.9 feet at the top. At the corners of the wall are towers with intricate roofs boasting seventy-two ridges, reproducing the Pavilion of Prince Teng and the Yellow Crane; they appeared in Song dynasty paintings. As a guess, there are approximately 9,999 rooms, including antechambers, in the Forbidden City, although this guesswork is not supported by survey tabulation. The Forbidden City was designed to reflect philosophical and religious principle and the majesty of imperial power.

The Forbidden City served as the home of emperors and their

households and the ceremonial and political center of Chinese government for almost five hundred years. It was designated a World Heritage Site in 1987, and listed by UNESCO as the largest collection of preserved ancient wooden structures in the world. According to a 1925 audit of the Forbidden City, more than 1.17 million pieces of art and other rare collections are stored in the Palace Museum of the Forbidden City.

These collections include valuable works of arts, paintings, ceramics, seals, steles, sculptures, inscribed wares, bronze ware, enamel objects and others. Based on an audit completed in 2016, the Palace Museum collection is presently on record as possessing 1,862,690 valuable objects.

The second day of our tour, we were driven to the site of the Great Wall. When we arrived, we were surrounded by souvenir kiosks, with merchants selling everything from food to Chinese apparel to Chinese garb you could purchase or dress up in to take photos.

While the souvenir items were available, I was more interested in the sites and scenes displayed by the Great Wall, as well as the historical significant of the structure that I had heard so much about.

The average height of the Great Wall ranges from four feet to nineteen feet, depending upon the location of the specific area of the wall.

The section of the Great Wall we visited was close to Beijing. It snaked up and down the mountain ridges just like a bow. This section of the wall was never renovated and retained its natural beauty for tourist to see. Owing to the steep mountains and great scenery, this section probably always was the ideal place for photographers and tourists to observe.

I walked halfway up the elevated walkway, which consisted of stone, brick, tamped earth, wood, and other materials. I walked upward on the rickety steps with the intention of reaching one of the watchtowers at the top of the wall. I walked halfway up to the watchtower but had to stop and turn around. The walkway became more difficult and harder to navigate the further up I walked. The steps leading to the tower varied in size, ranging from one small size to another smaller size, making it difficult to maneuver. Along the way, however, I took lots of photos of everything in sight.

The saga of the Great Wall is an interesting story. Several walls were built as early as the seventh century BC. Improvements were made as time passed. The majority of the existing wall is from the Ming dynasty (1368–1644). The wall was reinforced with watchtowers, troop barracks, garrison stations, and signaling capabilities. The Ming wall measures 5,500 miles, is made up of 3,889 miles of sections, has 223 miles of trenches, and has 1,387 miles of natural defensive barriers, such as hills and rivers. A survey found the entire wall is 13,171 miles, one of the most impressive architectural feats in history.

The Great Wall was built along an east-to-west line across the historical northern borders of China to protect the Chinese states and empires from raids and invasions of various nomadic groups (e.g. colonies of farming peasants in the area) of the Eurasian Steppe. There was a sharp cultural divide between Mongolia and China, and almost constant warfare existed until 1757. Mongolian nomads collected large amounts of tributes (mostly agricultural land, products grown, and livestock) from the Chinese dynasties in the steppe region.

A steppe regions is defined as an ecoregion of montane grasslands, shrub lands, and temperate grassland plains, without trees, apart from those near rivers and lakes. Steppes are characterized by a semi-arid and continental climate, with temperatures ranging from 113 degrees in the summer to 67 degrees below zero in the winter. This must have been an unusually difficult environment to imagine the existence and preservation of human life.

The Great Wall of China is known as one of the New Seven Wonders of the World. Visiting the Great Wall of China was one of the highlights of my tour to the Asian continent.

After leaving the Great Wall, we traveled through the valley of the Ming tombs, which displayed marvelous statues whose beauty could only be appreciated if you were there to see them in person. We walked along the Sacred Way or Divine Road, which means the road leading to heaven. This was a fantastic sight to see and for taking pictures of the statues of eighteen pairs of mythical animals and the legendary Chinese Ming emperors, whose bodies are buried on the Tombs grounds.

The statues were sculpted from whole stone and are larger than life-size; they led to a three-arched gate known as the Dragon and Phoenix Gate. These were gorgeously picturesque scenes, featuring the trees and manicured grass on either side of the Sacred Way. You would experience a time-honored and favorite pastime of the Chinese, imagining when they would go kite-flying. This was an ideal place to relax and just enjoy the moment. The Ming tombs were listed as a UNESCO World Heritage Site in August 2003.

The evening ended with a trip to the Tang Dynasty Theater Restaurant for a Peking duck dinner and the traditional Peking opera. We had dinner at the restaurant, served buffet-style on trays carried by waiters. This was my first dinner at which duck was served as the entrée. We enjoyed the Peking duck dinner.

The Peking opera was presented in four segments. The first segment was the instrumental titled the "King of Ever." The second segment featured four dances and different moods. The third segment presentation was titled the "Rainbow Costume Dance," a famous dance from the Tang dynasty. And the last dance in this segment was the "Warrior's Triumphal Dance." Then there was the finale; the final presentation was the "Tage," a clog dance, where heavy shoes are worn for hammering out the lively rhythm.

The Peking opera was very exciting as a cultural extravaganza, reflecting the grandeur and splendor of ancient China, and was a delightful experience. It was a dazzling performance, and the cast of performers was great. The music was stimulating. And the colorful costumes worn by the artists were captivating.

The next day we visited the UNESCO site of the Old Summer Palace. The Old Summer Palace is among the most noted classical gardens in the world.

The original construction of the Old Summer Palace began in 1707 and was significantly expanded in 1725. At that time, the imperial gardens at the Summer Palace were made up of three gardens—the garden of perfect brightness proper, the garden of eternal spring, and the elegant spring garden. The gardens collectively covered an area of 860 acres with hundreds of structures, such as halls, pavilions, temples, galleries, gardens, lakes, and bridges. Hundreds of examples of Chinese artwork and antiquities were stored in the halls, along with unique copies of literary works and compilations. Several famous landscapes of southern China were reproduced in the gardens.

The original palace was destroyed by the British and French expedition forces during the 1860s. It was sacked once again and nearly completely destroyed in 1900, although some of the components of the gardens survived the destruction.

The site was reclaimed by the Chinese in the 1980s and turned into a historical site, with additional restoration to follow. In the meanwhile, the ruins of the Old Summer Palace remained open to the public as an important tourist attraction in Beijing. The Chinese government is considering whether it should apply to include the Old Summer Palace on the UNESCO World Heritage Sites.

What we saw during our tour was the restored version of the Old Summer Palace. This included temples and other structures, lakes, waterways, gardens, statuettes, and museums with an assortment of collectibles.

We spent the entire day touring the reconstituted Old Summer Palace and all it had to offer. The local population frequently visits the grounds and structures of the palace, where they meet daily to exercise and play chess and other games. We noticed these activities taking place when we were there on tour.

On the fourth day, we visited the Temple of Heaven. It is a multifaceted and intricate combination of religious and philosophical traditions and concepts. It was constructed in Beijing between 1406 and 1420 by a Chinese king as the Forbidden City of China. The name of the Forbidden City of China was changed to Temple of Heaven by another king when he became the ruler of China during the sixteenth century. Three more temples were built: Temple of Sun, Temple of Moon, and Temple of Earth.

During the eighteenth century, more renovations to the Temple of Heaven were made. In 1914 a Chinese emperor took his oath of office in the Temple of Heaven. And four years later, the temple was open to the public.

The Temple of Heaven has become one of the most popular places for exercise because of its huge park. This is a place where Chinese emperors have worshipped their gods. Tai chi, a popular physical training workout, is routinely performed in the park.

The Temple of Heaven became a UNESCO site in 1988. It is described as a masterpiece of architecture and design and one of the prominent civilizations of the world.

As our tour continued, we were driven to a narrow street commonly referred to as hutong or neighborhood in a Chinese city. It was located near a canal. We departed from the bus and prepared to enter wooden canoes at a docking station for a trip up a canal waterway.

There were small canoes at the docking station. Each canoe could accommodate about six people. Our tour group found a canoe to board. Each of the canoes was propelled by an escort using a paddle. The escorts paddled the canoes up and down the canal, and on either side of the canal were merchants, shops, and other souvenir stands. The canoes made several stops on our journey. We departed our canoes to look over the items for sale, make some purchases, and re-board the canoes. When our canal tour ended, we departed the canoes. And then we got on rickshaws that were waiting to take us to one of the homes in a hutong neighborhood.

Our rickshaw had an overhead canvas to shield riders from the sun. The rickshaw was operated by a driver peddling a bicycle. The driver was helpful and appeared to enjoy operating the rickshaw. The ride was a unique experience that we all enjoyed on our way to the home of a family in the hutong neighborhood.

We toured one of the hutong neighborhoods. Hutongs are home to celebrities, business owners, and officials. Passageways in the hutongs were narrow but were lined on either side by spacious homes and gardens. Many of the ancient hutongs still exist, and a number of them have been designated as protected areas. Some of the older neighborhoods exist today, offering a glimpse of life in Beijing as it has been for generations.

Members of our tour group were invited to visit the home of a family living in a hutong neighborhood. The family prepared a Chinese meal for all of us; we sat around three or four tables. The lady of the house prepared Chinese dumplings while we were there and invited those who were interested to help her with the preparation. Of course, Jean's curiosity compelled her to get involved. Jean mixed one of the dumplings and was very excited about her accomplishments. We ate the Chinese meal to the delight of the Chinese family.

After this interesting outing, we boarded the bus and returned to the hotel, ending the day.

On the fifth day, we visited the most famous Buddhist temple in the world, the classic Wild Goose Pagoda. The Buddhist pagoda is located in southern Xi'an. The original pagoda was built around 649–83. It stood at a height of 177 feet at that time. The construction of rammed earth with a stone exterior façade collapsed in later years. A ruling Chinese empress rebuilt the pagoda in 704 and added five new stories. An earthquake in1556 massively damaged the pagoda and reduced it by three stories to its current height of seven stories.

The structure leans visibly several degrees to the west. The eighth-century Small Wild Goose Pagoda in Xi'an suffered minor damage in a 1556 earthquake. It was not repaired.

The Giant Wild Goose Pagoda was extensively repaired during the Ming dynasty (1368–1644) and renovated again in 1964. The pagoda now stands at a height of 210 feet tall, and from the top, it offers views all over the city of Xi'an. The pagoda is an enormously ostentatious structure. It was originally built to house Buddhist treasures.

Continuing our tour, we traveled to the museum that contained the excavation pit of the Terracotta Army. Viewing the display at the museum, we saw a collection of Terracotta sculptures presumably representing the Terracotta Army of Qin Shi Huang, the emperor of China. These works of art were portrayed to protect the emperor after he was buried sometime between 210-209 BC.

The figures were shaped to fit the size of the characters they represented, with the tallest being the generals. Also, there were warriors, chariots and horses on display. In the three pits we saw, there were a large number of sculptured Terracotta soldiers and smaller numbers of chariots, horses and cavalry horses on display.

The Terracotta soldiers were portrayed as life-size figures with uniforms and hairstyles that varied according to their ranks as soldiers. Creation of the figures was produced by government workers and local craftsmen. Pieces of their bodies were assembled separately and cemented together to form heads, arms and torsos and then placed in meticulous military formation regarding rank and duty status.

We were amazed by the sheer number of Terracotta figures and their detailed lifelike resemblance.

On the fifth day, we began the tour with a tai chi lesson. Tai chi is a highly revered Chinese martial art that is both invigorating and relaxing. The exercise was directed by a trained martial arts expert. He took time to work with each of us who desired special attention to ensure that we were doing the moves and postures correctly. He worked with us for an hour or more.

The tai chi lesson was a new way of exercising for us, and it will be remembered. Most of our group purchased tai chi souvenirs as evidence of this newly gained experience.

As we continued the tour, we traveled to the countryside to visit a rural village in Xi'an. We met with a local family who lived there. The family raised cattle for the government and was subsidized for it.

Not too far from their house was a cave home, and we were given a tour. Cave homes are common places to live in some rural communities in China. Typically, cave homes (known as *yaodong* in Chinese) have a long, vaulted room dug out of the side of a mountain, with a semicircular entrance covered with rice paper or colorful quilts. People hang decorations on the walls, often a portrait of Mao Tse-tung or a photograph of a movie star torn from a glossy magazine.

We were told that the cave homes are cool in the summer and warm in the winter. They are quiet and safe. They have a nice yard out front where the residents can exercise and sit in the sun. At certain times in China, more than thirty million Chinese people lived in cave homes. Some cave homes have more than one room. A one- room cave home without plumbing can rent for thirty dollars a month, with the resident relying on outhouses or "potties" that they empty outside.

The inside of the cave home we saw was beautifully decorated with bedding and a lantern for lighting. But I don't think anyone was living there at the time of our visit.

The Chinese family were gracious hosts. They prepared a typical Chinese meal for us consisting of rice, shrimp, eggplant, fermented tofu, vegetable stir-fry, and meat. It was a wholesome dining experience, served buffet-style.

Nearing the end of our tour in the rural village, we all stopped at a local elementary school. This stop turned out to be the highlight of the day. Class was in session. The students were surprised and excited to see us. We stayed at the school, interacting with them, for about an hour.

Jean, sitting with Chinese students at the elementary school in Zi'an, China

Some of the students spoke English. The students were eager to show us what they were working on. They explained everything they might have done during the school year.

Visiting the school was one of the memorable events of our trip. I took many photos of each of the students, as well as the various interactions between the students and members of our group.

The next day, we boarded a plane for a short flight to Shanghai. Shanghai is noted for its bustling trade port. It is the economic heart of China. It has futuristic skylines that are spectacular, leaving you speechless.

After arriving, we were led on a guided tour of the waterfront district, known as the Bund, which runs along the western bank of the Huangpu River. The Bund usually refers to the buildings and wharfs on the side of the road, as well as some adjacent areas. It is famous for its gorgeous colonial buildings. We felt as though we had stepped back into nineteenth-century Europe as we wandered among the impressive Gothic, Baroque, and Renaissance architecture.

The Bund waterfront district is one of the most famous tourist destinations in Shanghai. The buildings in the Bund district are designed in various architectural designs. The Bund is one of the most prominent features visible from the Shanghai World Financial Center in Pudong. Its observation deck is on the one hundredth floor. The World Financial Center is housed in a skyscraper that is the third tallest in the world.

We spent the night at the Renaissance Shanghai Zhongshan Park Hotel. On the eighth day, we enjoyed a full-day excursion to the water village of Zhujiajiao. Zhujiajiao is a southern town, known as "Venice in Shanghai." It is located north of the foot of the pictureque Dianshan Lake.

There are many creeks in this small town. Thirty-six ancient stone bridges that cross the canal run through the center of town. The creeks and bridges contribute to Zhujiajaio's historical interest. Numerous buildings from the Ming and Qing dynasties are scattered by the creeks—after more than one thousand years, these buildings still stand.

We visited the Shanghai Museum. The striking architecture and use of technology make the museum the most famous in China. The museum covers an area of about 3,600 square yards with a scale that surpasses the old museum several times. The exterior of the museum is in the shape of an ancient bronze cooking vessel called a ding with a round top and a square base. The structure and materials of the entire building, however, represent an accomplishment of the most modern technology.

Among the collectibles in the museum are superior works of art that are unique in the entire country. These include, in particular, the bronzes, calligraphy, paintings and Ming and Qing furniture. The subdued dark-green tone of the walls imparts an ancient atmosphere. The simple and elegant display cases and the lighting are carefully designed to enhance the experience.

Later in the evening, we were picked up at our hotel and driven to a restaurant for dinner. The dinner was followed by admission to a theater to see a Chinese acrobatic performance. The captivating performance of the acrobatic cadre was unbelievable. We were in awe watching the world-class skill of the acrobats as they performed a routine of compelling choreography that has been practiced over centuries. With their graceful agility and immense skill, it's no wonder the Chinese acrobatics have won hundreds of international competitions. The show was intriguing and absolutely amazing. I videotaped the entire performance from my strategically located seat in the theater.

On the ninth and last full day of our tour in China, we visited the Shanghai Changning Children's Palace. The palace was originally built as a home for Wang Boqun, former Chinese minister of communications. The forty-room mansion was built from 1932 to 1934 in the Victorian Gothic style. The house is currently used as a community children's center for art, music, and dance lessons.

From 1941 to 1944, during the Second Sino-Japanese War, the house was used by the head of Japan's puppet government. After the war, it became a prison and was used as an execution ground for Communist revolutionaries. In 1947 it was returned to China. China rented the house to the British Embassy for use as its Shanghai Consulate General and British Information Offices. From 1949 to 1960, the house was used for government offices, and eventually it was turned into the Children's Palace.

The remainder of the day was given way to leisure options. Some of us returned to the Shanghai Museum for more observation of the variety of collectibles on display and to purchase souvenirs. Others seized the opportunity to explore more of the city, snap a few more photos, and shop for last-minute souvenirs to bring back home.

Later that evening, our fellow travelers came together for a farewell dinner and to offer heartfelt goodbyes. We had become like family. We all had enjoyed being together throughout the entire tour.

I brought my video camera to dinner and filmed audiovisual messages. It was very interesting as I went from table to table, asking all members to state their names and where they were from and to offer any comments they wished to share with their fellow travelers about their remarkable tour of China. I got great responses from everyone.

I told everyone that I was going to set up a website when I returned home and that anyone who wanted copies of any of the more than four hundred photos I took could log on to the website and make copies of any photos they wanted. I instructed them on how to access the website. I informed them that I was going to make DVDs of the videos I'd recorded during the trip and they would be available to anyone who wanted a copy, but I would ask to be reimbursed for the minimal cost of producing the DVDs. (Only five members of our group took advantage of the offer to visit the website. Four travelers requested copies of the video.)

After our farewell dinner, we spent some cheerful time with our fellow travelers.

The next morning our tour ended. Following breakfast, the travelers from the USA boarded a bus for a short ride to the Shanghai Pudong airport. The two travelers from London left later for the airport, as they were extending their trip to include a tour of of Hong Kong.

The three of us from the DC area boarded United Airlines Flight 858 at 12:10 p.m. for the long flight to San Francisco International Airport, arriving at 8:04 a.m. After going through customs, we boarded United Airlines Flight 255 at 9:50 a.m. for the flight to the Dulles International Airport, arriving at 5:59 p.m.

After collecting our baggage at the airport, Jean and I were picked up by a Collette Sedan Service driver and taken to our home in southwest Washington, DC. Our traveler from Maryland collected her luggage and was picked up and driven to her home. Collette's prearranged service to and from the airport was great.

Chapter 30

Remembering the United States Coast Guard in 2017

LOOKING BACK ON MY JOB AT THE COAST GUARD YEARS LATER, I OFten wonder was what happening, especially with respect to the civil rights doctrine, the Coast Guard Academy, and some other civil rights issues. Were my efforts in vain? Did I do enough to inspire implementation of the civil rights doctrine?

There is an old saying: If you find a job you like, you will never work a day in your life. The position in the coast guard from which I retired was such a job. And I had mixed emotions about retirement at the time I did. I had just published a civil rights doctrine for the coast guard. This was the first such document promulgated for implementation throughout the service. I was concerned that my retirement might affect how the civil rights doctrine would be received, understood, and executed by the rank and file throughout the coast guard, although all coast guard program directors and the chief of staff had commented on it and concurred with its promulgation.

There was reason to be worried for a while until I realized that the civil rights doctrine was only a combined set of policies and principles, designed to integrate the policies and practices of the Civil Rights program into the coast guard's policies, practices, and operational missions. When implemented, the doctrine would become part of the culture of the coast guard. But the policies and principles governing the civil rights doctrine could be rescinded, modified, or strengthened and there was nothing I could do, as I had retired from the coast guard.

The civil rights dogma was an outstanding advancement for the coast guard, and it was a creditable operating philosophy. Such a doctrine had never been issued in the coast guard, nor had a civil rights doctrine ever been promulgated by any other agency of the federal government. The coast guard's civil rights doctrine was arguably an innovative exemplar meriting emulation by other agencies of the federal government.

The civil rights doctrine was one of my major accomplishments while serving as the assistant commandant for civil rights. I wanted the civil rights doctrine to continue guiding the civil rights activities in the coast guard and to enhance future outcomes in several areas, for example:

- Integrate the Civil Rights policies and practices into the military operational missions, policies and practices of the service
- Improve the status of minority civilians in the civilian workforce
- Improve the status of minorities in the enlisted and officer corps of the coast guard
- Reach out beyond traditional non-minority recruiting markets to attract more minorities to the Coast Guard Academy.

Based on actions taken by Admiral Thad Allen (commandant), management of the EEO program and telephone conversations with Captain Bob Mckenna (dean of admissions at the coast guard academy) and other information I've reviewed since my retirement, there is reason to believe that the civil rights doctrine is an inherent part of coast guard culture and is adding value to coast guard operational missions.

The chief of staff at the time of my retirement was Vice Admiral Thad Allen. I had consulted with him on numerous occasions when developing the final version of the civil rights doctrine. He was aware of the visionary direction of the Civil Rights program.

The president selected Vice Admiral Allen for advancement in May 2010 and appointed him as commandant of the coast guard for a four-year period. Early on during his tenure as commandant, he took steps to strengthen the civil rights doctrine. He modernized the civil rights office by centralizing all civil rights functions and employing full-time civil rights service providers. In addition, he discontinued the collateral duty position of civil rights officers and established full-time civil rights officers in all major organizations throughout the service.

Before retirement, I initiated actions to implement the EEOC MD 715 directive in all major commands that employed civilians. Now, Management Directive EEOC MD 715 is guiding actions to address the status of minorities in the civilian workforce. Major organizational components are performing annual self-assessments and developing strategic plans to remove workforce barriers to free and open competition in the civilian workforce. The results of annual assessments are posted on the internet and are transparent for the public to see. Transparency is the best course of action the coast guard could take to demonstrate that it is striving to solve real problems and become the desired federal agency in which to work.

The Coast Guard Academy has strategically expanded its outreach to recruit minorities. The academy's demographically recruiting outreach is attracting potential candidates from all segments of society for consideration for enrollment as cadets. A considerable number of minorities were enrolled for the class of 2020, including twenty-three African Americans, forty-eight Hispanics, and thirty-one Asian American Pacific Islanders, among the total of 304 cadets. This is a strong indication that the academy values diversity and is continually working to achieve a critical mass of minorities at the institution. It may be possible that as time passes a critical mass of minority cadets at the academy may attract other minorities to apply for admission as cadets. Concurrently, the creative steps taken to assemble the class of 2020 bode well for encouraging minorities to consider enrollment at the Coast Guard Academy.

Considering the foregoing activities, there is reason to believe the civil rights doctrine is playing a pivotal role in realistically addressing and solving problematic issues to improve the operation of coast guard missions. And I would speculate that what is happening in the coast guard, as a consequence of the doctrine, will not only create and sustain a model workforce for civilian and military members, but more importantly, add recognizable value to coast guard personnel readiness and operational mission performance.

Afterword

My Memoirs: Edifying Times was not easy to write. It is a story of growing up with dreams in an impoverished environment, performing public service to make a positive difference in the lives of ordinary people, living an enjoyable life after retirement, traveling abroad for curiosity and education, and remembering the coast guard after retirement. These memorable experiences are intertwined with one another.

I did not want to focus exclusively on myself. No one accomplishes anything alone, except perhaps individuals such as tennis players, golfers, swimmers, and the like, even though they have trainers to help perfect their athletic skills. I tried to write about growing up in an impoverished environment, and with the nurturing and guidance of my parents and the mentoring of others, unimaginable things were made possible.

I can't say enough about the coast guard and what it did for me. The coast guard was like a family organization. The organization challenged my intellectual capabilities (including my knowledges, skills, and ability) to be all I could be. The coast guard gave me an unimaginable opportunity to create a visionary civil rights doctrine that will make a positive difference in the lives of military and civilian members of the service. The experience acquired working in the coast guard helped shape my prospective outlook on life with respect to creating a better life for all members of our society.

I was born during the Great Depression, a time in our history when families like mine were struggling to make ends meet. My parents were always optimistic about the future, despite not having what it would take to guarantee a stable and predictable life. My family was poor, but we didn't think we were poor. I recognized this early on in my youthful years, while going to school and working menial jobs because I thought the money earned would help my parents.

At the same time, I was fascinated with baseball and had hopes and dreams of becoming a professional baseball player. Playing baseball in high school is partly what kept me there and out of trouble.

After graduating, I continued to pursue my baseball dreams by playing sandlot baseball and working at menial job that didn't seem to offer long-term employment. At my father's advice, I joined the United States Air Force and began to realistically think about what I should do to prepare for the future.

When my air force service was completed, I obtained employment in the federal government and enrolled in college classes in the evening. Taking college courses at night enabled me to acquire enough credits to graduate later in life with a bachelor's degree in business and economics.

After getting a college degree, my progression in the federal government seemed to rapidly advance. With the advice and mentoring of superiors in the federal government, I progressed from an entry-level job to a senior management position in ten years. Considering the competitive nature of what it would normally take to move up in the federal government, I believe my advancement was notably unusual.

Then in 1983, the coast guard commandant appointed me to a position in the Senior Executive Service (SES) as the national director for the coast guard's Civil Rights program. I never dreamed this would happen to me. This was a serious job with unimaginably complex challenges and opportunities.

In the coast guard, the civil rights terminology was referred to synonymously as equal opportunity. But to be clear, the term "civil rights" is defined as the basic rights of every person, regardless of race, gender, age, and/or other attributes. And the term "equal opportunity" is defined as the aggregation of policies and practices in employment and other areas that do not discriminate against persons on the basis of race, color, age, sex, national origin, religion, or mental or physical disability.

I studied the coast guard organizational structure, including its policies, practices, and operational missions. The Civil Rights program was shown on organizational charts as part of the organizational structure of the coast guard, but, in practice, it was not integrated into its policies, practices, and operational missions. There was an apparent disengagement between the coast guard operational missions and the civil rights operations.

I considered this disconnect between the coast guard operational missions and the civil rights operations as a major problem with respect to ensuring equal opportunity throughout the service. The responsibilities of the leaders administering operational missions were vague when it came to taking actions and making decisions to ensure equal opportunity. Most of the equal employment opportunity decisions regarding civilian activities (hiring, training, promotions, etc.) were made by human resources workers with limited input from coast guard senior managers directing operational missions. Issues regarding civilian disputes (of an equal employment opportunity nature) were handed off to the Civil Rights program to resolve.

The status of minorities in the coast guard was not proportionally equal to the prominence of non-minorities in the military service. The same disparity among the two groups existed in many civilian occupational areas. Why did this exist, and what could or should be done about the matter?

These questions begged answers and practical solutions to eliminate other equal opportunity issues. There appeared to be systemic equal opportunity issues that could not be fixed in the short run. Ensuring equal opportunity is a continual activity that required the involvement of everyone, including top leadership, managers, supervisors, and nonsupervisory personnel. To fix this archaic situation was something that had to be done during the twenty-one years I served as the USCG civil rights program director.

Collaborating with Coast Guard Headquarters and field program directors and commanders, as well as heads of external minority civil rights and education organizations, the civil rights office formulated and issued a visionary civil rights doctrine. The civil rights doctrine was the first set of guidelines ever issued for integrating the coast guard civil rights and equal employment opportunity policies and practices into coast guard operational policies and practices to improve the effective and efficient operation of coast guard missions. The successful development and promulgation of the civil rights doctrine was a monumental enterprise accomplished prior to my retirement.

Transition from retirement to another phase of life was seamless. There is an opportunity for an enjoyable life after retirement. When I retired from my job at the coast guard, I pondered what I should do next. Should I do what some people do and look for another job? This didn't go over very well, given that I had been working nonstop for a considerably long period of time—nearly fifty-four years. I did not want another job. If I wanted to continue working, I would have continued my work at the coast guard, doing something I enjoyed.

Jean had retired the year before I did. We talked about being active after retirement. We concluded that neither of us should seek another job but that we should do something just to enjoy life. That something was to travel and see parts of the world we had never seen before. So we decided on tourism.

Tourism has been one of the most interesting experiences of our lives. It is one thing to talk about places you have never been but to be there is another thing entirely. Being there and talking with new people introduces you to another aspect of education and curiosity. Curiosity led us, especially me, to research some of the places we visited and things we saw. The research added another perspective to everything and created another dimension of understanding in a historical context.

To learn more about the history of countries we visited was not only enlightening but academically enriching. The architecture we saw was stunning. Knowing more about the evolution of some of the buildings was unbelievable. And to personally observe the standard of living in other countries as compared to the United States offered an insight into the values, customs, and traditions of peoples living abroad.

Traveling abroad is one of the best ways to get to know and better understand other peoples of the world.

As I consider the nearly fitty-four years of performing public service, it has been a journey mixed with challenges, opportunities and jam-packed with memories of life experiences that I characterize as "My Memoirs – Edifying Times". I will never forget such occurrences for they have shaped my life for whatever it is, hopeful an advocate for making a positive difference in the lives of ordinary people. My public service, combined with tourism, has inspired me to never stop dreaming of what can be, but to let your intellectual curiosity and education determine your limitations. A combination of public service and traveling abroad has enriched my curiosity for education and persuaded me to write "My Memoirs – Edifying Times".

This is the second book I have written about various experiences in life. The only difference between the two books is that this second book contains more expansive information as it details more personal experiences. Also, it has chapters on tourism and other things in which Jean and I have been engaged in since retirement.

My first book, *My Autobiography: A Legacy of Public Service*, was a story of my public service career as the coast guard assistant commandant for civil rights. Much of the writing in the first book is contained in this book, *My Memoirs: Edifying Times*. Also my first book was printed in color, with photos, and perfect bound. It was a souvenir version primarily for family members and friends.

Appendix
Awards and Recognitions

United States Coast Guard Recognitions

1. United States Coast Guard certificate in recognition of selection as a member of the Senior Executive Service of the United States of America (1983)
2. Coast Guard Academy Board of Trustees (1997–2004)
3. United States Coast Guard Senior Executive Service performance bonuses/cash awards for outstanding performance (1993 and 2000)
4. United States Coast Guard Distinguished Career Service Award (2004)
5. US Department of Homeland Security certificate for fifty-four years of service to the people of the United States of America (2004)

Medals

1. Syngman Rhee Presidential Medal for Service in Korea (1952– 1953)
2. United States National Defense Medal for service in Korea (1952–1953)

Certificates

1. Federal Executive Institute certificate for completion of Senior Executive Education program (1975)
2. Civil Service Commission/Office of Management and Budget certificate in recognition of successful participation in the Federal

Executive Development Program and for contributions toward improving management in the federal service (1975–1976)

3. Washington, DC, H. D. Woodson Senior High School certificate for outstanding support as Partner in Education (1992)

Awards, Proclamation, Key to City

1. Department of Transportation Secretary's Gold Medal Award for outstanding support of the Garrett A. Morgan Transportation and Futures program that inspired more than one million students to gain knowledge and skills needed to join the transportation workforce of the twenty-first century (1999)
2. Maritime and Science Technology Academy Award in appreciation of support of the first United States Coast Guard JROTC MAST Academy (1991–1992)
3. National Association for Equal Opportunity in Higher Education's special award
4. National Association for the Advancement of Colored People Benjamin L. Hooks Distinguished Service Award (1993)
5. National Association for the Advancement of Colored People Roy Wilkins Meritorious Service Award (1987)
6. Minority Access, Inc. Role Model Award (1996)
7. Proclamation from the city council of the City of New Orleans
8. Key to the City of Franklin, Kentucky (1992)
9. University of Maryland University College Distinguished Alumnus Award (2008)

Department of Defense Board, Council, and Task Force

1. Department of Defense Human Relations Education Board (1983–1985)
2. Department of Defense Equal Opportunity Council (1986–1992)
3. Department of Defense Task Force on Discrimination and Sexual Harassment (1994–1995)

Memberships

1. National Urban League President's Club (charter member)
2. Washington Urban League (life member)
3. National Association for the Advancement of Colored People (two life memberships—Golden Heritage and Diamond)
4. University of Maryland University College Alumni Association
5. Blacks in Government (life member)
6. Veterans of Foreign Wars (life member)
7. National Association of Human Rights Workers

www.ingramcontent.com/pod-product-compliance
Lightning Source LLC
Chambersburg PA
CBHW071721120626
46550CB00001B/327